The Holy Spirit as Communion

The Holy Spirit as Communion

*Colin Gunton's Pneumatology of Communion and
Frank Macchia's Pneumatology of* Koinonia

I. Leon Harris

☙PICKWICK *Publications* · Eugene, Oregon

THE HOLY SPIRIT AS COMMUNION
Colin Gunton's Pneumatology of Communion and Frank Macchia's Pneumatology of *Koinonia*

Copyright © 2017 I. Leon Harris. All rights reserved. Except for brief quotations in critical publications or reviews, no part of this book may be reproduced in any manner without prior written permission from the publisher. Write: Permissions, Wipf and Stock Publishers, 199 W. 8th Ave., Suite 3, Eugene, OR 97401.

Pickwick Publications
An Imprint of Wipf and Stock Publishers
199 W. 8th Ave., Suite 3
Eugene, OR 97401

www.wipfandstock.com

PAPERBACK ISBN: 978-1-4982-9749-3
HARDCOVER ISBN: 978-1-4982-9751-6
EBOOK ISBN: 978-1-4982-9750-9

Cataloguing-in-Publication data:

Names: Harris, I. Leon.

Title: The holy spirit as communion : Colin Gunton's pneumatology of communion and Frank Macchia's pneumatology of koinonia / I. Leon Harris.

Description: Eugene, OR : Pickwick Publications, 2017 | Includes bibliographical references and index(es).

Identifiers: ISBN 978-1-4982-9749-3 (paperback) | ISBN 978-1-4982-9751-6 (hardcover) | ISBN 978-1-4982-9750-9 (ebook)

Subjects: LCSH: Holy Spirit. | Gunton, Colin E. | Macchia, Frank D., 1952–.

Classification: BS2545.H62 H36 2017 (print) | BS2545.H62 H36 (ebook)

Manufactured in the U.S.A.   09/14/17

Dedication

To Jesus Christ, who revealed Himself to me as the Son of the Father and gift of the Holy Spirit. To my parents, Ivory and Vernice, whose early love and support still lives with me to this day; I miss you both. To my wife, friend, and biggest supporter, Joyce, whose continual love, support, and encouragement kept me motivated throughout our entire journey to Scotland and back; my journey would not have been possible or the same without her. To my sister, Sister, who displays unconditional love and support. To my great friends, Jerald, Jerome, and Stanley, whose friendship and constant conversations kept me invigorated. To the Dorsey/Coffey family, thank you for your support and familial love. To my Scottish family of King's Community Church, Aberdeen, your kindness will not be forgotten; especially the Duthie family who treated us as one of their own. To Alan Gomes, I greatly appreciate your encouragement and advice; may God continue to bless you. And finally, to my supervisor Phil, one of the most patient Christians that I have had the pleasure of knowing; thank you for your advice, instructions, and unending patience. To John Webster, you are missed—see you in heaven.

Contents

List of Figures | viii
Introduction | ix

Colin Gunton: Pneumatology as Recovery of Relationality | 1

Chapter 1   The Doctrine of God: Being as Being-in-Communion | 13
Chapter 2   Pneumatology of Communion: Particularity as Being-in-Relation | 38
Chapter 3   A Pneumatological Christology | 65
Chapter 4   Ecclesiology: The Church as Pneumatic Community | 99

Frank D. Macchia: Pneumatology as Justification | 117

Chapter 5   Toward a Spirit-Baptized Ecclesiology | 128
Chapter 6   Christology: Christ as the Spirit Baptizer | 149
Chapter 7   Pneumatology as Baptism in the Spirit | 166
Chapter 8   Doctrine of God—The Spirit-Baptized Divine Life | 190

Conclusion | 202
Bibliography | 223
Author Index | 235
Subject Index | 237

List of Figures

Figure 1: Traditional View of Hypostatic Union | 94
Figure 2: Gunton's Pneumatological Christology | 95

Introduction

THE PRIMARY GOAL OF this work is to outline the theologies of Colin Gunton and Frank Macchia with a focus on their doctrines of the Holy Spirit. I am not simply concerned with constructing a Pneumatology that is an addendum to Christology; I desire to develop an account of the Holy Spirit which portrays His active agency in a way that emphasizes His personhood. The Holy Spirit is not only transforming the believer's moral qualities; the Holy Spirit is transforming the entire created order towards its divine goal of a full relationship with God. This means that within the doctrine of creation, redemption, and eschatology, there must be an account of the Spirit as an active agent in the same manner as the Father and the Son. In following the Reformation and the Enlightenment, the Spirit has been expressed using individualistic soteriological terms as the agent who awakens faith in the believer toward a life of sanctification. Karl Barth avers that, for liberal theology,

> to speak about God meant to speak about humanity . . . this divine God was in danger being reduced to a pious notion: the mythical expression and symbol of human excitation oscillating between its own psychic heights or depths, whose truth could only be that of a monologue and its own graspable content.[1]

When the Holy Spirit is perceived in these terms, it resulted in the Spirit being relegated to the interior working of the doctrine of sanctification, which led Western theology to emphasize personal piety and a type of Christian autonomy that is grounded in individual confessions of sin and faith. Sanctification is construed as personal moral improvement towards a Christ-like existence without a consistent engagement with ecclesiology. Wilson Varkey says,

---

1. Green, *Karl Barth*, 48.

There are three things that are important when dealing with the pneumatology of Luther, as follows; firstly, the Holy Spirit is a central doctrine in the theology of Luther; secondly, his theology expresses his personal experience of conviction of sin and forgiveness, the testimony of the Holy Spirit that he has been rescued in Christ by faith, and finally the Holy Spirit comes through the physical means of the Word and sacrament.[2]

There is a sense in Luther that all the interesting work of God is in the past, in the work of Christ; the Holy Spirit is active in the sense of pointing the believer back to the saving work of Christ. While this is true, there must be an eschatological component to God's redemptive activity which gives room for the active and continual work of the Holy Spirit. In general, "Reformation theology viewed faith as the decisive work of the Holy Spirit, the later development of Reformation soteriology . . . was expressed more in Christological than in pneumatological terms."[3] Pannenberg sums it best when he says that "theology has often neglected the relation between the soteriological operations of the Spirit in believers and his activity as the Creator of all life and also in its eschatological new creation and consummation."[4] The point is that just as the Father's love is described as personal and active in sending the Son to redeem; and the Son's love is described as personal and active by willing to become human, suffer and die on the cross; the Holy Spirit should also be viewed in terms of personal active love.

This thesis will critically examine two contemporary systematic theologians, whom each has a particular distinctive emphasis upon the Holy Spirit as an active personal agent who completes the divine Trinity in the immanent life; in creation; in redemption; and in the final consummation. The Holy Spirit is not simply the external power who awakens faith in humanity, and then grows that faith in sanctification. Basil says, "And in the creation bethink thee first, I pray thee, of the original cause of all things that are made, the Father; of the creative cause, the Son; of the perfecting cause, the Spirit."[5] This perfecting action of the Spirit is an eschatological action that is experienced in our history, but is not yet fully consummated. Basil also connects the work of the Spirit to creation in such a way that creation itself becomes an eschatological work of the Holy Spirit. Therefore, an account of Pneumatology must not limit the work of the Holy Spirit to a

2. Varkey, *Role of the Holy Spirit in the Protestant Systematic Theology*, 40.

3. Kärkkäinen, *Pneumatology*, 84–85.

4. Pannenberg, *Systematic Theology*, 2. Later, Pannenberg says "In contrast, Reformation theology viewed faith as the decisive work of the Holy Spirit, though then followed by the gift of the Spirit himself for sanctification" (ibid., 2–3).

5. Basil of Caesarea, *On the Holy Spirit* XVI.38.

passive role in relation to the transaction between the Father and the Son; otherwise a binitarian view of creation, soteriology and eschatology will develop because of a lack of the eschatological perfecting work of the Spirit. Both Colin Gunton and Frank Macchia are theologians who are consciously aware of and advocate strongly for recognition of the Holy Spirit's role of perfecting the immanent life and work of the Trinity: a work that takes place in creation, in redemption, and in the final consummation of the Kingdom of God. So we now turn to a brief introduction to both theologians in order to explicate the reason for their inclusion, as well as their specific contribution to this work.

Colin E. Gunton

The inclusion of Gunton as a conversation partner is due to his particular Pneumatology that is shaped by his Trinitarian approach to theology. In his introduction to Colin Gunton's theology, Lincoln Harvey says that "Colin Gunton helped to rekindle the discipline of systematic theology in England."[6] Gunton's commitment to shaping theology through the doctrine of the Trinity has a strong impact on his pneumatology. Since the Trinity is at the basis of creation, redemption, and the final consummation, the Holy Spirit is conceived as an active agent in all theological categories. But in order to develop the place of the Trinity in theology, Gunton's approach is to begin with the revelation of scripture as the place to discern and as the basis on which to define the nature and persons of the Trinity. It is not from metaphysical speculations or from experience but from the economic activities of God that defines God.

In other words, Gunton begins his theology from within the revelation of scripture in order to determine the attributes of God. In a way, Gunton redefines the attributes of God based on the divine activity as witnessed in the incarnation of Christ. For example, when determining the attributes of the two natures of Christ, Gunton says that "we cannot decide what they are simply a priori, but have to ask what they are in the case of the particular divine and human action which encounters us here."[7] Even though the doctrine of God is first in Gunton's theological presentation, it is the divine action attested in and by the scriptures which has priority in determining the divine attributes. Those attributes of God which are derived from speculative reason based on apophatic or anthropological thinking still have usefulness; it is just that God's activity in the incarnation has priority as a determinate

6. Harvey, *The Theology of Colin Gunton*, 1.
7. Gunton, *Act and Being*, 152.

when defining the attributes of God. So instead of omnipresence being defined as the ability of God to be present everywhere simultaneously, Gunton says that Jesus' "life is the taking place of the capacity of the creator of time and space to be freely present to it."[8] This way, God's omnipotence is defined within God's activity in the incarnation; for Jesus' "life is the expression of God the Father's omnipotent dealing with his creation through the life and death of his incarnate Son."[9] Instead of searching for the Spirit's activity in sanctification alone, all theological *loci* aid in defining the activity and attributes of the Holy Spirit. The reason is that biblically speaking, creation, redemption, and sanctification "are attributed to the Father and mediated by both the Son and the Spirit."[10] So what we are after in Gunton is an account of the Holy Spirit that is taken from the revelatory action as revealed in the narrative account of the incarnation of the Son. The reason is that,

> we need an account of the kind of person that the Father is in creating, redeeming and sanctifying—and anything else essential to an account of the economy of the divine action—and the kind of persons that the Son and the Spirit are in mediating that action as the Father's "two hands" and therefore as the Father himself in action through their particular action.[11]

So through Gunton we are able to account for the active personal agency of the Holy Spirit in all theological categories because of his commitment to different *kinds* of divine action as witnessed in the scriptures based on the inseparable and trinitarian economic activity of God.

This way, the Spirit is defined within the economic activity instead of within the subjective experience of the believers—as in sanctification or various gifts (e.g. healing, miracles, etc. (c.f. 1 Cor. 12)). In reference to the Spirit, Gunton says "that we must avoid talk of *individual*—non-perichoretic—agency . . . The Spirit is neither an individual power nor a subjective feeling, but a person sent by the Father through his ascended Son."[12] What we see in Gunton is a theologian who stresses the Trinity so that the Son and the Spirit are not deprived of their reality as *particular* agents. The point being that the scriptures demonstrate that the Holy Spirit is a person who acts both actively and passively in relation to the Father and the Son. This divine action of the Holy Spirit is also witnessed in the economy as an active and passive action in relation to the world, because the Holy Spirit

8. Ibid., 153.
9. Ibid.,
10. Ibid., 139.
11. Ibid.,
12. Ibid., 144.

liberates the Son to obey the Father, and He also liberates creation to learn obedience to the Father. Therefore, Gunton's Trinitarian theology does not necessarily comport well with the traditional doctrine of appropriations; where the "attributes which are essential to the divine nature are assigned to one of the persons of the Godhead, or when one of these persons reveals himself by attributes of the divine nature."[13] Typically, power, wisdom, and love are attributed to the divine nature in general; "but *per appropriationem*, power is assigned to the Father, wisdom to the Son, and love to the Holy Ghost."[14] Gunton disagrees with this model, for it is the distinctive *kinds* of actions of each person in relation to the other two—originating, becoming incarnate, and perfecting—which establishes the active personal agency for each divine persons. The theologian should investigate the Biblical narrative to determine the *kind* of action that each divine person exhibits in power, wisdom, and love. Hence, the tension between the attributes of God and the appropriations to the person is reduced, in that, God is power, wisdom, and love; while simultaneously, the Father, Son, and Holy Spirit are equally involved in working out the divine attributes of power, wisdom, and love. At this early stage, it seems safe to conclude that for Gunton the Holy Spirit is the personal divine agent of eschatological perfecting action of power, wisdom, and love.

Gunton's designation of the Holy Spirit as the 'perfecting cause' affords him the conceptual space to interrelate pneumatology and eschatology. Salvation becomes a here-and-now reality, instead of simply a causal connection to Christ's past work on the cross. The Holy Spirit is seen as the eschatological perfecting agent who was given by the risen Christ from the Father to bring about redemption in the created order. Gunton says that "the Spirit is the one who enables the whole creation to anticipate its eschatological destiny."[15] The Holy Spirit is not that power which indwells human beings only for the sake of an inward moral transformation, but the agent who completes the Father's will of transforming creation as a downpayment of what is to come. The Holy Spirit perfects in the here-and-now by perfecting the fellowship of creation with its Creator, as well as relations between creatures. This is the reality of community—a term that becomes his primary designation of the Spirit's work of reconciliation. The Holy Spirit constitutes a new community due to the work of Jesus Christ. But as the risen Christ, Jesus' work is not confined to the past or the present, but is also a future reality, i.e. a reality that is being propelled forwards by the

---

13. Twesten, "The Trinity," 44.
14. Ibid., 44–45.
15. Gunton, *Act and Being*, 142.

work of the Holy Spirit so that creation will reach its final destiny according to the will of the Father.

Lastly, Gunton has influenced many theologians over the years, primarily due to his contributions to the recent resurgence in Trinitarian theology. Gunton's seminal work *The One, The Three and the Many*, along with others, not only established him as a theologian who took the Trinity seriously, but also as one who searched in particular for a more adequate conception of Pneumatology. John Webster states that "Gunton was deeply impressed by Barth's dogmatic achievement, and shared many of his instincts."[16] Gunton is both a Reformed scholar and a theologian who represents theology after Karl Barth. Gunton is well known for the "aspects of his work [that] revolve around his conception of the Trinity and how the Trinity acts as a hermeneutical key that shapes the content and nature of theology."[17] Gunton is also known for his particular reading of the problem of the 'one and the many' which establishes this two-fold scheme as a foundational hermeneutic for his interpretation and analysis of philosophy and theology. Gunton stresses that a properly construed Pneumatology has the potential to alleviate the historic privileging of the one over the many. So my selection of Gunton is not without merit. Gunton's construal of pneumatology is committed to viewing the Holy Spirit as an active agent within all theological *loci*, especially within the doctrines of God proper, creation, redemption, and eschatology. Since the Holy Spirit is fully divine and yet a distinct person, it is necessary to define the attributes of the Spirit from the revelatory event of the Incarnation in order to locate His perfecting eschatological action.

Frank D. Macchia

Frank D. Macchia is a Pentecostal scholar who, as of this writing, is a professor of theology at Vanguard University in Costa Mesa, California. Macchia received his doctorate degree from the University of Basel, Switzerland, and has served as the editor of the international Pentecostal journal *Pneuma*. In commenting on Macchia's work, *Baptized in the Spirit*, Clark Pinnock said that "we have before us a significant volume in Christian theology written by a leading American Pentecostal scholar."[18] Macchia has authored several books and many articles; his primary works are *Justified in the Spirit* and *Baptized in the Spirit*. Both works are an attempt to contribute to the development of Pentecostal theology both systematically and ecumenically.

16. Webster, "Systematic Theology after Barth," 258
17. Whitney, *Problem and Promise*, 1.
18. Pinnock, "Review of Frank D. Macchia's *Baptized in the Spirit*," 1.

Macchia is an important voice because of his theological commitments and ecumenical concerns; but it is that he represents a self-consciously Pentecostal scholar that is of most interest to me. Pentecostals are known as the people of the Spirit; but it has also been noted that, according to the *World Encyclopedia of Christianity*, approximately a quarter of the world's Christians fit this description. Remarkably, whereas in 1970 less than 10 percent of Christians identified with Pentecostalism, by 2025, fully one-third may be Pentecostal."[19] The rising interest and global impact of Pentecostal theology led me to engage with a Pentecostal scholar. Macchia is an ideal conversation partner due to his Pentecostal identity and related Pneumatological commitments.

First, Macchia's personal commitment to Pentecostalism is well documented; he is writing as an insider of his particular Pentecostal theology. Macchia says, "I came to cherish most from my Pentecostal heritage its strong sense of calling from God toward some form of gifted ministry . . . "[20] The Pentecostal distinctive of Spirit baptism is normally a reference to a personal encounter with the divine that is either transformative or salvific, or both. Macchia's theological background does not necessarily overshadow this important element in his account of Pentecostal theology, for he says that Spirit baptism is a " . . . participatory metaphor of our relationship with God that is to have a significant experiential effect."[21] This way, Macchia is truly a Pentecostal scholar and not a scholar of Pentecostalism. As a theologian, Macchia is also attempting to develop a systematic account of Pentecostal theology that takes into account the tradition of the Church, recent revival in Trinitarian theologies, and a more systematic approach to the Holy Spirit.

Another reason for including Macchia is that he develops an account of the Holy Spirit which places an emphasis on the active personal agency of the Holy Spirit in the immanent and economic life of God. Macchia desires to move Pentecostalism beyond a subjective empowering approach to Pneumatology, towards a theology which stresses the active personal agency of the Holy Spirit. This he does by developing the metaphor of Spirit baptism. That is, Macchia derives his theology from the foundational experience of salvation so that Spirit baptism is construed as "a metaphor of life in the Spirit."[22] The Spirit is not a passive participant who simply imparts divine energy placed at the disposal of the individual. The Spirit is an active agent

19. Miller and Yamamori, *Global Pentecostalism*, 18.
20. Macchia, *Baptized in the Spirit*, 13–14.
21. Ibid., 32.
22. Ibid., 91.

who acts in a free manner in creation to redeem it and prepare it as God's future dwelling place. Macchia's Trinitarian theology is shaped primarily by our experience of salvation, and not from commitments to creeds or human reasoning. After the Word is received, the Holy Spirit moves us to receive the Gospel in faith. So even prior to deep theological reflection, but after faith, the doctrine of the Trinity is simply implied as a matter of the Christian faith. The Trinity is implied when we recognize Christ as our redeemer and during our worship of Him. The Trinity is implied when we acknowledge the "Holy Spirit as God's presence among us and in our assumption that God is a circle of love into which we come for fellowship."[23] As we will see later, Macchia's metaphor of Spirit baptism is appropriated as the bond of love between the Father and the Son; as that which empowers the incarnated Christ; and as that which the risen Christ empowers his believers. The point being that for Macchia, none of this takes places unless the Holy Spirit is recognized as an active personal agent who is given as a gift between the Father and Son, who in turn redeems creation as a gift from the Father to bring creation into the loving embrace of the divine communion.

Secondly, the inclusion of Macchia is that he also believes that Pneumatology must be a formative part of all theological *loci*. Macchia construes justification in broader aspects than a moment in the *ordo salutis*; without the Spirit as part of justification, as the very substance of justification, there cannot possibly be a proper Trinitarian view of the doctrine of justification. This is because, "justification as a Trinitarian act must be accessed by the Spirit and in relationship to the Son."[24] Justification is forensic, but also experiential, it is imputed and imparted to us. This way, justification involves an experiential element of the Spirit so that Spirit baptism expands the role of the Holy Spirit as an active agent in all areas of other doctrines. Jesus is the Spirit baptizer, the one who has the right from the Father to baptize creation with the Holy Spirit. This way, through a soteriological lens, Macchia is able to define the deity of Christ in Trinitarian terms that also emphasizes the agency of the Holy Spirit. In other words, it is not reasoning about the two natures of Christ, but the presence of the Spirit in Jesus' baptism that aids in determining the deity of Christ. This tracks Pannenberg's view that,

> The involvement of the Spirit in God's presence in the work of Jesus and in the fellowship of the Son with the Father is the basis of the fact that the Christian understanding of God found its developed and definitive form in the doctrine of the Trinity and not in a biunity of the Father and the Son . . . If the Spirit were

23. *The Trinity*, xii.
24. *Justified in the Spirit*, 294.

not constitutive for the fellowship of the Son with the Father, the Christian doctrine of the deity of the Spirit would be a purely external addition to the confession of the relation of the Son to the deity of the Father.[25]

The point being, because Jesus saves by pouring out the Spirit by the will of the Father, his deity is reliant on the divine agency of the Spirit to return creation back to the Father. Macchia's Trinitarian commitments leads him to the logical conclusion that each member of the Trinity is a necessary and active agent at all points in the unfolding of salvation, for that is the way it is experienced. Only God the Creator can save: the Father is divine since He is the source of all living things and saves through the Son and the Holy Spirit; the Son, Jesus Christ, is divine because He saves through His conquering death and giving new life through the agency of the Holy Spirit; "The Holy Spirit is divine because the Spirit perfects salvation by making all things new, in the Son and to the glory of the Father."[26] The Holy Spirit is an active personal agent in all areas of Christian life considered by theology, especially in the doctrines of creation, redemption and the final consummation.

Macchia's theology fulfills the eschatological requirement for Pneumatology because the Holy Spirit is acting in our present reality to prepare creation to be fully indwelled in the eschaton with the presence of God. The goal is that Christ "fill all things" (Eph 4:10), and that God be "all in all" (1 Cor 15:28); this way the metaphor of Spirit baptism allows for eschatological movement in which creation will become the temple of God's presence. Macchia maintains a Pentecostal distinctive of Spirit baptism and eschatological focus by stating that "eschatology is an aspect of Spirit baptism—and not the other way around."[27] Therefore, a major concept for Macchia is that the eschatological goal of creation is becoming the habitation of God (cf. Eph 4:7–10; rev. 21:3–5). So, "in the meantime, humans experience Spirit baptism as the Spirit is manifested to their experience in moments of ecstasy and of self-giving. Ecstasy is not only an emotion but is also a sense that one can transcend oneself in embracing God and the neighbor."[28] Therefore, Macchia's Pneumatology has a strong emphasis on the eschatological role of the Holy Spirit as the agent who completes the Father's will of redeeming His creation by fully indwelling it at the consummation.

---

25. Pannenberg, *Systematic Theology*, 1:268.
26. Macchia, *The Trinity*, 40.
27. *Justified in the Spirit*, 94.
28. Ibid., 97.

So, discussion of Macchia's theology in this work, as with Gunton, is strategic. His particular re-interpretation of Pentecostal theology leads him to a unique systematic approach, an approach that defines the Holy Spirit as a personal divine agent, and not simply a description of God's presence in the believer. The Holy Spirit is an active agent in the doctrine of God proper, creation, Christology, and eschatology. As we will see, Macchia construes Pneumatology in a similar manner as Gunton, primarily because Macchia is motivated by reflection upon Pentecostal personal experiences of salvation, whereas Gunton is attempting to begin with the revelation of scripture and the tradition.

Our concentrated study of Gunton and Macchia is further justified in that both theologians draw strong inferences from the movement of the Holy Spirit within ecclesiology—that is the new community that is formed by the Holy Spirit. The church of Christ is an expression of the Holy Spirit's work in concrete form; the Holy Spirit creates a new community of reconciliation that reflects the church's communion with the Trinity. Gunton stresses the constitutive action of the Holy Spirit in forming the community; it is an eschatological perfecting action that perfects the will of the Father through Jesus Christ. For Macchia, the church is the new community that reflects the divine *koinonia* that is brought about in creation by Jesus Christ when he baptizes creation with the Holy Spirit. Gunton begins with the revelation of God and moves to the community, whereas, Macchia begins with soteriology and ecclesiology because it is in the church where salvation through the Word happens. So both theologians' Pneumatology culminates in relational terms as expressed in the *koinonia* of the community, as a reflection of the divine life of God and the economic work of the Trinity with an accent on the eschatological perfecting work of the Holy Spirit.

Since Gunton and Macchia have both been influenced by the theology of John Zizoulas, it is of no surprise that personhood and Pneumatology are integral in shaping their understanding of what it is to be a person. The recent interest in relationality as constitutive of our reality, including the person, seems to require that a theologian must at least interact with relationality when developing a systematic account of theology. Ernest Simmons says that, "the basic vision of reality shifted from giving priority to permanence to that of change. Substantive ontology was dead, and relational ontology was born."[29] Both Gunton and Macchia are theologians who take relational ontology quite seriously. Typically, the term 'person' in modern usage is non-relational, it is a referent to the individual autonomous self. But due to the influence of individuals like Kant, Einstein and John Macmurray, many

---

29. Simmons, *The Entangled Trinity*, 35.

theologians adhere to a view of 'person' in relational terms. The shift to a relational ontology results in a theological model that constructs the constitution of the person in relational terms. Gunton's pneumatology creates two types of relations for the Holy Spirit, one active and one passive. The active relationship is seen as the Spirit is a person who constitutes the relation of the Father and Son, but is simultaneously passive in that the He is also constituted by His relation to the Father and Son. The Father and Son are who they are because of their relation with the Holy Spirit, and the Holy Spirit is the Spirit due to His relation with the Father and Son. This way, the Spirit perfects personhood, while having His personhood constituted by His relation with the other two divine persons. As the constitutive perfecting agent of personhood-in-relation, the Holy Spirit's role in redemption becomes concrete when communities are being formed in an onto-relational manner. Communities that reflect the work of the Holy Spirit are formed by distinctions but yet are constituted by relationships with God and with others. Both Gunton and Macchia understand the Holy Spirit as the perfector of community, of *koinonia*: both terms reflect the idea that the individual person is constituted by the relations which take place in the community of Christ. The 'person' of the Holy Spirit is both constitutive and transformative; constitutive in the sense that the Holy Spirit is constituted as a divine person by relations; and transformative in the sense that the "person" of the Holy Spirit is transforming creation's reality towards community. This way, Gunton and Macchia provide the theological currency in Reformed and Pentecostal theologies to express the transforming power of the Holy Spirit to bring about *koinonia* in the Godhead (albeit in a logical, non-temporal sense) and within God's created order.

Goals

In what follows, I review and analyze accounts of the Holy Spirit offered by Gunton and Macchia across the theological categories of the doctrine of God, Pneumatology, Christology, and Ecclesiology. The goal is to engage in a sympathetic exegesis of their material, albeit with a critical assessment and evaluation of the success of their endeavors. The ultimate aim is to ascertain and demonstrate the place of the active personal agency of the Holy Spirit as an essential aspect of their treatment of all theological *loci* within their works. I will argue that as both Gunton and Macchia make patent, Pneumatology cannot be an afterthought, but is an essential doctrine to Christian theology. I will argue, by using Gunton and Macchia as conversation partners, that the Holy Spirit is not a passive participant or merely an empowering force that awakens the subjective in humanity, but is an active personal Trinitarian agent in creation, redemption, and eschatology. I will demonstrate that the Holy Spirit is necessary for God to be God; and that the Holy Spirit plays an active role in Christology; and finally, that the Holy Spirit is an active and essential personal agent in the creation, sustaining and perfecting of the church. Finally, I will also demonstrate that the Holy Spirit is necessary in order to conceive of salvation as a cosmic reality, meaning that the entire created order is being redeemed by God in Christ.

Outline and Format

I have chosen to develop this paper in a chiastic structure in order to remain faithful to Gunton's and Macchia's contrasting orders of exposition in their theology. It is Barth's assertion that God's attributes must be defined from within the divine revelation of God as Father, Son and Spirit that serves as the basis of Gunton's theological project. This way, the revelation of scripture is revelatory when viewed as the *acts* of God as Father, Son and Spirit in history.[30] God reveals Himself as a subject, and not as an object. So the order of theological presentation for Gunton is to begin with the doctrine of God as Father, Son, and Holy Spirit because the economy of God reveals God; and then he moves through the remaining theological categories with a thorough systematic account of God as our Triune redeemer.

On the other hand, Macchia is not overly concerned with epistemological issues, or a proper ordering of theological *loci*. Emil Brunner says that "revelation is not only the means through which God shows us Himself, as He is; but revelation is the flowering of the Divine Nature itself.[31] So for Macchia, revelation is a Trinitarian event which culminates in the experience of baptism in the Holy Spirit. For Brunner, revelation is associated with God's attribute of love; when God reveals Himself he also reveals that "He is the One who loves."[32] Macchia comments that "divine love is not an intellectual concept but an event: the event of the incarnation, the cross, the resurrection, and the outpouring of the Spirit on all flesh."[33] For Brun-

---

30. Barth says, "If we really want to understand revelation in terms of its subject, i.e., God, then the first thing we have to realise is that this subject, God, the Revealer, is identical with His act in revelation and also identical with its effect. It is from this fact, which in the first instance we are merely indicating, that we learn we must begin the doctrine of revelation with the doctrine of the triune God" (see Barth, *The Church Dogmatics*, I/1:296).

31. Brunner, *The Christian Doctrine of God*, 188.

32. Ibid.,

33. Macchia, *Baptized in the Spirit*, 262.

ner and Macchia, God's revelation is God's self-communication of Himself. For Macchia, Baptism in the Holy Spirit is a Pentecostal metaphor that is multi-layered. In the context of revelation, baptism in the Spirit is a reference to the personal experience of the believer when they come to faith in Christ. This way, "Spirit baptism implies a 'baptism' in or with the very breath or Spirit of God, indicating a participatory metaphor of our relationship with God that is to have a significant experiential effect."[34] The 'participatory metaphor' indicates that Spirit baptism is a personal experience but one that takes place within the *koinonia* of God's self-communication. A *koinonia* which is experienced in the body of Christ as it is constituted by the Holy Spirit. Since *koinonia* is the place where revelation is first experienced, it seems both appropriate and faithful to Macchia's project to begin where the experience of revelation first takes place—within the new community of Jesus Christ. So returning back to theological categories, we will begin Macchia's account with Ecclesiology and work back to the doctrine of God. This will be more in-line with a theology that accents personal experience, while giving proper space and weight to the revelation as received in scripture and church tradition.

Also, I have chosen to associate the term 'communion' with Gunton, and '*koinonia*' with Macchia in order to stress their respective theological epistemologies–Gunton fundamentally stresses the place of revelation and Macchia stresses soteriology. In other words, Gunton shapes his theology from the divine action of God within the incarnation as revealed in scripture; and Macchia begins with the experience of salvation through the Word and Spirit, and then through theological reflection and induction determines the shape of his theology. Chapters 1 and 8 will explore the doctrine of God and the way the Holy Spirit is a necessary person who perfects God's *being*. In chapters 2 and 7, I will engage with Pneumatology proper in order to demonstrate that the Spirit is the personal agent of eschatological perfecting. In chapters 3 and 6, I will review Christology in order to develop a type of Spirit Christology that is faithful to Chalcedon but also accents the approach of the theologians. Finally, in 4 and 5, I will show that ecclesiology which is shaped by Pneumatology requires a communal and relational approach. So for both theologians, it is within Ecclesiology where their particular Pneumatology will find its most concrete expression. The chiastic structure allows for the accommodation of each individual theologian, while expressing the emphasis on the eschatological role of the Holy Spirit to constitute a community that has a proper relation to God and others.

34. Ibid., 32.

Colin Gunton: Pneumatology as Recovery of Relationality

Introduction

"Have we in the West of Christendom effectively forgotten the Trinity, so that we need to be reminded?"[1] With these words, Colin Gunton establishes the basis of his theology as decisively grounded in the Triune God. The doctrine of the Trinity is not simply an afterthought, or an appendix, but the essence of theology for Christianity; it provides *the* foundation and basis for all the categories of theology. Gunton cites a recent study by the British Council of Churches, which concluded that both the New Testament and the early Fathers grounded worship and prayer of the church in Trinitarian language;[2] as such, the Trinity is not relegated to theological discourse alone—it is necessary for an understanding of the Creator and his creation.[3] It is the doctrine of the Trinity, as an indispensable revelatory concept, that shapes all of Gunton's theology, hermeneutics, and philosophy. It is out of his concern that the doctrine of the Trinity has a logical priority in Christian epistemology that Gunton finds the basis for developing a proper account of Pneumatology. The Holy Spirit is not to be conceived as an afterthought to Christology or soteriology, but as an indispensable agent of both Christology and soteriology; for that matter, the Holy Spirit is indispensable in every theological category. In this work, we are not concerned so much with how Gunton develops his Trinitarian

---

1. Gunton, *Father, Son, and Holy Spirit*, 4.
2. Heron, *The Forgotten Trinity*,
3. Rahner says "[t]here must be a connection between Trinity and man. The Trinity is a mystery of salvation, otherwise it would never have been revealed" (Rahner, *The Trinity*, 21).

theology, but with how he shapes his Pneumatology in relation to the doctrine of God, Christology, and the church.

It is Gunton's Trinitarian theology that shapes his theological presentation, his ontological understanding of both divine and human persons, and his account of epistemology in relation to revelation and reality. For Gunton, our epistemological process involves God's acts because "that is the order of knowing: we know God (by his ostensive self-definition) from and in his acts. We know *who* God is from what he does."[4] As we will see later, it is Gunton's particular conception of the doctrine of revelation that shapes his doctrine of God, Pneumatology, Christology, and Ecclesiology. Revelation is the central idea in Gunton's theology that establishes the order of knowing and presentation because priority is given to the self-revealing God. This allows God's acts of revealing to precede and determine human reason as a gift and a guide to develop a proper account of reality which begins with an acknowledgement that God is our Creator. In order to distinguish Gunton's conception of revelation from others, and to ensure that the word "revelation" is not misconstrued due to it being pregnant with various meanings and interpretation, we will designate it as "mediated personal revelation."

Revelation begins with God because it is God's *self*-communication. It is not humanity's discovery of God, or an existential exercise whereby humanity discovers itself by conceptualizing God. Gunton says that "Revelation is God making h*imself* knowable; more than that, it is making the human intellect able to appropriate this knowledge."[5] Barth's understanding that God's attributes must be defined from within the revelatory acts of God as Father, Son, and Spirit is the basis of Gunton's theological project. The revelation of scripture is construed as the *acts* of God as Father, Son, and Spirit in our history which reveal God's nature. Barth states:

> If we really want to understand revelation in terms of its subject, i.e., God, then the first thing we have to realise is that this subject, God, the Revealer, is identical with His act in revelation and also identical with its effect. It is from this fact, which in the first instance we are merely indicating, that we learn we must begin the doctrine of revelation with the doctrine of the triune God.[6]

For our purposes, what matters is not merely that God is simply the source of revelation, but that he reveals *himself*. This knowledge from God is not an immediate type of knowledge which is given to the receiver directly by the Father, rather it is always on Gunton's account mediated knowledge,

---

4. Gunton, *Act and Being*, 97.
5. *Revelation and Reason*, 24.
6. Barth, *The Church Dogmatics*, I/1:296.

knowledge afforded by the Father's two hands (i.e. the Son and the Spirit) in our creaturely reality. Christoph Schwöbel observes that "mediation is a central implication of Gunton's theology."[7]

Paul Cumin is correct when he states that "when we recall the centrality of the concept of mediation for Gunton we have the key of understanding the connection between [Christ and creation]."[8] In the context of revelation, mediation allows for God's hiddenness while revealing his nature to creation through the acts of the Son and the Holy Spirit. Mediation is an event that begins and ends with God as a Trinitarian being; and it is also an indirect event that God brings about through creaturely means. It is a Trinitarian event in that mediation engages both Christological and Pneumatological aspects of theology. Regarding mediated knowledge, Gunton says that "central to this is John's pneumatology, which makes it clear that knowledge is being brought into relation with God the Father through the mediation of Jesus Christ: the Spirit leads into all truth."[9] This way, the actions of God in the Incarnation is the Father's ultimate expression of this self-communication of himself to creation. Gunton says,

> in sum God's being is known in and through his action, his triune act. God's action is triune in the sense that it is the action of Father, Son and Spirit, whose *opera ad extra* are inseparable from one another, though they are distributed, so to speak, between the three persons: the Father being the originating source of action, which he performs through the Son's involvement in the created world and the Spirit's perfecting of created things in anticipation of and on the Last Day.[10]

Mediation is also an economic act in that God indirectly communicates himself to creation through creaturely means. God communicates through the human nature of Christ; through the use of human writers who were inspired by the Holy Spirit; through the selection of the canon by the church; and also by the reading of the text by the individual. In the context of revelation and the economic acts, this means that central to Gunton's thought is that the proper order of knowing comes about through God's mediated revelation which begins with the free acts of the Triune God. Those acts which are witnessed by creation in the economic activity of God which finds ultimate expression in the Incarnation. To repeat our earlier claim, for Gunton our human epistemological processes involve God's acts because

7. Schwöbel, "The Shape of Colin Gunton's Theology," 197.
8. Cumin, "The Taste of Cake," 72.
9. Gunton, *Revelation and Reason*, 20.
10. *Act and Being*, 113.

"that is the order of knowing: we know God (by his ostensive self-definition) from and in his acts. We know *who* God is from what he does."[11] The expectation is that as finite creatures we will not be able to fully comprehend the impenetrable nature of God. But that does not mean that revelation is not related to reality; truth does not have to be exhaustive for it to be true. So, we can add to our understanding of revelation as a free act of God to reveal himself to his creatures through the mediation of the Son and the Holy Spirit who are free to use creaturely means to communicate God's self. At this point, it is necessary to review how Gunton understands revelation to be true without being exhaustive.

Gunton is defining revelation against two streams of thought, one philosophical, the other theological. Historians of philosophy tend to categorize British and continental philosophy as rationalist or empiricist. Kenny explains that "the continentals were rationalists, trusting to the speculations of reason, and the British were empiricists, basing knowledge on the experience of the senses."[12] Gunton's assessment of the history of philosophy leads him to categorize most non-theistic epistemologies as rationalistic. The rationalism of Descartes, the empiricism of Hume, and even the logical positivism of the Vienna Circle, were all described as giving priority to human reason as the arbiter of reality.[13] It is not simply the priority of reason, but that the rationalist, empiricist, and logical positivists deny truth unless it adheres to their strict rules of rationalistic certainty. So philosophically speaking, modern philosophy denies revelation as a valid source of truth; instead it privileges human reasoning as the valid source and arbiter for truth. On the other hand, theologically speaking, Gunton finds that the view of revelation in liberal theology tends towards an immediacy which gives priority to the subjective over the objective revelation from God. In a summation, Gunton says that we meet, "in the person of Kant, a rationalism of the moral agent…[and] with Schleiermacher, a form of rationalism of experience, the effect of which is to emasculate traditional doctrines of the atonement, destroying their base in the historic redemptive action of God and producing a reductionist account of their language."[14] Then when he describes Hegel, he says that "we come to what is best called conceptual rationalism, which is a third way of limiting and narrowing the way in which

---

11. Ibid., 97.

12. Kenny, *A New History of Western Philosophy*, 127.

13. For example, Lowe states that "the logical positivists condemned as meaningless all 'metaphysical' statements which failed to reduce either to logical tautologies or else to empirically verifiable claims of the sort that science supposedly deals with" (Lowe, "Metaphysics," 448).

14. Gunton, *The Actuality of Atonement*, 16.

words may be conceived to express meaning and truth."[15] What we see is that Gunton interprets those theologies which have their roots in Schleiermacher and the left-wing Hegelians as reducing the role of propositions and the traditions of the Church in favor of internal feelings of an immediately given revelation.[16] So philosophically and theologically speaking, there is a tendency in the West to promote rationalistic thought or subjective inner feelings as the ultimate source of knowledge about reality. In order to overcome the deficiencies of rationalistic certainty and a liberal theological account of revelation which degrades both propositions and the traditions as primary sources of mediated revelation, Gunton adopts Locke's ideas of "nominal essence" and "ostensive definition."

In the case of Locke's nominal essence, Gunton is concerned with *definitions* themselves. Gunton says, "A definition can be open, in the sense of indicating some of the things characteristic of a person or thing, but never exhaustive—[thus] Locke's nominal essence."[17] Gunton is not concerned with Locke's preoccupation with scholasticism's realist metaphysics[18], but with his ability to allow for one level of understanding to be based on an unknown, but real, existence. For Locke, a "nominal essence" is created by the human mind, but nevertheless, it corresponds in some way to reality.

Gunton is not attempting to endorse a type a nominalism, he is developing a concept of *definition* which allows him to know something about a given object without the requirement of Cartesian certainty. In reference to Locke's usage of universals, Gibson says that, "Generality, however, though it is 'something imperfect, which cannot exist,' has its foundation in experience and in reality."[19] For Locke, universals are a product of our mind, our understanding. So, for Gunton, Locke developed a method for grounding our *understanding* of the essence of something in the reality of our experience. Again Gibson: "The general idea, that product of the mind's own workmanship, does not falsify the reality presented to us in experience,

---

15. Ibid., 16–17.

16. Roles says that "the rejection of a transcendent God and the identification of God with man underline the extreme humanism that characterized not only Strasuss' thought but the thought of all the Young [i.e., Left] Hegelians" (Nola, "The Young Hegelian," 292). The point is that the Left Hegelians stressed the thought of humankind as defining religion, especially Christianity. There is nothing *out there* to send a revelation; revelation is a construct *from* and *of* the human mind.

17. Gunton, *Act and Being*, 95.

18. Gibson says that Locke's "criticism is directed against what he regarded as an implication of scholastic Realism" (see Gibson, *Locke's Theory of Knowledge and Its Historical Relations*, 202).

19. Ibid.

but furnishes an indispensable instrument for our comprehension of it."[20] Gunton adopts Locke at this stage because of his stress on the particular and his anti-Cartesian epistemology, both of which led Locke to conclude that our general concepts are based on reality: nominal essences coexist with real essences.[21] What this means is that our understanding of reality does not have to comport with rationalistic philosophies that require *a priori* or empirical approaches that require absolute certainty for knowledge to be true knowledge.

This leads us to the second epistemological concept Gunton takes up for his own theological purposes, namely "ostensive definitions." W.E. Johnson was one of the early adopters of the term "ostensive definition"; so we will turn to his work for an insight into Gunton's usage of the term.[22] Johnson describes the use of "proper names" and "articles" in his work *Logic*. Johnson defines two types of *names*; descriptive and proper. A descriptive name is adjectival or relational, in that it has an indefinite connotation; where a proper name has a more definite connotation. What Johnson is explaining is that even within descriptive names (e.g., "the 43rd President of the United States") there must be an element of the proper name for the referent to have any meaning. In this way, a proper name is directed to an object "which is identical with the object to which it may have been previously understood as applying in another proposition."[23] So for Johnson, since a descriptive phrase can actually refer to a proper name, " . . . what it factually indicates is indistinguishable from what it means." Johnson, *Logic*,[24] Johnson's work is more nuanced and involved, but it is necessary to give a brief summation of

---

20. Ibid.

21. "By this real essence, I mean, that real constitution of any thing, which is the foundation of all those properties that are combined in, and are constantly found to co-exist with, the nominal essence; that particular constitution which every thing has within itself, without any relation to anything without it. But essence, even in this sense, relates to a sort, and supposes a species" (see Locke, *An Essay concerning Human Understanding* 3.6.6; p. 323).

22. "Johnson invents phrases and also attaches new meanings to familiar words. His terms determinate, determinable, occurrent, continuant and ostensive definition have entered the philosophical lexicon. Some of his innovations are largely forgotten" (see Sanford, *Determinates vs. Determinables*).

23. Johnson, *Logic*, 83.

24. Ibid., 93. Johnson develops four basic categories of articles: Indefinite Indefinite (or, Alternative Indefinite); Definite Indefinite (or Instantial Indefinite, or Introductory Indefinite); Indefinite Definite (or Contextual Definite); Definite Definite (that is, the understood referent is not dependent on context). Johnson determines that "this" and "that" are special forms of his Indefinite Definite, or contextual definite article. "This" and "that," when used as demonstratives, serves to point out, or identify, an object to the senses, in an unambiguous manner.

his purpose for using "ostensive definitions." First, Johnson concludes that "it seems legitimate or possible to define a proper name as a name which *means* the same as what it factually indicates."[25] Secondly, in respect to "ostensive definition" as a pointer to factuality, a proper name usually applies to an object whose existence takes place over some period of time and in some region of space. So, the appearance of this object to our senses provides the conditions for our imposing a name during the process of identification, or presenting that object as that which the name is being applied. For Johnson, this process of identification or presentation is what constitutes an ostensive definition. It must be kept in mind, that the object must be present in some form for an ostensive definition to take place; the object must be available to receive the definition imposed on it. It is not so much the process that Johnson is ultimately concerned with, but the notion that definitions are not limited to verbal absolute certainty to be valid. Ostensive definition of an object is just as valid. Kotarbinska states:

> In a broader interpretation, however, what is essential for ostensive definition is not the pointing gesture but the result which we want to obtain thereby. The aim is to distinguish in our surroundings a certain definite object and to draw to it the attention of the addressee of the definition in question.[26]

So, an "ostensive definition" is a valid tool that acts as a sign indicating something in reality, without having the burden of absolute rationalistic certainty.

Returning to Gunton's account of revelation, in light of the concepts of "nominal essence" and "ostensive definition," we find that together they allow for revelation as an external activity that impacts upon the human mind and they authorize propositions and traditions to serve as mediators of revelation. We find that a nominal essence corresponds, or coexists, with a real essence in such a manner that a definition is possible without obtaining absolute knowledge of the object. This allows Gunton to retain a hiddenness when defining God's attributes, but simultaneously say something about God that is true regarding his essence. On the other hand, we find that an "ostensive definition" is simply a sign that indicates a certain definite object to our senses, either visually or through verbal descriptions. Gunton combines these two ideas to describe how the narratives in scripture can

25. Ibid., 93–94.
26. Kotarbinska, "On Ostensive Definitions," 2. Kotarbinska also states, "And that can be done in various ways, not only by pointing at the object with the finger or by lifting that object or handling it in some other way, but also in a purely verbal manner, by mentioning its individual name in the definition statement" (ibid.).

lead to an epistemological discovery of God's attributes without completely revealing God's essence in totality. Gunton says, "generalizing, we can say that in scripture God is presented both narratively and creedally: in narratives of actions and in creedal summaries of the meaning of those actions."[27] For Gunton, the narratives in the Bible correspond to Locke's "nominal essence" in that they coexist with God's real essence; and methodologically, the narratives are ostensive in that they are signs pointing to a certain object, God.[28] In other words, "nominal essence" and "ostensive definition" are being used to express the connection between God's being with his revealed acts. As with Locke's "nominal essence," the revelation is a real revelation but not exhaustive.[29] In this case, the supreme revelation in scripture is found in Jesus Christ, which is primarily a narrative account of an interaction between the Father, Son, and Holy Spirit to redeem creation.

By using the narrative accounts of scripture, Gunton concludes that "the essence of God is known pre- and extra-trinitarianly; once that is sketched in, we treat the attributes deriving from the persons."[30] So the acts of God are considered an "ostensive definition," which indicate God's "nominal essence"; and both taken together actually correspond to God's triune being. For in Christ, the acts of God are revealed by their "ostensive definition" of God as Father, Son, and Holy Spirit; so God's self-revelation is his "nominal essence" as Father, Son, and Holy Spirit. But, this "nominal essence" coexists with his "real essence," so that we can confidently claim that God revealed himself as Father, Son, and Holy Spirit through his ostensive

27. Gunton, *Act and Being*, 96.

28. Haight expresses a similar idea. He states that "[t]he medium through which religious experience takes place may also be called a symbol, making all religious knowledge symbolic knowledge. A symbol is that through which something else is made present and known; a symbol mediates a perception and knowledge of something other than itself . . . Thus when one experiences God in any finite situation or medium or symbol, God is experienced as utterly transcendent, beyond the symbol, and other than the symbol. Yet one must also say that insofar as God is experienced in and through any given symbol, God is present to the symbol and through it to human consciousness" (Haight, "Spirit Christology," 263).

29. For some, without a complete exhaustion in the description of an object (in this case God), or at least knowledge that adheres to rules of reason, there is no real knowledge of the essence of the object (in this case God). For example, A. J. Ayer says, regarding the possibility of religious knowledge, "that this possibility has already been ruled out by our treatment of metaphysics. It is now generally admitted, at any rate by philosophers, that the existence of a being having the attributes which define the god of any non-animistic religion cannot be demonstratively proved . . . If the conclusion that a god exists is to be demonstratively certain, then these premises must be certain . . . [for] it is only *a priori* propositions that are logically certain" (Ayer, *Language, Truth and Logic*, 119).

30. Gunton, *Act and Being*, 96.

acts because he really is Father, Son, and Holy Spirit. The result of this discussion is that God's revelation through propositional knowledge, while not being exhaustive, is still factual and based in the reality of the object who gives the revelation. But this is not enough for Gunton, for there is a knowledge that is superior to propositional and rational knowledge—that is personal knowledge.

Gunton now encapsulates his mediated revelation within the further suggestion that revelation is *personal*. The idea that revelation is personal knowledge performs a wide undertaking in regards to theological epistemology. Personal knowledge involves the self-giving of a subject to another subject, in this case God is the person who is revealing himself. Gunton says that "this knowledge has to be understood as knowledge in relation, in relationship."[31] Revelation is mediated through relationships: it is mediated through the relations human beings have with the risen Christ, the Holy Spirit, the Biblical text, and the Church. This personal knowledge is based on faith and is superior to factual knowledge alone. Faith is not merely an ascent to facts, but a trust in God which is expressed by the individual's life and finds its expression in worship. Gunton states that "Christians are in a form of relationship, rightly characterized as "knowledge" which is the gift of the eschatological Spirit, and therefore not necessarily shared by those without that faith."[32] So based on knowledge as an "ostensive definition," revelation is also God's self-disclosure as indirect mediated personal knowledge.

Since revelation is God's self-disclosure and is personal knowledge, revelation must begin with God. Gunton explains that God reveals himself to his creatures through strict limits which he established: "[t]he Creator is known only insofar as he interacts with the creation."[33] Since revelation begins with God himself, all areas of theology are therefore bound to God's self-disclosure: Revelation points to God, while simultaneously, revelation originates with God. Gunton explains that, "revelation is therefore of a God who creates, conserves, saves, calls into the community of praise, and redeems; although, given that things are as they are, he is primarily and centrally revealed through his saving action."[34] Since God personally saves, revelation requires an initiative by God himself. This way the character of divine revelation is both Christological and Pneumatological. It is Christological because Jesus Christ is the ultimate expression of God's

---

31. *Revelation and Reason*, 20.
32. Ibid., 22.
33. Ibid.
34. *A Brief Theology of Revelation*, 112.

self-communication to his creation. It is Pneumatological in that a personal mediated knowledge requires relationship and openness. This means that the eschatological work of the Holy Spirit is necessary in order for revelation to remain a continual work of God as a gift to creation: revelation is eschatological; it is an awaiting for the future revealing of Jesus Christ.

So, we can now define Revelation as a free act of God whereby he freely discloses himself to his creatures through the mediation of the Son and the Holy Spirit who are themselves free to use creaturely means to communicate God's self; this act gives rise to propositional statements as ostensive signs that point to God's essence while simultaneously maintaining the hiddenness of God; all of which culminates in a mediated personal knowledge of God as Father, Son, and Holy Spirit. This revelation is propositional in form and related to reality, but is ultimately relational because it is a function of the relation that begins with the Triune God and involves participation by humanity in the divine communion through the saving acts of Jesus Christ and the life-giving Spirit. Since God's acts cannot be separated from his being, and his revelation is his self-communication, it is safe to assert that a mediated personal revelation is the foundation for Gunton's theological project. If we want to know about God, we have to look to his revelatory acts in scripture by means of which he gives himself to us and upholds us in personal relationship with him. Gunton's logic is that 1) revelation is mediated; 2) scripture has the capacity to inform us about God's being; 3) and revelation is open—meaning the Church's doctrines over the years are part of God's continual revelation; 4) therefore, God as Father, Son, and Holy Spirit is defined *within* his revelation. Gunton will not allow *a priori* rationalistic conception about God to have priority over the acts of God, especially as expressed in the incarnation. As we will see later, Macchia's Pneumatology is more concerned with the experience of salvation. By contrast, Gunton's Pneumatology is an extension of his particular theological epistemology. The Holy Spirit is approached and understood with consistent reference to those redeeming acts of God attested in scripture, to the life of the Church, to the creeds and to wherever else it is that the Spirit appropriates to reveal truth. So, the order of knowing begins with God's revelation of himself, which has a direct impact in both the order of being and presentation. Without God actively and willingly informing us about himself, we would not be able to discern God's triune existence. Since God is the Creator, and the self-revealing One, it seems proper to begin with God when presenting a theological account of God and his activities. This way, revelation is behind Gunton's account of theology, in that the acts of God, which come about in our historical existence, is where we are to learn about God. Therefore, the doctrine of God, Pneumatology, Christology, and

Ecclesiology are all defined and shaped by Gunton's doctrine of revelation as a mediated personal revelation event.

What we will find is that for Gunton, the doctrine of God shapes his theology, because for Gunton, God's being is grounded in the communion of the Father, Son, and Spirit. It is the relation between the three persons, which is expressed using *perichoresis,* which determines not only God's being, but also his actions *in* and *towards* his creation. Relationality becomes a key determinate for shaping his theological and philosophical content to the point that "relation" is conceived as an ontological category for Gunton— the ultimate expression of reality is to be found in communion. It is the perfecting and eschatological action of the Holy Spirit to bring communion to creation. The Holy Spirit is the agent who provides the "bond of love" between the Father and the Son, thereby providing God with divine power to reach out to his creation establishing a communion between God and his creatures. Since for Gunton the doctrine of God is essential, we will examine how communion is a constitutive element in his social trinitarian model.

Next, we will examine how communion also shapes Gunton's construction of Pneumatology proper. The Holy Spirit is not simply an addendum for other theological categories, but he is essential in completing all theological categories. We will see that Gunton is not interested in proving the deity or equality of the Spirit, but providing a paradigm that gives theology the tools necessary to locate the work of the Spirit in all categories of theology. The Holy Spirit is the eschatological perfecting agent of God's being and all his economic works in relation to creation. Gunton demonstrates the necessity of the Spirit to God's being, which is a being-in-communion, by perfecting that communion through free relations. This divine action of the Spirit is also seen in creation as the eschatological agent of perfecting communion; communion with God and within creation itself—the Holy Spirit perfects communion.

Also, since the Father mediates his works in creation with his two hands, it is essential that we examine Gunton's Christology in order to determine how the Holy Spirit shapes the life of Christ. The Holy Spirit for Gunton liberates Jesus Christ's humanity to be *that* particular messiah by maintaining a free relationship between the Father and Jesus Christ. Gunton ultimately borrows elements of Spirit Christology from John Owen and Edward Irving to reconfigure Christology so that the Spirit is an empowering presence to Christ's humanity so that the human nature of Christ is liberated from the effects of sin, which results in the freedom to be obedient to the Father's will.

Finally, Gunton's ecclesiology will demonstrate the concrete reality in creation where the Spirit's work as the perfector of communion takes place.

The Spirit works in creation, but for Gunton that work is best expressed in the church. The church is where new networks of relations are created and shaped by the Spirit through the Word of the Father. The Spirit is a down payment to the church that presents an instance in the present of the future reality that God will complete. A future that is a perfection of the vertical communion with the Triune God, and the horizontal communion with other human beings and the created order.

We are not interested in developing a full-blown account of Gunton's doctrine of God, creation, and theology; mostly because space will not permit, but also because there are other accounts that have attempted this task. The goal of examining Gunton's Pneumatology is to demonstrate that communion is an essential part of Pneumatology, and that the Holy Spirit must be conceived as an active and necessary agent in God's divine life, creation, redemption, and the *eschaton*. So, we will turn to Gunton's doctrine of God in order to demonstrate that his Pneumatology is the grounds of communion. In other words, in respect to Pneumatology, Gunton's doctrine of God is based on God's self-revelation as a divine triune communion, then this same self-disclosure and self-communication by God establishes the ontological basis of communion.

Chapter 1

The Doctrine of God: Being as Being-in-Communion

Introduction

THE DOCTRINE OF GOD is that which shapes our understanding of creation itself, and our place within creation; but it also shapes our understanding of Christian theology, especially God's economic activity. Herman Bavinck says that

> the knowledge of God is the only dogma, the exclusive content, of the entire field of dogmatics. All the doctrines treated in dogmatics, whether they concern the universe, humanity, Christ, and so forth, are but the explication of the one central dogma of the knowledge of God. All things are considered in light of God, subsumed under him, traced back to him as the starting point. Dogmatics is always called upon to ponder and describe God and God alone, whose glory is in creation and re-creation, in nature and grace, in the world and in the church. It is the knowledge of him alone that dogmatics must put on display.[1]

The doctrine of God is a central theme throughout Gunton's corpus: for if God is the creator of our reality, then it follows that God's self-revelation of himself should have an impact on how we develop an account of creation itself. The doctrine of God is only possible because of God's self-disclosure through his acts in creation. This way, what we know about God begins with God's free will decision to give of himself in revelation to us. Hans Schaeffer's states, "Colin Gunton's theology can be summarised as a quest for a Trinitarian ontology."[2] Schaeffer continues his evaluation of

1. Bavinck, *Reformed Dogmatics*, 2:29.
2. Schaeffer, *Createdness and Ethics*, 27.

Gunton by averring that the doctrine of God serves as the means to evaluate and resolve problems in those earlier accounts of the Trinity which limited the role of the Holy Spirit. The doctrine of God, which really means the doctrine of the Trinity, is that which serves as the relation between God and his creation; we learn about ourselves by learning about God. William Whitney's survey of Gunton's doctrine of creation argues "that for Gunton, if one is to understand the triune nature of God, then one must grasp the unity of divine action in the created order, and this includes God's action in salvation and eschatological perfection."[3]

Gunton does not break any new ground regarding our knowledge of God as Father, Son, and Spirit; the tradition of the Church has established the Triune nature of God. For Gunton, it is the understanding of God as triune that gives shape to all Christian theology in such a way that the doctrine of the Trinity has a logical priority in the order of knowing about God and his relation to creation. It is not just the doctrine of the Trinity, but the immanent Trinity that has logical priority. The economic points to the immanent life of God, which in turn has logical priority over the development of the rest of Christian doctrine. Gunton says that "because God is, 'before' creation took place, already a being-in-relation, there is no need for him to create what is other than himself."[4] The economic activity of God reveals that God is a being-in-relation, and this must have decisive bearing on theology. Gunton says that "it is the Incarnation that determines both the reality and the limits of the knowledge of God. Therefore, we must accept that the limits to the knowledge of God are set Christologically, not philosophically."[5]

The doctrine of God has logical priority in Christian theology because God is the basis of creation's existence. Since God is the basis of creation's *being*, there should be some indication within creation of its Creator: "or said another way, who God is in his movement and relations towards the created order is who God is in his eternal being."[6] For Gunton, the relations between the infinite and the finite are to be found in his concept of "open transcendentals." Gunton states that,

> the error of imposing a priori philosophical categories on the being of God must also be avoided. If there are transcendentals, they have their being in the fact that God has created the world

---

3. Whitney, *Problem and Promise*, 2–3.
4. Gunton, *The Promise of Trinitarian Theology*, 142.
5. Gunton, *Revelation and Reason*, 23.
6. Whitney, *Problem and Promise*, 101. Whitney also says that "Gunton never tired of championing this point" (ibid.).

in such a way that it bears the marks of its maker. They are not then the "forms through which being displays itself," because that might suggest a priority of "being" over God, but notions which can be predicated of all beings by virtue of the fact that God is creator and the world is creation.[7]

The doctrine of God has priority because the divine transcendentals are conceived by Gunton as a means of relating God to his creation—eternity meets time, infinity meets the finite. What we know about God is revealed in history through God's action in the incarnation, but once that knowledge is apprehended, then Christian theology can develop a systematic approach that is grounded in the revelation of God as Father, Son, and Spirit. Gunton says that "we cannot say it too often: Genesis presents an account of the knowledge of God the creator, not by negation but by affirmation of his power and absolute creativity, incomparable with anything attributed to the pagan gods."[8] God reveals himself not *in* creation, but *within* his economic acts of creation. Irenaeus, to whom Gunton repeatedly returns, says, "there is one only God, the Creator . . . he is Father, he is God, he the Founder, he the Maker, he the Creator, who made those things by himself, that is, through his Word and his Wisdom—heaven and earth, and the seas, and all things that are in them . . . he is the Father of our Lord Jesus Christ."[9] Gunton interprets Irenaeus to be determining God's attributes by reference to his act of creation, instead of philosophical speculation alone. It is the divine action of God that determines our way of being, and which in turn determines our understanding of God. Gunton says,

> Barth's project to bring revelation and being together is an implicit, and often explicit, reproach to much of the tradition. It establishes an important principle: that treatments of the being or essence of God must be trinitarian from the outset and that it must be trinitarianism which is based in, and a drawing out of the implications of, the economic Trinity: of how God reveals himself to be in the narratively identified economy of creation, reconciliation and redemption.[10]

So, it is God's acts in creation that determine our knowledge of God, because God's essence cannot be separated from his enacted being. Barth states,

7. Gunton, *The One, the Three, and the Many*, 136–37.
8. Gunton, *Act and Being*, 55.
9. Irenaeus of Lyons, *Irenaeus against Heresies* 2.30.9 (ANF 1:406).
10. Gunton, *Act and Being*, 98.

> but we have consistently followed the rule, which we regard as basic, that statements about the divine modes of being antecedently in themselves cannot be different in content from those that are to be made about their reality in revelation. All our statements concerning what is called the immanent Trinity have been reached simply as confirmations or underlinings or, materially, as the indispensable premises of the economic Trinity. They neither could nor would say anything other than that we must abide by the distinction and unity of the modes of being in God as they encounter us according to the witness of Scripture in the reality of God in His revelation. The reality of God in His revelation cannot be bracketed by an "only," as though somewhere behind His revelation there stood another reality of God; the reality of God which encounters us in His revelation is His reality in all the depths of eternity. This is why we have to take it so seriously precisely in His revelation.[11]

John McIntyre explains Barth at this juncture by saying that "a right understanding of the elements of the doctrine of the economic Trinity, especially as it relates to the activity of the God who is Father, Son and Holy Spirit as recorded in Scripture, commits us to the component elements of the doctrine of the immanent Trinity."[12] What all this means is that Christian theology must begin with a proper account of the doctrine of God that is grounded and shaped by the revelation of God as Father, Son, and Holy Spirit.

Gunton postulates that transcendentals, conceived trinitarianly, elucidates the relationship between God and creation. Transcendentals are those marks of being that are derived from the revelation of God as Trinity. The Incarnation reveals God's action in creation, redemption, and eschatology. Gunton learned from Barth that those actions cannot be separated from God's being. This way, the divine action, as revealed in the incarnation of the Word, is where God relates to his creation; the determinants of open transcendentals as found in Christ are also the determinants of the relation between God and his creatures. Therefore, the doctrine of God includes the idea of transcendentals as marks of being which are also applicable in creation, but as marks of created being. Julián Marías comments that "Hellenic philosophy had striven to solve the ap*oria* . . . of making the *Entity*—one, immovable and eternal—compatible with the th*ings*—*m*anifold, variable and transitory."[13] The problem of the "one and the many" is an underlying

---

11. Barth, *The Church Dogmatics*, 1/1:479.
12. McIntyre, *The Shape of Pneumatology*, 144.
13. Marías, *History of Philosophy*, 44.

concern for Gunton which represents the fundamental problem that is resolved by his particular doctrine of the Holy Spirit. Green says, "Gunton takes the perennial philosophical problem of the one and the many as the key theme of chapter 1 of *The One, the Three and the Many* (and it can be argued that this theme underpins Gunton's overarching theological program)."[14] In his work, *The One, The Three and The Many*, Gunton develops "trinitarian transcendentals"[15] in order to provide an ontology grounded in God's being and also relevant to creation. For Gunton "trinitarian conceptuality enables us to think of our world, in a way made impossible by the traditional choice between Heraclitus and Parmenides, as both, and in different respects, one and many, but also one and many in relation."[16] More than this, Gunton argues that a general Trinitarian solution is not enough: a proper account of the Spirit is necessary to overcome the problem of the one and the many. To this end, p*erichoresis*, substantiality, and relatedness form the nexus of Gunton's concept of "open transcendentals," which ultimately serves the purpose of relating creation to the triune God. Therefore, we will examine how Gunton describes and resolves the problem of the "one and the many" with the assumption that this is also of paramount significance for his view of personhood as constituted by the Spirit.

Gunton says that the shape of *The One, The Three and The Many* is "chiastic, because the reconstruction takes its orientation from the final chapter of the first part, in which the intellectual outcome of modernity, with its decline into various relativisms and subjectivisms, is charted."[17] The chiastic structure of the book corresponds to the structure to Gunton's theology; and also shapes his underlying theme of trinitarian transcendentals. Here is a summary of Gunton's chiastic structure, based on each chapter's content:

A—Chapter 1: "The problem of the one and the many in modern life and thought"

   B—Chapter 2: "The problem of the particular in modern life and thought"

      C—Chapter 3: "The problem of relatedness in modern life and thought"

         D—Chapter 4: "The problem of meaning and truth in modern life and thought"

---

14. Green, "Colin Gunton and the Theological Origin of Modernity," 167; bold emphasis added.

15. Gunton, *The One, the Three, and the Many*, 7.

16. Ibid.

17. Ibid., 5.

D'—Chapter 5: "Towards a theology of meaning and truth"

C'—Chapter 6: "Towards a theology of relatedness"

B'—Chapter 7: "Towards a theology of the particular"

A'—Chapter 8: "Towards a theology of the one and the many"

I propose to evaluate each part of the chiasm as a single unit with the purpose of demonstrating that Gunton's "trinitarian transcendentals" have an inherent and tacit quality within his theological project. In other words, Gunton's use of "trinitarian transcendentals" is the impetus for grounding his theology in the doctrine of God and creation; for the universal marks of being are to be found in God's self-disclosure as the Creator who is related to his creation through the mediation of the Son and the Holy Spirit.

Therefore, the two parts taken together as A/A' represent Gunton's understanding of God's threeness and unity; that is, his doctrine of God. The goal of Gunton's doctrine of God is not simply to explicate the Trinity, but to demonstrate that God's being is constituted by communion, a communion that is guaranteed by the divine action of the Holy Spirit.[18] Then in part B/B,'

---

18. Throughout Gunton's corpus, the words "constitute," "constituted," and "constituted by" are used with contextual fluidity. In light of God's nature, Gunton uses "constituted" and its variants in order to express that God's divine essence is not a stand-alone substance, but only exists with the three divine persons. Gunton is concerned that a static divine substance has an ontological and logical priority over the persons. Gunton says that, "in the case of God, [person] means that to speak of the *koinonia* or communion in which the being of God consists provides a concept of divine oneness in which the individuality of the particular persons is also stressed, because Father, Son and Spirit in their interrelatedness make God to be the God that he is" (*Father, Son, and Holy Spirit*, 46). Gunton feels that some Trinitarian theologies have been affected by Augustinian analogies which are based in neoplatonic thought, and that the outcome is . . . a view of an unknown substance *supporting* the three persons rather than *being constituted* by their relatedness" (*The Promise of Trinitarian Theology*, 42–43).

By stressing "constituted" over "subsistence," Gunton is not implying that God somehow derives his being from the three persons, in a causal manner. Instead, he is attempting to maintain the idea that the persons subsist in the divine nature, while simultaneously, the divine nature is constituted by the three divine persons. Gunton does not want a naked divine substance acting as a subject in which the divine persons are conceived as accidents or predicates. When the Trinitarian persons are conceived as subsisting *intrinsically* in the eternal Being of God (cf. Torrance, *Trinitarian Perspectives*, 27), Gunton asks, if they "really subsist, we may ask, but as what?" (Gunton, *Father, Son and Holy Spirit*, 47). This way, Gunton is in agreement with Zizioulas, who states, "No substance or nature exists without person or hypostasis or mode of existence. No person exists without substance or nature, *but* the ontological 'principle' or 'cause' of being—i.e. that which makes a thing to exists-is not the substance or nature but the *person* or hypostasis. Therefore being is traced back not to substance but to person" (Zizioulas, *Being as Communion*, 42–43).

Gunton's concern for particularity is developed. Particularity, theologically speaking, is construed within the framework of freedom and relationality. In this way, the doctrine of God characterizes what it means to be a person; in that, particularity is intimately connected with freedom in relation. But for Gunton, it is the divine action of the Holy Spirit—who perfects both the freedom and relationship of the Father and Son—that secures personhood in the divine life of God and in created reality. Finally, in parts C/C' the idea of relations is addressed, which ultimately leads to a definition of relation as an ontological category and a marker of being, i.e., transcendental. For Gunton, a proper account of Pneumatology will locate relationality within the work of the Holy Spirit; as a work of perfecting relationality that is grounded in the immanent life of God as the communion. We will not discuss part four, because it is related to epistemological issues, and our focus is on the revelation of God through mediated personal knowledge. The purpose of surveying Gunton's work on the Doctrine of God then is twofold: first, to demonstrate that God is a being-in-communion; and second, that the Holy Spirit is identified and understood to be perfector of the divine communion.

Also, the chiastic structure of the analysis of the "one and the many" indicates that the reader must be vigilant to keep in mind Gunton's "trinitarian transcendental" model, otherwise it is possible to misunderstand Gunton's meaning. Schwöbel explains that Gunton's quest is to understand transcendentals as "generated from the Trinity in which the one and the many, the particular and universal and the relationship between temporality and eternity are mediated in the communion of person which God is."[19] We will now turn to examine part A/A' in order to explicate Gunton's doctrine of God as a revelation that is derived from God's economic act which reveals God as a being-in-communion, which results in a view of creation that recognizes relationality as an ontological category.

Gunton is allergic to "subsistence" language due to his perception that it is related to substance metaphysics, which grounds the divine nature in notions of static divine nature. God is a dynamic being-in-communion: "This 'being in becoming' makes it impossible to conceive God in the old substantial categories" (Gunton, *Becoming and Being*, 143). If God's *being* is conceived as "being-in-becoming," Jüngel says "in that case one cannot think of God's being as subsistence in the sense in which Plato conceives οὐσία [being]" (Jüngel, *God's Being Is in Becoming*, 108). Zizioulas explains that "outside the Trinity there is no God, that is, no divine substance ... The personal existence of God (the Father) constitutes His Substance, makes it hypostases" (Zizioulas, *Being as Communion*, 41). The point of the discussion is to show that "constitutes" language is not causal or used to exemplify derivation from a prior source, but it is Gunton's method to give proper place to the three divine persons as a dynamic communion of mutual relations intrinsic to the divine substance.

19. Schwöbel, "The Shape of Colin Gunton's Theology," 200.

A. The Doctrine of God: An Ontology of Communion

The purpose of this section is to review Gunton's doctrine of God in order to determine the purchase that it affords his Pneumatology. Gunton's doctrine of God defines the basis of created ontology due to God's self-disclosure in his economic acts that establishes the markers of creaturely *being*. This way, transcendentals are conceived out of our knowledge of God in Christ. So ultimately, Gunton's approach to the doctrine of God not only impacts his theology proper, but also has implications for his doctrine of creation. The doctrine of God is approached as a revelatory enterprise; God's attributes are derived from God's acts throughout redemption history that culminates in the incarnation of Christ. By using transcendentals based on God and his creative and redemptive activity, Gunton creates a system where God and creation, or eternity and time, can be open to relations beyond the construal of God as a primary cause. At this stage, Gunton is concerned with establishing God's nature as communal; and then to flesh out the implications for creation.

Gunton uses the Doctrine of God to address the problem of the one and the many by developing an ontology in which the one and the many are not opposed but integrated into one conceptual model of being. Gunton views modern culture's drive towards homogeneity as stemming from a stress upon the one over the many. He proposes that the revelation of God as Father, Son, and Spirit will alleviate the privileging of the one over the many because God's being is constituted by communion—a communion that maintains unity and distinction. Communion is the ontological ground of being because, by his very nature, God is communion; therefore, communion is also the ground of being in creation because it is a created reality by the Triune God. This way, communion understood as a marker of being is conceptually linked to the relation between God and his creation. So Gunton formulates the phrase "*Trinitarian* transcendentals" to denote his method for resolving the problem of the one and the many within the revelation of God as Father, Son, and Holy Spirit. The problem is that from Parmenides to Aquinas it was "unity, but not plurality, [which] is transcendental."[20] This means that transcendentals are "notions which can be predicated of all

---

20. Gunton, *The One, the Three, and the Many*, 138. Guthrie (to whom Gunton frequently refers) stresses Gunton's point that Greek philosophy trended toward unity when he says that "Plato posited a permanent reality outside the physical world. It is usually assumed (*a*) that these opinions were Heraclitus' own . . . and (*b*) that although they are explicitly confined to the sensible world, this for Hercaclitus constituted the total sum of reality" (Guthrie, *A History of Greek Philosophy*, 468).

THE DOCTRINE OF GOD: BEING AS BEING-IN-COMMUNION

being by virtue of the fact that God is Creator and the world is creation."[21] These markers of being are transcendentals; not just any transcendentals, but transcendentals that are based on God's being as triune.

In an epistemological context, Gunton says that "to seek for a transcendental is to seek for those features of our language and experience by means of which reality at its most fundamental makes itself known to us."[22] In other words, transcendentals are basic to our being, a being that derives from God who is its cause and sustainer. So instead of transcendentals being conceived historically as primarily grounded in some form of unity, transcendentals should be conceived as "open transcendentals" in order to provide a scheme that solidifies the relation between the Creator and creation. The relation is based on God's nature as a communal *being*; meaning he created according to his nature—communally. Creation's existence is due to the communal creative activity of the Triune God which leads to the conclusion that creation exists as a created communal reality. A reality given to it by its Triune Creator. So communion *is* an "open transcendental." By "open" Gunton means that theology is open to the eschatological work of the Spirit in revealing the universal marks of being. He explains that "an open transcendental is a notion, some way basic to the human thinking process, which empowers a continuing and in principle unfinished exploration of the universal marks of being."[23] Here, Gunton is concerned "very much with the doctrine of creation, and in particular with what light the doctrine of God throws on our understanding of created reality."[24] A proper transcendental must "enable us to understand something of how things are with our world as the creation of God."[25] As we will see, relation is also an open transcendental, so that "of both God and the world it must be said that they have their being in relation."[26] The point is that relation is a fundamental structure of being but it is open to new understandings and definitions as the Holy Spirit opens our minds to deeper understanding of God in theology, the sciences, and philosophy. Therefore, Gunton purports that a proper doctrine of God is essential to developing transcendentals that are able to hold in tension the apparent unity and plurality as experienced in the world. This view of open transcendentals means that the doctrine of God will have a direct and decisive impact on how we view our reality.

21. Gunton, *The One, the Three, and the Many*, 137.
22. Gunton, *Father, Son, and Holy Spirit*, 185.
23. Gunton, *The One, the Three, and the Many*, 142.
24. Ibid., 150.
25. Ibid., 162.
26. Ibid., 230.

Gunton's initial assessment of our modern conundrum is formulated within the framework of his trinitarian theology, especially his doctrine of God.[27] Gunton believes that theology in the West took its cues from Hellenistic philosophy, which stressed homogeneity or unity over the many. In this way, relationality as a foundational part of reality was lost, and relations were conceived more as mere accidents instead of essential properties of substances. But for Gunton, reality is conceived "through a focus provided by the doctrine of the God made known in Christ and the Spirit."[28] Ultimately, the resolution to the problem of the "one and the many" in light of the doctrine of God is to be found in relationality; that is a proper relation between the one and the many that is constitutive of each. Gunton states that by relation he means "the belief that particulars, of whatever kind, can be understood only in terms of their relatedness to each other and the whole."[29] His understanding of God's existence as a being-in-relation becomes the overarching convention that guides his system of thought towards the resolution of the problem of the "one and the many." Gunton states, "the many can find their true being and be understood only as they are related to each other and to the One, but the main streams of neither antiquity nor modernity have been able to conceive the patterns of relation adequately."[30] The solution is the doctrine of the Trinity because God eternally exists as an interrelatedness of persons. For "the unity of God has been stressed at the expense of his triunity, and to that extent the modern critique must be understood as a recalling of theology to its own trinitarian roots."[31] Reflecting on the work of social critics such as Václav Havel and Robert Pippin lead Gunton to conclude that instead of creating a truly autonomous society, the

27. The use of the term "modern" can be misleading because of its relative nature; what is modern to one generation is not modern to the next. But in this usage, Gunton is referring to his era which was still under the influence of the German Enlightenment, especially Kant and Hegel. For Gunton, "modern" is a condition of complexity and above all paradoxes. Gunton states, "modernity is the realm of paradoxes: an era which has sought freedom, and bred totalitarianism; which has taught us our insignificance in the vastness of the universe, and yet sought to play god with that same universe; which has sought to control the world, and yet loose forces that may destroy the earth" (ibid., 13). The term "modern" for Gunton connotes "a view that the pressures of modernity are pressures toward homogeneity" (13). In his article on Gunton, Terry says that, "at the start of the twentieth century, debates about the doctrine of atonement in Britain had become sharply polarized by the rise of modernism" (Terry, "Colin Gunton's Doctrine of Atonement," 131). The term "modern" seems to indicate the conflict during the middle of the twentieth century between Liberal and (Neo)Orthodox theologies.

28. Gunton, *The One, the Three, and the Many*, 11.
29. Ibid., 37n53.
30. Ibid., 37.
31. Ibid., 39.

displacement of God produced a need for homogeneity, which resulted in the stress and location of the "one" apart from the triune God.[32] In other words, society displaced God as the source of the infinite (or absolute) in favor of an existential autonomy. But instead of autonomy, they created a need for some type of unity, or homogeneity, which resulted in defining unity or oneness apart from God: society created a man-made absolute. Therefore, in order to resolve the tension, a correct doctrine of God must be recovered; a doctrine which recognizes God's inherent, complete and self-determined being-in-relation. Relationality then becomes a universal mark of being as such—that is, a transcendental, grounded in God's very being, and whose recognition is a sign of creation's dependence on God. In some way, theologians must include a recognition of relationality as an ontological category that incorporates and holds in tension the one and the many.

Gunton proposes that "the being of God is not a blank unity, but a being in communion."[33] Gunton owes much to Zizoulas, who says, "so, whenever the question of the ontological relationship between God and the world is raised, the idea of *hypostasis*, from now on ontological in an ultimate sense, must be completed with that of substance if we do not wish to fall back into ontological monism."[34] God's *ousia* is derived from the persons, beginning with the person of the Father, otherwise the substance would be a "blank" unity not reliant on personhood. For Gunton this also accords with the biblical passages where the term "God" is a reference to the Father, especially when the triune persons are juxtaposed in a particular passage. By grounding God's *ousia* in the person of the Father, God's *being* is apprehended as inherently relational and as defining the ontological category of being in a relational manner. Gunton frames his idea this way: "We may say that to think of divine being is to have one's mind necessarily drawn to the three

32. Neither Havel nor Pippin are theologians; they did not stress social problems in relation to the Trinity. With that said, both philosophers did see a problem in modern society that is related to autonomy and some type of displacement of relationality. For example, in reference to the industrial age, Havel states that "it is a symbol of an epoch which denies the binding importance of personal experience–including the experience of mystery and of the absolute-and displaces the personally experienced absolute as the measure of the world with a new, man-made absolute, devoid of mystery, free of the 'whims' of subjectivity and, as such, impersonal and inhuman" (Havel, *Open Letters*, 251). Pippin understands the problem with modernity as dissatisfaction with the results of the promise of autonomy. Pippin says, "I have suggested that the philosophical problem at stake in such dissatisfaction might best be examined as the problem of autonomy, or more specifically, the nature of both the independence and the dependence or finitude of modern communities and individuals" (Pippin, *Modernism as a Philosophical Problem*, 148–49).

33. Gunton, *The One, the Three, and the Many*, 214.

34. Zizioulas, *Being as Communion*, 89.

persons, to think of the three to be led ineluctably to a concept of shared, relational, being."[35] God is a relational being; a being-in-communion. Our realization of this will have an impact upon our concept of *being* itself.

Gunton defines human existence within a proper understanding of God without collapsing into a univocal concept of *being* derived from our creaturely existence. Returning to Zizioulas, he says that "creaturely truth is dependent upon something else, in which it participates; this is truth as *communion by participation* (as compared with God, who is truth as *communion without participation*)."[36] For Gunton, this means that the analogy between God and creation is not a direct one between the immanent Trinity and human society. The creature participates in the perichoretic activity of the triune God as revealed in the economic history of salvation. This way, *perichoresis* is primarily used of God's being-in-communion, but when perichoresis refers to creation it refers to an economic gift of creation by God in the work of the Son and the Spirit, thereby giving creation its particular shape. T. F. Torrance expresses it this way, "we must think of God, rather, as '*personalising Person*,' and of ourselves as '*personalised persons*,' people who are personal primarily through onto-relations to him as the creative Source of our personal being, and secondarily through onto-relations to one another within the subject-subject structures of our creaturely being as they have come from him."[37] For Gunton, "perichoresis" simply denotes "a dynamism of relatedness."[38] More on this will be stated later, but for now, the point is that God's *being* is a *being-in-communion*, which relates to creation in diversity of dynamic ways through the Son and the Spirit. But it is only when a proper doctrine of God is established—one that conceives of God *perichorectically* as relatedness-in-unity, and then who is involved with his creation in the same manner—that the problem of the one and the many will be able to find resolution. This means that since the persons of the Father, Son, and Holy Spirit have been revealed in the economy as a communion of mutual interpenetration, then it is expected that the same mutual penetration exists in the immanent divine communion. Since God's activity is grounded in his very being, and creation is part of God's act, then the divine *perichoretic* existence should have some bearing on creation itself. For it is the creative action of the Son and the Spirit—the two hands of the Father—which gives creation the room to participate in the perichoretic action of God, which is actualized in relationality. Creatures are constituted

---

35. Gunton, *The One, the Three, and the Many*, 214.
36. Zizioulas, *Being as Communion*, 94.
37. Torrance, *The Christian Doctrine of God*, 160.
38. Gunton, *The One, the Three, and the Many*, 165.

by what they receive from God, and then what they give and receive from other creatures. Gunton realizes that the relation between God and creation is only an analogical one, but it is a reflection of God in creation which takes place by Jesus Christ through the Spirit.[39]

The trinitarian persons are constituted by divine perichoresis inherit in the nature of God. On the other hand, the particulars of creation are constituted by perichoresis as a divine gift. The point is that by creating an analogy between God and creation, Gunton feels that there will be a recovery of relationality as a transcendental.[40] Robert Solomon says that

> when the social is reduced to second-rate status, and the individual will and universal principles take priority, we lose what would seem to be the primary ground of ethics, our membership in a community and interaction with others. Instead of

---

39. There is a certain implicit concern within Gunton's writings that the link between God and the creatures is not associated too closely; any analogy between God and creation is always asymmetrical as best. Gunton asks regarding transcendentals "how the concepts may be considered to apply analogously to God and the world" (ibid., 153–54). His answer is that analogies are "extreme" generalities that are "both unfathomable and infinitely suggestive." Gunton's doctrine of God is very close to a social Trinitarian model, but he insists that we must be careful not to push the social analogy between God and human life too far: "When we come to speak of human sociality, we once again speak by analogy. We are not what we are eternally because we are . . . constituted in a network of relations that takes shape within our boundedness in time and space" (ibid., 214). In other words, God is an eternally self-sufficient communion of persons; but the creature's communion is first reliant on God and other creatures–there is an analogy but an infinitely different analogy. In a way, Gunton argues against his own work. In *The One, The Three and the Many* he proposes that the doctrine of the Trinity argues against individualism and collectivism. He states that even though he has argued this point, that "for all the value of such arguments from analogy, they tread a slippery slope" (*Father, Son, and Holy Spirit*, 24.). Then he adds that "it remains true that the moves from the immanent Trinity to the created world are not obvious, and are fraught with dangers of idealizing and projection" (*ibid.*, 25). Gunton's desire is to maintain the Creator creature distinction, but allow analogies regarding God to serve as a means to maintain a relation between the two without collapsing the doctrine of God into some type of pantheism.

40. Gunton understands there to be a certain loss of "relationality" in modern philosophy and theology, which is primarily due to the displacement of Triune God as the basis of transcendentals. This loss of "relationality" impacts epistemology and ontology because personhood is no longer envisioned in terms of relationality, but individuality. The result is an overstressing of the "one" over the "many," which alters humanity's understanding of what it is to be a person. Gunton engages with Robert Solomon, who says Rousseau argued that "in the state of nature . . . the individual is free and independent." (Solomon, *Continental Philosophy since 1750*, 19). Solomon acknowledges that Rousseau battled between individualism and the self as a social being, but he concludes that "Rousseau emerges as the champion of free and natural living" (ibid., 20).

morality we have cosmic self-righteousness—the transcendental pretence.[41]

Gunton responds to Solomon's summation by saying that "the key is once more to be found in a trinitarian doctrine of creation and theory of transcendentality."[42] Gunton explains that, "the theology of the Trinity as a dynamic personal order of giving and receiving is, in the idea of sociality that it suggests, the key to the matter of transcendentality that we are seeking."[43] In this way, creation is "inextricably bound" with the immanent life of God—as revealed in the economy—that provides creation its ground of *being*. This way, creation takes the shape it does due to the *perichoretic* life and action of the triune God. God's *perichoretic* life is one of free relations, of give and take, between the triune persons. Creation's existence is therefore grounded in the free and gracious act of God who gives it freedom to be; that is, the freedom to be what God intended as a community in relation to its Creator and with others. This way, "trinitarian transcendentals" are based on the saving act of God as Father, Son, and Holy Spirit toward creation that gives creation its meaning—the freedom to be a community-in-relation to God and with others. So, for Gunton, both *perichoresis* and relationality are transcendentals because they flow from the foundational doctrine of God as a being-in-communion who acts according to his *being* as revealed in his economic acts.

The doctrine of God is the determinant for "open transcendentals" as markers of *being* for creation. Our study of Gunton's doctrine of God demonstrated that communion and relationality are not only grounded in God's being, but also provide the grounds of being for created reality. The Holy Spirit for Gunton is the perfector of communion within God and creation, so it is necessary to first establish God's being as communion, and then demonstrate that God's creative activity is trinitarianly conceived. Creation must display signs of relationality and communion, but given and perfected by the divine action of the Holy Spirit. This will be fleshed out more in the section on Pneumatology, but for now, we will examine Gunton's use of "particularity" as related to God, creation and the Holy Spirit.

---

41. Ibid., 40.
42. Gunton, *The One, the Three, and the Many*, 225.
43. Ibid.,

B. Transcendentals—Perichoresis and Relationality Determine Particularity

In the previous section, the doctrine of God solidified communion as a necessary component of *being*. Now we will investigate Gunton's idea of "particularity," which corresponds to the idea of otherness-in-relation. Particularity is formulated by Gunton when he develops *perichoresis* and relationality as universal markers of *being*. Gunton developed three transcendentals—substance, *perichoresis*, and relationality—which he based on God's triune being.[44] Gunton first argues that relationality is a necessary component of *being* by examining the relationship between eternity and time. Eternity and time corresponds to the primary levels of reality, which are God and creation respectively. So in order to create a system where the eternal God can relate to his temporal creation while maintaining the integrity of both, "time" cannot be conceived as a transcendental; otherwise, the age old philosophical problem of relating eternity to time, or the timeless to the temporal, is still left unresolved.[45] Since "time" is not a transcendental, Gunton constructs a system where *perichoresis* and relationality are the universal marks of being instead of "time and space." The aim for Gunton is to develop *perichoresis* and relationality as transcendentals in a way that is conceptually shaped by God's *being* and gives room for the perfecting agency of the Holy Spirit. We will first examine Gunton's development of relationality as a transcendental, and then proceed to *perichoresis*.

In part C/C,' Gunton returns to the theme of the "one and the many" in order to appraise and resolve the problem of relatedness. The historic

---

44. For Gunton, substantiality is based in the "particulars" because God's being is based on particulars-in-unity, therefore, "particularity" provides a way of resolving the "one and the many" because the "particular" is given equal priority (and some may argue more) in respect to the "one." Substantiality is not a static something underlying reality, it is particularity that is encapsulated in freedom and eschatology that is only possible with a relationality that is with and from God. The Spirit creates substance by perfecting freedom, unity and eschatology of the Godhead as an internal action; and provides substance in the same manner for creation as an outward action of grace. In this way, substantiality is viewed as a transcendental by Gunton because it originates in God, and is given by God in Christ through the Spirit. The Holy Spirit gives particularity because he gives authentic substantiality to creation; a substantiality that is grounded in the particularity of each creature, but that is a particularity-in-relation. This way, the Spirit perfects the substance and the particular person in such a way that neither has priority over the other; there is no substance without the person, and no person without the substance.

45. Succinctly stated, "eternity" is ontologically different than "time." Thomas Aquinas says "It is manifest that time and eternity are not the same . . . for eternity is the measure of a permanent being; while time is a measure of movement" (Thomas, *Summa Theologica* I.10.4; in Thomas, *Basic Writings* [trans. Pegis]).

influence of Aristotelian metaphysics caused eternity to be conceived as a static domain that is completely opposed to our temporal world. Gunton says, "I shall be concerned almost exclusively with time, because it is the main factor by which the many may be conceived to be bonded historically."[46] Gunton means that time is the "place" where the distinction of the many in this world takes place, but since our culture has difficulty relating time and eternity, either the "one" or the "many" is displaced. So the result is the loss of the *relation* between the one and the many, in parallel to that of eternity and time. Therefore, "the interest shifts to the matter of relationality: of how the universe is bonded together, and how we indwell and so participate in that relationality."[47] This inability to maintain a proper relation between eternity and time results in a drive towards privileging the 'one' over the 'many.' Gunton cites Wolfgang Achtner, who states that "ever since Plato made the fundamental distinction between time . . . and eternity . . . in Timaios and Parmenides, the relation between time and eternity has been an issue of philosophical and religious dispute."[48] Bernard Reardon says that "it is this idea of the infinite in the finite which furnishes the basic motif of German romanticist philosophy, in which nature and human history alike are conceived synoptically as forms or manifestations of one infinite Life. We also have it, very signally, in Schleiermacher, whose *Reden über die Religion* gave it such telling expression."[49] The point being that modern thought and theology began to turn to the infinite as the true source of reality, at the expense of the integrity of creation. On the other hand, there are aspects of our thinking that is a "this-worldly culture. Our time and space and not some distant heaven is the important reality."[50] Pannerberg gives us additional insight into Gunton's concern when he states, "Barth in particular vigorously attempted a revision of the traditional opposing of time to eternity. But he was not the only twentieth-century theologian to do so. There is widespread agreement that eternity does not mean timelessness or the endlessness of time."[51] The point is, for Gunton, in the history of Western thought, time and eternity have been set in opposition to the point

---

46. Gunton, *The One, the Three, and the Many*, 76.

47. Ibid., 78.

48. Achtner, "Time, Eternity, and Trinity," 268. Achtner later states that, "in late antiquity this debate entered into a new realm when Neo-Platonic Plotinus and Platonic St. Augustine associated time with the human consciousness. From this time onward the relation between time and eternity could be thought of as a feature of the human consciousness" (ibid.).

49. Reardon, *Religion in the Age of Romanticism*, 4.

50. Gunton, *The One, the Three, and the Many*, 75.

51. Pannenberg, *Systematic Theology*, 1:407.

that the relationship between the two has been severed; the dissolution of the relationship has resulted in the stress of the infinite as the real. In order to overcome this deficiency, there must be a recovery of the integrity of the particular, or in this context, time.

Since particularity is conceived as a "this-worldly" problem in as much as theology and philosophy tends towards eternity as the place where the true definition of reality is located, Gunton wants to revive "time" as the locus of redemption.[52] He says, "put theologically, the truth seems to be that for the representative Greek mind time was not the realm in which to find redemption."[53] On various occasions, Gunton refers to Plato's *Timaeus* to indicate that Greek philosophy conceives time as the "image of eternity;" meaning that time is less real. For example, in regards to the "father-creator" creating the universe, Plato states,

> But the being that served as the model was eternal, and it was impossible for him to make this altogether an attribute of any created object. Nevertheless, he determined to make it a kind of moving likeness of eternity, and so in the very act of ordering the universe he created a likeness of eternity, a likeness that progresses eternally through the sequence of numbers, while eternity abides in oneness.[54]

In his introduction to Plato's *Timaeus*, Benjamin Jowett explains that in Plato's cosmology, the Father-creator created time's "past," "present," and "future," as an image of eternity; and that "all [three] apply to becoming in time, and have no meaning in relation to the eternal nature, whichever is

---

52. Gunton refers to this as the "West's double-mind," meaning that at times our creaturely existence in time and space is viewed as that which will be redeemed, and at other times eternity is proclaimed as the location of real existence. This double-mind is also seen in Calvin. Blocher says, "One dimension of our created being seems even more humbling than the other: our *bodiliness*. On countless of occasions, Calvin refers to the body as a 'prison,' and he can paint a very grim picture of our physical life" (Blocher, "Calvin's Theological Anthropology," 75). On the other hand, he later quotes Richard Stauffer and comments: "The problem of the *imago dei* is one of the most difficult in Calvin's theology. The texts that deal with it are as numerous as they contradict each other" (Stauffer, *Dieu, la Création et la Providence dans la Prédication de Calvin*, 201; trans. Blocher), and he criticizes Niesel and Torrance for unilateral systematization" (Blocher, "Calvin's Theological Anthropology," 79). This criticism could be applicable to Gunton as well. But Blocher concludes by saying that, "Though one can glimpse 'sparks' of the image of God in the human body, Calvin has no doubt that its seat is in the *soul*, or heart, or mind, or spirit" (ibid., 80).

53. Gunton, *The One, the Three, and the Many*, 79–80.

54. Plato, *Timaeus* 37d (trans. Waterfield, 25).

and never was or will be."[55] For Gunton, it is the alienation of our "past" against our "future" which causes a disruption with our present; the past, present, and the future are viewed as only causally related and less than real in comparison to eternity. By not maintaining a proper relationship between time and eternity, salvation is either an other-worldly conception, or grounded in "this-world" apart from eternity. In other words, salvation is either found in eternity as a rescue from our fallen temporality; or salvation is found in *our* future, a future that is brought about by our human ability to progress towards greater fulfillment. As a result of time (and space) being conceived as true transcendentals, eternity and time are perceived as products of human rationalization.[56] For Kant, time and space were viewed as being beyond our reality because our knowledge of reality is grounded in the categories of time and space. Time and space became universals and transcendentals which our mind uses to shape the world; time and space are now separated from the *being* of our reality: the unity-in-relation between time and eternity was irrevocably lost because eternity has no relation to our reality, only time does.

Gunton says, "By using the concept of time, we are able to relate things as before and after, and thus as belonging in some kind of order."[57] Time and eternity must be approached in a type of dialectic that allows for distinction and unity. Time is not defined as a lesser subset of eternity that is awaiting its return to eternity in order to find completion. Time must be free to be itself, but also conceived as having its being in relation to eternity. Time as such is not a transcendental.[58] Gunton interprets Kant's transcendental idealism as shifting the transcendentals away from God to the human subject, which severs the relationship. On the other hand, he finds that much of historic Western theology shifted transcendentals away from the temporal towards eternity which "appeared to deny due reality to the created order."[59] Therefore, in order to allow time to be itself, that is, as an actual created reality, theology and philosophy must "conceive

---

55. Jowett, Introduction to Plato, *Plato's Timaeus*, 20.

56. Gunton has in mind Kant's transcendental idealism.

57. Gunton, *The One, the Three, and the Many*, 155.

58. Martin says, "If we try to keep within the framework of what can be proved by the Kantian argument, we can say that it is possible to demonstrate the empirical reality of space and time, that is to say, the objective validity of all spatial and temporal properties in mathematics and physics. But this empirical reality involves transcendental ideality; space and time are forms of human intuition, and they can only be proved valid for things as they appear to us and not for things as they are in themselves" (Martin, *Kant's Metaphysics and Theory of Science*, 41).

59. Gunton, *The One, the Three, and the Many*, 156–57.

both eternity and time in their interrelatedness."[60] By eliminating time (and space) as a transcendental, Gunton develops alternate transcendentals that are based on the action of the triune God. This way, God's time (eternity) and creation's time (temporality) maintain their integrity while also safeguarding the relatedness between the two. The Biblical concept of "economy" acts as a bridge between God's time and creation's time. God has revealed in his economic activity a *taxis* which culminates in the action of the Holy Spirit: the Spirit is the agent who provides the liberation for time to be itself while maintaining the relationship with God. In this context, the word "economy" is not just a reference to God's triune redemptive activity; it signifies God's entire relation with his creatures—eternity and time in relation. "Economic" language signifies a transaction that originates from the generous activity of the triune persons, but a transaction that takes place in our time and space. Gunton says, "The concept of economy became a way of integrating a plurality, of maintaining the richness and diversity of the ways of the one God towards and in the world."[61] So "economy" indicates God's action in our history by which eternity and time are both afforded distinctive freedom but also the freedom to be in relation.[62] Gunton says, "creation, fall, redemption and eschatology all therefore had due part, though together in their distinctness, but not separateness, and interrelatedness."[63] Gunton is refining the meaning of "economy" to include the idea of unity-in-relatedness. If time is not conceived as having its own integrity and fully realized as a product of God's creation activity, then time will either be given too much weight as a transcendental, or it will be viewed as less than real in relation to eternity. In Gunton's view, the Holy Spirit is the divine agent who perfects particulars by liberation and the gift of relationality. Time, like all created realities, is brought to perfection by the Holy Spirit, becoming what God intended as a location of renewed relationship with God's own realm of eternity. Before we complete our discussion of the relationship between time and eternity, and since time and

---

60. Ibid., 157.

61. Ibid., 158.

62. Gunton has in mind Ireneaus's conception of "recapitulation," which takes place in creation by the one whom Created and redeems it. Ireneaus states, "[A]nd as the protoplast himself, Adam . . . was formed by the hand of God, that is, by the Word of God . . . so did He who is the Word, recapitulating Adam in Himself, rightly receive a birth, enabling Him to gather up Adam [into Himself]" (Irenaeus, *Irenaeus against Heresies* 3.21.10). Also, regarding eschatology, "God recapitulated in Himself the ancient formation of man, that He might kill sin, deprive death of its power, and vivify man; and therefore His works are true" (3.18.7).

63. Gunton, *The One, the Three, and the Many*, 158.

space both serve as a part of Kant's transcendentals, it is necessary to give a brief account of the way Gunton theologically renders "space."

Where the language of "economy" designates relatedness in respect to time, the language of *perichoresis* signifies relatedness in respect to space. The *perichoretic* action of the immanent Trinity, for Gunton, is seen as a theological equivalent to the "space-time" of relativity in physics; the internal relatedness of God is conceived as simultaneously eternal (time) and personal (space). Gunton incorporates *perichoresis* into the doctrine of God by explaining that "the concept of *perichoresis*: [is] a metaphor of spatial motion which introduces a dynamism into the eternity in which the persons are what they are in and through one another."[64] At this stage, instead of limiting the usage of *perichoresis* to the persons of the imminent trinity, Gunton advances an analogical model of *perichoresis* in respect to created reality. Based on his understanding that the "economic" activity of God is a relation between eternity and time, Gunton says that *perichoresis* "is a concept heavy with spatial and temporal conceptuality, involving movement, recurrence and interpenetration . . . it is an *implication* of the unity-in-variety of the divine economic involvement in the world."[65] There is an overlap between the twin concepts of "economy" and "*perichoresis*" in Gunton's project in that they both refer to God's eternal existence and bear upon his relation to creation. *Perichoresis* focuses on the space of the other to be him/herself, but as an existence constituted in relation. This way, Gunton is able to explain that "the central point about the concept is that it enables theology to preserve both the one and the many in dynamic interrelations."[66] Gunton constructs an ontology of God that is grounded in an internal relatedness between the three trinitarian persons: "God is not God apart from the way in which Father, Son, and Spirit in eternity give to and receive from each other what they essentially are."[67] It is easy to be overwhelmed by Gunton's ontological thrust, and his revising the doctrine of *perichoresis* from an explanation of the unity of the persons towards an account of God's very being as constituted as a unity-in-relation. What is easy to overlook is that Gunton is using the concept of *perichoresis* to resolve the tension between the one and the many. Gunton says that the language of *perichoresis*—that is, "dynamic interrelations"—allows for "a particular kind of relational diversity, or rather non-Heraclitean flux."[68]

64. Gunton, *The Promise of Trinitarian Theology*, 134.
65. Gunton, *The One, the Three, and the Many*, 163.
66. Ibid., 163–64.
67. Ibid., 164.
68. Ibid.

Where the language of "economy" for Gunton maintains the relational tension between time and eternity, *perichoresis* aids in resolving the relational tension of being: *perichoresis* has a logic of its own which Gunton construes as being-in-relation.

So, for Gunton, the language of "economy" deals with the relation between God and creation; but it is not a universal mark of being because the "economy" begins and ends with God. Creation only exists because of the economic activity of God; creation does not have its own "economy" in the theological sense. But, the doctrine of *perichoresis* is a universal mark of being—that is, an open transcendental based on the creative action of the triune God. It is open because, in Gunton's estimation, transcendentals must be conceived eschatologically as a work of the Holy Spirit. *Perichoresis* is a transcendental because the Spirit that perfects the personal relations in the imminent life of God, also perfects relations (albeit not in the same manner of interpenetration of the divine persons) between particulars in creation—*perichoresis* in the divine nature is eternal and uncreated, but temporal and created in creation. Gunton is continuing his goal of maintaining a dialectical stasis between the "one and the many," which requires an ontological account of relatedness. To summarize our earlier findings: in the course of developing *perichoresis* as a transcendental, Gunton begins with the doctrine of God in order to develop an asymmetrical but analogous relation between the *being* of God and the *being of* his creatures. God is revealed as an ordered and free life of internal *perichoretic* activity in the shape of Father, Son, and Holy Spirit. Barth is instructive here: he says, "Eternity is God in the sense in which in himself and in all things God is simultaneous, i.e., beginning and middle as well as end, without separation, distance or contradiction."[69] This means that God's temporality is one of eternal relations that are also a reflection of *perichoretic* activity. So, in the same way for Gunton, *perichoresis* is fundamental in explaining God's reality, so that "to speak theologically of the economy is to speak of the way in which God constitutes reality: God is what he is by virtue of the dynamic relatedness of Father, Son and Spirit."[70] In this way, the foundation for all reality has an order; *perichoresis* specifies that creatures are "dynamically related to each other in time and space."[71]

Perichoresis is the heart and soul of Gunton's doctrine of relation, in that it is an encompassing mark of God's economic activity towards the world—from creation to redemption and to eschatology. Relatedness for

---

69. Barth, *The Church Dogmatics*, II/1:608.
70. Gunton, *The One, the Three, and the Many*, 165.
71. Ibid.

Gunton becomes a soteriological concept because the Creator gives—of himself—to creation a particular shape of relatedness. So redemption is a recovery of the lost relatedness—between Creator and creature, and creature to itself—that was and is its intended destiny. Gunton says,

> the dynamism of a mutual constitutiveness derives from the world's being a dynamic order that is summoned into being and directed towards its perfection by the free creativity of Father, Son and Holy Spirit. That orientation of being is, of course, distorted and delayed by sin and evil, and returns to its directedness only through the incarnation and the redeeming agency of the Spirit.[72]

In this way, economic language indicates that the world is what it is due to its relation to God's activity in Christ and the Spirit. Gunton says, "the difficulty will be eased by the fact that, as we have seen, perichoresis is a concept which, because it derives from reflection on the involvement of God in time and space, is not conceptually foreign to createdness."[73] In other words, *perichoretic* language also indicates something fundamental of creation's own internal relatedness: "its way of being distinctively what it is."[74] Gunton proposes that "if the world is creation, then it has its own particular being, even if that being is not separable from its relation to its maker and redeemer."[75] The premise that creation has its own particular being, but in relation to its maker and redeemer, leads Gunton to conclude that *perichoresis* is a universal mark of being because of its inherent relatedness which is grounded in the dynamic life of the Triune God. The persons of the Trinity exist in an eternal relationality of interpenetration between the persons; in Gunton's scheme, it is the Spirit who gives the divine persons the "space" to be themselves. The same perfecting action of the Holy Spirit, as the giver of life, gives creation its *being*. As a work of the Spirit, creation is what it is because of its relation to God and what it gives and receives from other creatures. Gunton says that "a doctrine of human perichoresis affirms . . . that persons mutually constitute each other, make each other what they are."[76] Therefore, *perichoresis* is understood as a universal mark of being because it is a divine action of the Spirit eternally perfecting the relationships within God's very being. It is also understood as eschatologically constituting the *being* of creation by perfecting relationships. This way,

72. Ibid., 166.
73. Ibid., 167.
74. Ibid., 166.
75. Ibid., 167.
76. Ibid., 169.

THE DOCTRINE OF GOD: BEING AS BEING-IN-COMMUNION   35

both God and creation are liberated by the Spirit to be free, albeit creation's freedom is given to it by the triune God.

For Gunton, *perichoresis* is *only* an analogous concept in respect to creation and the divine nature. When it is used in reference to God, it defines God's absolute eternal being-in-relation that explicates the perfect communion between the Father, Son, and Holy Spirit.[77] But when used in reference to the creature, *perichoresis* is *only* an analogy because "to be created involves spatial and temporal limitation,"[78] which defines createdness as well as the limitation of each creature being *perichoretically* bound up with other creatures. In this way, the temporal and spatial aspects of creation are accounted for in the concept of *perichoresis* because they determine that created *being* is an existence of relatedness with others (spatial) and with our past, present, and future (time). In explaining Gunton's use of open transcendentals, Lincoln Harvey explains that "on the basis of the single Christological economy, perichoresis becomes an open transcendental, which means that the pattern of being found in God can also be found *alongside* God in the creaturely realm."[79] God's love creates and redeems freely, "giving to the world a perichoretic reality which in different ways reflects within the structures of the temporal and spatial the perichoresis which is God in eternity. It is not therefore some*thing* which hold things together, but some*one*: the one through whom, in the unity of the Father, and the Spirit, all things have their being."[80] Therefore, when Gunton develops his "open transcendentals," it is with the philosophical problem of the "one and the many" in view; *perichoresis* takes into account the relationship between eternity (one) and time (many); between God (unity) and his creatures (many); and finally the individual (one) and the others (many). Gunton concludes from *perichoresis* and communion (or substantiality) that relationality is also a transcendental. Now we will examine Gunton's third "open transcendentals" of relationality.

Relationality is a transcendental because it follows logically from the transcendentals of *perichoresis* and substantiality (which is a product of particularity). All three concepts find their perfection in the work of the Holy

---

77. Heppe defines *perichoresis* "in the divine persons is the completely close union, whereby one person is in another, not like an accident in a subject, but in the way in which one person permeates and embraces in every direction the whole of another always and inseparably because of the numerically one and the same essence, the whole of which the separate persons possess" (Heppe, *Reformed Dogmatics*, 113).

78. Gunton, *The One, the Three, and the Many*, 170.

79. Harvey, "The *Double* Homoousion," 92.

80. Gunton, *The One, the Three, and the Many*, 179.

Spirit.[81] As we will see in the section on Pneumatology, the Holy Spirit is not the relation between the Father and Son, but is the divine person who perfects the relation. For Gunton, the same divine action of the Spirit is also seen in the created realm; the Spirit of God constitutes and perfects the particulars in and "by many and various forms of relation."[82] Again, to quote Gunton, "Relationality is thus the transcendental which allows us to learn something of what it is to say that all created people and things are marked by their coming from and returning to the God who is himself, in his essential and inmost being, a being in relation."[83] Gunton is consistent within his doctrine of God because all three transcendentals are derived from God's revelation as a *being*-in-communion. Randal Lyle is correct in his assessment when he says, "for an ontology to be based upon the Trinity, Gunton believes that it is crucial to see relations as an ontological category."[84] For Gunton, relationality accommodates both ontology and soteriology in that the Holy Spirit crosses boundaries between uncreated and created realities in order to destroy opposition. Jenson says that "each of the inner-trinitarian relations is then an affirmation that as God works creatively among us, so he is in himself."[85] This expresses nicely Gunton's purposes for establishing relationality as an ontological category: as God is in himself, there is a reflection in creation of his activity. Moltmann expresses a similar view of relationality this way,

> Our starting point here is that all relationships which are analogous to God reflect the primal, reciprocal indwelling and mutual interpenetration of the trinitarian perichoresis: God *in* the world and the world *in* God; heaven and earth *in the* kingdom of God, pervaded by his glory; soul and body united *in* the life-giving Spirit to a human whole; woman and man *in* the kingdom of unconditional and unconditioned love, freed to be true and complete human beings. There is no such thing as solitary life . . . All living things—each in its own specific way—live in one another and with one another, from one another and for one another.[86]

---

81. Gunton states that relationality is a transcendental because it "enables us to incorporate the insights gained from the discussion of the other two transcendentals, perichoresis and substantiality" (ibid., 230).

82. Ibid., 229.

83. Ibid.

84. Lyle, "Social Trinitarianism as an Option for 21st Century Theology: A Systematic Analysis of Colin Gunton's Trinitarian Paradigm," 135.

85. Jenson, *The Triune Identity*, 107.

86. Moltmann, *God in Creation*, 17.

The point for Moltmann, as for Gunton, is that relations are the primal being of things. For Gunton, relationality derives from God's own *being*—as revealed in those divine acts of creation and redemption—and is given to creation by God in a manner that reflects his nature: the Father originates, and the Son creates and the Holy Spirit perfects the relations in creation. This way, God as a being-in-communion creates the creaturely transcendentals which are related, in their own way, to the idea of communion. As we will see in the section on Pneumatology, communion, theologically speaking, is only what it is by the perfecting action of the Holy Spirit.

Chapter 2

Pneumatology of Communion: Particularity as Being-in-Relation

Introduction

GUNTON'S THEOLOGY CENTERS ON the idea of communion because he believes that the incarnation represents God's ultimate expression of his self-revelation; and in the incarnation we find God's fullest expression of his Triune nature. Since God has revealed himself as a tri-unity, that is, a communion of persons, theology should begin with God's *being* as constituted by communion of the three divine persons. The idea of "particularity" is important because it affords him the conceptual space to maintain real distinctions while conceiving subjects as constituted by relations. In other words, beings are particulars-in-communion. Hohne explains that for Gunton

> particularity of persons or things [was] understood as the consequence of mutually constitutive relations. More than this, because the discussion is theological not merely philosophical, the perfection of particularity (concrete substantiality) in creation is the eschatological work of the Spirit of the Father, through the Son.[1]

The point is, that for Gunton, particularity expresses the individuality of a thing that comes about from a set of ontological relations. Concrete substance is also expressed in terms of particularity, because individual substance exists through a given set of relations. There is not an underlying substance in which the relations inhere; without particulars, there are no relations, and without relations, there are no particulars. So the Holy Spirit is essential because he perfects communion and gives concrete

---

1. Höhne, *Spirit and Sonship*, 8.

reality to particulars in a manner reminiscent of the divine *taxis* in the immanent life of God.

Gunton's Pneumatology is where his concept of particularity finds its fullest expression. For the purposes of presenting Gunton's Pneumatology in a systematic fashion, we will examine first, how the Spirit perfects communion in the inner life of God; then second, in creation; and thirdly, in the human creature. The logic for this ordering is that Gunton begins his theology from the revelation of God—which establishes our understanding of the divine communion—then he moves to the personal aspects of creation, and finally humanity. Gunton's logic is that theology should begin from the doctrine of God, so that creation is properly related to the very being of God's communal life. Since humanity is part of the created order, and is the personal part, it also follows from the doctrine of creation that human beings are also shaped and related to the divine life of God. The final outcome of Gunton's logic is that regardless of the substance—divine or created—the Holy Spirit is the agent who perfects the communion, which in turn perfects the substance. Now we will examine how Gunton develops his Pneumatology in reference to God, creation and humanity; but first, we will briefly examine his motivation for developing a doctrine that is based on particularity-in-communion.

A. The Loss of Particularity

Gunton says that the doctrine of the Trinity "takes us wider and deeper into the mystery of what it is to be a human being in the world."[2] He is reacting against those philosophers who have shifted the locus of true humanity away from God towards humanity itself. Per Gunton's estimation, Don Cupitt expresses the sentiment of the Enlightenment period that in order for human beings to be authentic, they must have complete autonomy of their own self-definition. Unfortunately, Cupitt has completely misunderstood reality, the scripture, and the Triune God; but above all the fallenness of humanity.[3] Instead of defining humankind properly as the finite in relation *to* and *with*

---

2. Gunton, *The Promise of Trinitarian Theology*, 29.

3. Cupitt says that "the principles of spirituality cannot be imposed upon us from without and cannot depend at all upon any external circumstance. On the contrary, the principles of spirituality must be fully internalized *a priori* principles, freely adopted and self-imposed. A modern person must not any more surrender the apex of his self-consciousness to a god. It must remain his own" (Cupitt, *Taking Leave of God*, 9). Notice how Cupitt expresses spirituality: "That is, on our account the religious imperative that commands us to become free spirit is perceived as an autonomously authoritative principle which has to be freely and autonomously adopted and self-imposed" (ibid., 98).

the infinite, humankind is defined from within its own existence. Gunton criticizes Cupitt on this point because Cupitt does not take into consideration humanity's fallenness—that our existence is in a state of sin and evil. The finite becomes an isolated reality, which is really a condition of unrecognized fallenness due to the loss of relationality; that is, the loss of the relation with the infinite. By Gunton's estimation, there is such an inward turn towards humanity that relation as an ontological category is lost. The result is that the relation with the true Creator, as well as the relation with the rest of the created order, is no longer necessary when discussing ontology. So instead of freedom in relationship, philosophies like Cupitt's have created an enslavement of the individual who is no longer defined by relations with the other. In Gunton's estimation, this results in a loss of particularity, which results in the loss of a proper construal of the human person.[4]

Gunton agrees with W. J. Hill, who states that "the full understanding of creaturehood itself is disclosed in the light of the Trinity, for only thus is it clear that world or universe . . . bears a trinitarian imprint."[5] Personhood is defined in relation to the nature of the Triune God; personhood is not an individually isolated autonomous self. Since particularity is intimately associated with otherness-in-relationship, to view the individual apart from the communion with the triune God is a loss of particularity. The loss of particularity has wide implications for Gunton's theology, especially soteriology. Salvation is not a matter of redemption from a perishing world, but it is the advent of the Triune God to redeem this world by restoring the relationship with him. This way, particularity is recovered through the restoration of the relationship that defines what it means to be truly a human creature. Since redemption involves "the notion of God's faithfulness to his entire creation,"[6] the economic action of the Trinity is at the core of what it is to be human and what it is to be human in the world.[7] The doctrine of the

---

4. It should be recalled from our earlier discussion that "particularity" for Gunton is defined in terms of relations; the quiddity of particulars come from what they give and receive from and in relations with others.

5. Hill, *The Three-Personed God*, 273. When Hill uses the word "imprint" he is referring to the idea that creation and that salvation/redemption are Trinitarian events experienced within the history of the world.

6. Gunton, *The Actuality of Atonement*, 103.

7. Gunton views God's redemptive action as a holy love that is shaping and giving meaning to humanity, and our history. Forsyth says, "The power of God unto salvation is the revelation and the energy of the righteousness of God . . . It is holy love at work in final judgment (i.e., in the rectification of all things). The Cross of Christ creates in faith the assurance that the whole course of the world which entailed it is, before everything else, the explication of His work–a vast means for man's separation from his sin and union with his God" (Forsyth, *The Justification of God*, 124).

Trinity itself is not enough to secure a proper account of what it is to be a human person; ultimately it is Gunton's contention that a proper account of the Holy Spirit is necessary to develop a proper doctrine of the human person; that is, the recovery of pneumatic particularity. So first we will briefly look at how Gunton develops the notion of "person" within the immanent life of God, and then in turn how that corresponds with his understanding of the human person via Pneumatology.

B. The Holy Spirit as Perfector of Divine Communion: Richard of St. Victor

Gunton's Pneumatology is dependent on the idea that the Holy Spirit perfects communion within the divine life of God. The problem is that Gunton never fully develops the actual philosophical and theological line of reasoning for this assertion; as John Webster stated earlier, "when [Gunton's] theology does not persuade, it is usually . . . because he assumes the viability of his presuppositions and presses ahead to draw corollaries."[8] In order to understand Gunton's proposal regarding the Holy Spirit as the perfector of God's divine life, we will turn to Richard of St. Victor. As we will see below, Richard of St. Victor is an important figure for Gunton because he serves as a corrective voice to that of Augustine.[9] We will examine his proposal for presenting the Holy Spirit as a necessary person in the life of the Godhead by first reviewing germane metaphysical concepts; and secondly examining the attributes, relations, and action of the Holy Spirit in the Godhead; and thirdly, we will review Gunton's Pneumatology in light of Richard to

---

8. Webster, "Systematic Theology after Barth," 262

9. There has been enough attention given to critiquing those who critique Augustine in recent scholarship that it does not warrant another discussion of the merits of Augustine, and Gunton's alleged deficient reading of the historical Augustine. It seems Jenson is correct when in respect to Augustine he avers, "Did Gunton overdo it? Probably. Maybe I did too–once or twice. But was Gunton just wrong? I think not, and for an understanding of Gunton's theological choices, it is important to see that he was not wrong. Let me therefore, insert a general comment on the current polemics against those who criticize Augustine's Trinitarianism . . . What is *not* done by those who bash us Augustine-bashers is to face up to the truly disastrous propositions Augustine did in fact emphatically and insistently lay down, propositions that became maxims of subsequent Western theology" (Jenson, "A Decision Tree of Colin Gunton's Thinking," 11–12). Jenson's sentiments seem to express Gunton's thought elsewhere, for Gunton states, "A work, however, is to be judged not by what it sets out to do but by what it achieves" (Gunton, *Act and Being*, 49). So yes, Gunton probably did read Augustine incorrectly, but he is correct that the tradition has used Augustine in a certain manner; a manner in which recent scholarship is attempting to correct.

illuminate Gunton's use of "outward movement," "freedom," "communion" and "particularity" in relation to the Holy Spirit as perfector.

Richard of St. Victor

So far, we have indicated that Gunton's theology begins with his doctrine of God as a being-in-communion; and that particularity has the connotation that a particular substance is constituted by relations with others. The question at this point is: why use Richard of St. Victor? Gunton typically invokes Irenaeus in order to give due weight to the Spirit. But he usually limits his interaction with Irenaeus to the doctrine of creation; little attention is given to Irenaeus' conception of the immanent Trinity. Gunton frequently engages the Cappadocians, especially Basil, in order to demonstrate a proper ontology. But the ontology that the Cappadocians are reflecting is the ontology of the divine substance and persons overall; there is not a special reference to the Holy Spirit. But it is my contention that Richard of St. Victor supplies the necessary theological *locus* to account for Gunton's understanding of the role of the Holy Spirit. Bradley Green recognizes the importance of Richard of St. Victor in his work with a dedicated section titled "Anselm, Richard of St. Victor, and Aquinas."[10] Christoph Schwöbel comments that for Gunton, and in respect to Augustine, "Richard of St Victor serves as a better guide for understanding the love between two as perfected only when it turns outward towards a third."[11] It is of no small coincidence that Gunton quotes and engages Richard in what are arguably Gunton's most important works, *The One, The Three and the Many*; *Father, Son & Holy Spirit*; *The Promise of Trinitarian Theology*; and *Theology through the Theologians*. In these, Richard is primarily used as a corrective against Augustine—at least the way Gunton reads Augustine. For example, Gunton says, "Richard of St Victor argued that the third person of the Trinity is essential if there is to be true otherness in the Godhead."[12] There are many statements regarding Richard in Gunton's other works,[13] but there is one that is particularly pertinent to our discussion. In *Father, Son & Holy Spirit*, Gunton says that "Richard of St Victor, provided the basis of a correction

10. Green, *Colin Gunton and the Failure of Augustine*, 11. Green states that "Richard's attention is more centered on the role of the *persons*, and on the three persons as agents of divine love" (ibid., 12).

11. Schwöbel, "The Shape of Colin Gunton's Theology," 196

12. Gunton, *The One, the Three, and the Many*, 190.

13. For example, *The Promise of Trinitarian Theology*, 92; *The One, the Three, and the Many*, 190; Gunton, *Theology through the Theologians: Selected Essays, 1972–1995*, 172; and "The Trinity in Modern Theology," 951.

by making it possible to suggest that the Spirit is the focus of a love beyond the duality of Father and Son, of a love outwards to the other."[14] Before we proceed, a few preliminary comments are in order. First, Gunton only references Book III of Richard's *De Trinitate*. Richard's full work had not been translated into any modern language; and it was only as recently as 1990 that it was published in French and Italian.[15] In 2011, Ruben Angelici published Richard's complete *De Trinitate* in English; unfortunately, this was not available to Gunton. But in keeping with Gunton's usual motif of selectively reading those primary sources he deemed most influential, he probably would have still used just Book III because that is Richard's most influential book.[16] Now we will examine Richard's early discussion, which establishes the framework of his metaphysical understanding of key ideas that are critical when he discusses the triune persons.

At the outset, it should be stated that Richard is a theologian who considered himself to be working within the received tradition, so his explication of the doctrine of the Trinity follows the pattern of those before him, especially Augustine and Aquinas. Angelici states that Richard "starts with the demonstration of divine *unity* and *afterwards*, through the analysis of substantial attributes, he defines God's Trinity."[17] Even though Gunton decries against Augustine and Aquinas for beginning with the one God and moving to the threeness, Richard adopts the same scheme, but apparently with results more in line with Gunton's thinking. Richard lays the foundation for his metaphysics by establishing God's substantial *unity* in Book I, and only then does he discuss God's attributes. By establishing God's substantial *unity*, Richard identifies God as supreme in being and existence, "and it is God who identifies with power and wisdom."[18] Richard moves through a

---

14. Gunton, *Father, Son, and Holy Spirit*, 86.

15. Angelici says that "the De Trinitate has never been translated into English or German" (see Richard of St. Victor, *On the Trinity*, 7).

16. For example, Lyle is critical of Gunton's understanding of the Cappadocians; primarily on the grounds that Gunton did not read them thoroughly. Lyle says, "after examining his understanding of the Cappadocians, however, this writer finds that Gunton has based his concepts on very little of what the Cappadocians wrote since he interacts very little with the primary sources" (see Lyle, "Social Trinitarianism," 115). Another example is that in Gunton's works, *The One, the Three, and the Many; The Promise of Trinitarian Theology; Father, Son & Holy Spirit; Theology through the Theologians;* and *The Triune Creator*, Gunton has over fifty-five references to Augustine's *De Trinitate*, but less than thirty for all other works of Augustine combined. Lyle seems correct, in that Gunton relied on secondary sources for his knowledge of Augustine, while focusing on the key texts as a primary source.

17. Angelici, Introduction to Richard of St. Victor, *On the Trinity*, 24.

18. Ibid., 1.17.85.

series of arguments which begins with God's *unity* as the basis for assigning to God the attributes of "all-power" and "all-wisdom" to the conclusion that God must be *supremely good*.[19] That God is *supremely good* becomes an essential part of Richard's argument for the necessity of construing the Holy Spirit as a third person vis-à-vis the first and second persons.

Richard contends that fullness and perfection of all goodness are contained in the *supremely good*. Therefore,

> true and highest love cannot be absent where fullness of all goodness is found, since nothing is better or more perfect than charity-love. Yet, none is said to possess charity-love in the truest sense of the word if he loves himself exclusively. It is, thus, necessary that love be aimed at someone else in order to be charity-love. If a multiplicity of persons is absent, there can be no place for charity-love.[20]

The concept of "charity-love" becomes the focal point in arguing for the necessity of a third person. When Richard says that love must be aimed at someone else, this corresponds to Gunton's complaint that Augustine's "bond of love" "is in danger of leading us to think of God as a kind of self-enclosed circle."[21] Gunton means that there must be some sense that God is reaching out towards another. But the question at this stage is: does not the Father love the Son, who is another person? Richard addresses this by arguing that the love between two parties is not perfect charity-love, but a reciprocal love. The love between two persons is the beginning of charity-love, but not its perfection. Since God is *supremely good*, meaning perfect in himself, then love must be a perfected love. So Richard's argument must fulfill the requirement of perfect love within God, while simultaneously incorporating God's revelation as Triune.

In order to develop God's triunity in perfect love, Richard extends his argument to show that the "fullness of goodness" requires charity-love, and that charity-love requires at least two divine persons. By analogy, "fullness of happiness" also requires charity-love, which requires a plurality of persons. For God to be completely worthy of his glory, God must exist in complete "fullness of happiness," which requires that his happiness is shared.

---

19. Richard says, "He who really is omnipotent cannot lack any of the desirable attributes. Where omnipotence resides, no fullness and no perfection can be absent . . . Nothing can be better, nothing can be greater than that which is full and perfect under every aspect. Regarding the omnipotent being, then, it is clear that he is the highest good and thus he is–for himself–his own good" (2.16.104.).

20. 3.2.116.

21. Gunton, *Father, Son, and Holy Spirit*, 86.

This way, multiplicity of persons is proven, because fundamentally, God consists of perfect goodness, happiness and joy: all three attributes require the ability and willingness for God to share his perfect glory. So for Richard, perfect goodness necessitates perfect joy and happiness. Out of perfect goodness, joy, and happiness comes the conclusion that "there is nothing more glorious, nothing more splendid than being unwilling to possess a single thing that one should not want to share [also with others]."[22] In other words, there must be a free will that moves one person to love the other, and then the free will to reciprocate that love. The love between the Father and the Son is an authentic love for Richard, but it is not the perfect and supremely highest form of charity-love; something is missing that is necessary to complete his conception of perfect love.

After a series of arguments about God and humanity, Richard returns to the question at hand. Richard says, "And before anything else, if possible, let us ask supreme charity-love what it can testify on this specific topic."[23] So at this stage in his argument, supreme-love served as the basis for a multiplicity of persons in the Godhead, but not a triunity of persons. For supreme-love to be absolutely perfect, it cannot lack the highest greatness or excellence. Richard then states that "in authentic charity-love the greatest excellence seems to be this: to will that someone else be loved just as we are."[24] Richard means that charity-love only comes about when the one giving love and the one receiving and reciprocating that love both freely desire to share their love with an*other*. Richard states it this way, "The arguments expounded up to this point demonstrated that if those two reciprocally loving beings are absolutely perfect, both of them—for the same reason—must necessarily will that another being be [also] associated [with them] to share the love of which each of them is the object."[25] Richard concludes that for love to be a perfect charity-love that a trinity of persons is necessary. The reason is that perfect happiness and joy is of the shared sort, and not just a reciprocal type; two perfect persons will desire to share their happiness and joy—that is the nature of happiness and joy, the desire to share it. Richard concludes that "in order to be authentic, charity-love needs a plurality of beings; equally, in order to be perfect, it requires a Trinity of persons."[26]

Once Richard has determined that in order for charity-love to be perfected it requires a trinity of persons, he establishes both freedom and

22. Richard of St. Victor, *On the Trinity* 3.6.120.
23. 3.11.125.
24. Ibid.
25. 3.11.126.
26. 3.13.128.

communion as necessary attributes of divine persons. His argument is that since each divine person is omnipotent, and each person is perfect in happiness, and for happiness to be perfect it must be able to share its joy; therefore, an omnipotent person—being perfect-in-happiness—can and will share with an*other*. Then Richard argues that in each person, the attributes are perfect, and since goodness is an attribute in each person, each person has goodness in a perfect way. Since goodness includes the free desire to share love, then each person must share with an*other*, and also is willing to share *that* reciprocal love with a third. Richard states, "It must be rightly underlined that in the divine persons the perfection of one [of them] required the addition of the other. And consequently, between the two [persons], perfection of both requires the association of a third one."[27] Richard completes the picture of communion with the introduction of "co-love," *condilectio*.[28] Richard's argument can be simplified by stating that a subject loving an object is love, but not "co-love." A subject loving an object, and in turn, the object returning love to the subject is a reciprocal love, but not "co-love." So, "co-love" is when a third object (i.e., another divine person) is loved by the two objects participating in reciprocal love.[29] Obviously, the persons in Richard's arguments refer to the three persons of the trinity so that the Holy Spirit becomes the essential person that determines and perfects "co-love." Richard appropriates but moves beyond Augustine's "bond of love" by reconfiguring the metaphor "bond of love" as something that happens as a subject-object relation between each of the three persons (i.e., Father-Son, Father-Holy Spirit, Son-Holy Spirit). In this way, the "bond of love" is multiplied three times and is not limited to the Father-Son relationship. Richard says,

> if we analyse [this] concord, [we notice] that the bond of love is multiplied three-fold in it, so that where the suspicion of a lack of love could have risen more easily, certainty [of love] is confirmed by a more profound union. Then, in this way, because of the addition of the third person of the Trinity, it happens that

---

27. 3.15.129.

28. In a footnote, Angelici states that "the original, Latin word *condilectio* has been rendered as "co-love." The idea of co-love is ultimately the central theme of Richard's argumentation. Co-love is neither self-addressed love, nor reciprocal love, but it is ultimately what makes plurality harmoniously coexist in unity. It is love in harmony between the first and the second person that cannot but be directed also at a third person" (ibid., 132n10).

29. "[We rightly speak of co-love] when the two [persons'] affects are fused so to become only one, because of the third flame of love" (3.19.132.).

charity-love is in agreement, and that love is communitarian everywhere and never exclusive.[30]

In other words, the Holy Spirit is the one that perfects unity and brings communion to the Godhead. We now turn to Gunton in order to determine how Richard's understanding of the Holy Spirit's role informs and illuminates Gunton's Pneumatology.

Gunton's Pneumatology of Communion

It is no secret that Gunton lays the blame for deficient Pneumatology on Augustine. Gunton says, "Augustine called the Spirit the bond of love between the Father and the Son, but this is in danger of leading us to think of God as a kind of self-enclosed circle."[31] Based on our examination of Richard of St. Victor, when Gunton says "self-enclosed circle," he is equating this with Richard's conception of reciprocal love between the Father and the Son. This is an authentic love, but it is not Richard's perfect charity-love or "co-love." In Richard's scheme, the love between the Father and the Son is a love that exists only between them and does not have any movement towards any other person. Since it is an absolute love between two persons, it is only a reciprocal love—it is not yet a charity-love. Since the "bond of love" that exists between the Father and Son is a *reciprocal* action, the Holy Spirit is not *that* "bond of love" because Richard located the Spirit within *perfected* charity-love. In a sense, Richard has developed a dualistic view of love—love itself and a perfected love; but charity-love includes at least three subjects.

This would be problematic for Gunton if Richard terminated love in the reciprocal form, which would result in the Holy Spirit being associated with an action between the Father and the Son; metaphysically speaking, the Holy Spirit would be a relation defined as an action of reciprocal love. Gunton says that "the baneful Western tendency, whose root was in Augustine, [is] to define the person as a relation."[32] Also, in reference to Augustine's use of the term "person," Gunton explains that "despite his avowed reason for the use of the term, he had prepared the way for the later, and fateful, *definition* of the person as a *relation*."[33] Based on Richard's scheme, it seems that Gunton understands the love between the Father and the Son as a relation of love that exists between them as reciprocal love. This way, reciprocal

---

30. 3.20.133.
31. Gunton, *Father, Son, and Holy Spirit*, 86.
32. Gunton, *Becoming and Being*, 229.
33. Gunton, *The Promise of Trinitarian Theology*, 40.

love is a relational term that is predicated to a subject. This reciprocal love is conceived as a property that the subject possesses, albeit an eternal essential property. To put it differently, assuming that subject A is fifty years old and subject B is twenty years of age, it can be said that subject A is older than subject B. The term "older" is a relational term that exists between the two subjects, but it is an attribute that is predicated to subject A in relation to subject B. In this sense, for Gunton, "bond of love" is not a "person" but a relational term. In this case, the Holy Spirit is not really a "person," but a relational attribute of both the Father and the Son. But Gunton endeavors to recognize the Holy Spirit in strictly and fully personal terms.

Richard's scheme allows for a stronger construal of the Holy Spirit in fully personal terms because in order for reciprocal love to be perfected, it must become a shared love; that is, a charity-love. Only when the Father and Son freely share their reciprocal love with a third does that love become a perfect love. This has several ramifications on Gunton's Pneumatology. First, the reciprocal love between the Father and the Son is no longer between them, but is shared with another, creating new networks of reciprocal love, which are defined as "co-love." By creating these new networks of reciprocal love, in which the Father-Son network becomes Father-Son, Father-Holy Spirit, Son-Holy Spirit, Gunton can define God's love as a movement towards an other. Instead of viewing the Spirit as closing the divine circle of love—that is, as the closed relation of reciprocal love between the Father and Son—Gunton can perceive the Holy Spirit "with an orientation outwards, so that corresponding to the Spirit's constitution of the otherness in relation of the Father and Son in the eternal Trinity is an orientation to the other which is the created world."[34] This way, the Holy Spirit is the one who perfects the divine life of God and opens the circle of love towards the other—first towards the other divine persons and then towards creation.

The second ramification is that the Holy Spirit can now be conceived as the perfector of the divine nature. Gunton asks "may we say . . . that the Spirit perfects the life of the eternal Trinity by so relating the Father and the Son that together the three are one being in communion?"[35] Again, in Richard's scheme, the Holy Spirit perfects charity-love, which establishes the perfection of the divine substance. The Father and the Son share an authentic reciprocal love, but in order to have a perfect supreme love, charity-love is necessary. In order to be wholly perfect, charity-love must be in their possession, and since charity-love requires sharing of reciprocal love, the Holy Spirit is necessary to perfect the Father and the Son. This is also faithful to

---

34. Gunton, *Act and Being*, 120.
35. Ibid., 103–4.

the *taxis* of the trinity as revealed in scripture; the Father is the originator of the love, and the Son is the recipient, or the one begotten of the love, and the Holy Spirit is the final perfecting recipient of the Father's originating love and the Son's reciprocating love (which is conceived in a secondary sense)—this is not a chronological ordering, but an eternal logical *taxis*. Gunton says, "One of the many good reasons for rejecting the doctrine of the *Filioque* is that in the economy, the Son is also the gift of the Spirit, who is the one by whose agency the Father begets Jesus in time, empowers his ministry and raises him from the dead."[36] In this way, the Holy Spirit is not only the perfector but receives perfection from the Father through the Son because he shares in a reciprocal relationship of love with both the Father and the Son separately, while simultaneously sharing the reciprocal love of each with the other person. So, within the *taxis* of the Godhead, the Holy Spirit is conceived of third in the order of perfect "co-love;" the Spirit is designated as the eschatological perfector of the divine nature. In Gunton's estimation, the *filioque* creates an eternal subordination of the Spirit, but Richard's charity-love completes the *taxis* by locating the Spirit *within* the divine communion as the agent who is required to perfect it—the Holy Spirit gives to both the Father and Son, as well as receives from them.

Lastly, Richard's scheme has ramification on Gunton's Pneumatology in that the Holy Spirit can be described as giving particularity to the Father and the Son. In reference to Richard, Gunton says, "There must be three if there is to be a true outwardgoingness and diversity in God."[37] This corresponds to Richard's charity-love that completes the reciprocal authentic love. Gunton then argues, "in that sense, we may say that the Spirit's function in the Godhead is to particularize the *hypostases*."[38] Now we have additional insight to what Gunton means by the term "particularize"—to develop a constitutive relationship that simultaneously allows the subjects to retain their distinct identities. The Holy Spirit fulfills the role of the particularizing agent in the following manner as based on Richard's scheme, who says,

> divinity—which as we have observed there, cannot be shared by multiple substances—here, is common to multiple persons. Yet, if every perfection is shared by those who love each other reciprocally, as we have said, it is clear and certain that if one of them is omnipotent, the other one is omnipotent as well; if one is immense, the other one is immense as well; if one is God, the other one is God as well.[39]

---

36. Gunton, *Father, Son, and Holy Spirit*, 72.
37. Gunton, *The One, the Three, and the Many*, 190.
38. Ibid.
39. Victor, *On the Trinity* 3.8.122.

So Richard circumscribes the distinction between substance and persons in such a manner that each person must fully possess each of the divine attributes. In chapter XV, Richard concludes, "it must be rightly underlined that in the divine persons the perfection of one [of them] required the addition of the other. And consequently, between the two [persons], perfection of both requires the association of a third one."[40] For our purposes, it is the claim that "perfection of both requires the association of a third one" that underlines Gunton's view of particularity. The Father and the Son, being divine persons, must share completely in the divine attributes, especially in perfect love; but they must retain their respective relations of origin, that is, begetter and begotten.

The Father and Son must be constituted by a third relationship in order to create Richard's "co-love." So putting all these qualifications together, particularizing is the act of the Holy Spirit whereby the Father and the Son attain perfection and retain their distinctions. The Father's perfection is actualized when his relationship with the Son is perfected when it is shared with the Holy Spirit. The Son's perfection is likewise only truly actualized when the love he received from the Father is shared with the Holy Spirit. The distinctions of the Father and the Son are maintained because the Father is ever the source of the reciprocal love, and the Son's love is begotten by the Father's love. In this way, the Father is the originator and the Son is originated eternally. The personhood of the Father and the Son are each perfected because the Holy Spirit takes the reciprocal love they share, and completes it by allowing it to become a charity-love. The Holy Spirit's distinction is also maintained because he receives love from the Father and the Son. There is a logical *taxis*, but not a temporal one; the activity of love between the Father, Son, and Holy Spirit is an eternal activity. So "to particularize" for Gunton is the *action* of the Holy Spirit which allows the Father and Son to maintain their original reciprocal love while perfecting their authentic love so that it becomes the perfect and ultimate charity-love. So instead of the Holy Spirit as the "bond of love" between the Father and the Son—which is really the original reciprocal love—the Holy Spirit established a multiplicity of bonds. Once love is perfected by sharing with a third, there is a "bond of love" between the Spirit and the Father and between the Spirit and the Son; and by sharing the original reciprocal love, it is apprehended as a perfected "bond of love." This way, instead of the Holy Spirit being the "bond of love," He perfects the "bond of love" between persons.

By explicating the Holy Spirit in terms of the perfecting eschatological agent who perfects the "bond of love," Gunton gains much currency for his

---

40. 3.15.129.

theological project. First, there is a sense of movement outwards for God's love because the love between the Father and the Son moves beyond the reciprocal love towards the other. Gunton explains it thusly,

> the Spirit is indeed to be understood as the one who completes the relations of Father and Son. The difference is that the introduction of the eschatological note changes radically the way in which the relationship is understood: not a closed circle, but a self-sufficient community of love freely opened outwards to embrace the other.[41]

This movement outwards gives impetus to God's reaching out to that which is not God in a loving embrace of his creation. Secondly, explaining the Holy Spirit as the eschatological agent, Gunton develops a divine futureness in God and his activities towards the world. The Spirit's work is logically third, and brings perfection; which leads to some type of divine temporality. Eternity describes God's internal activity, an activity that the Holy Spirit completes, but only after the logical expression of the Father's and Son's relationship. In his *Becoming and Being*, Gunton turns to Jenson for assistance with divine temporality and the Holy Spirit.[42] In Jenson's *God After God*, he criticizes Barth's lack of attention to the Holy Spirit by saying that "Barth displays the doctrine that the Father is 'the fount of the trinity.' But that the Trinity also has a goal in the Spirit remains a mere occasional assertion."[43] Jenson concludes that "the futurity of the triune God must be made plain."[44] In other words, the Spirit, as that which brings perfection to God, as the third successive person, "is the goal of the Trinity, and this doctrine must be given the function which had belonged to the doctrine that the Father is the 'fount of the Trinity.'"[45] Gunton is in agreement with Jenson[46] because "the Spirit's action is perfecting, eschatological action"[47] that finds its basis in the action of perfecting within the Godhead. So Richard's scheme allows Gunton to conceive the Holy Spirit's action in terms

---

41. Gunton, *Theology through the Theologians: Selected Essays, 1972–1995*, 128.
42. Gunton, *Becoming and Being*, 171–85.
43. Jenson, *God after God*, 173.
44. Ibid.
45. Ibid.
46. Gunton says, "The orientation of Barth's theology to the past has given many critics the impression that everything has already happened in eternity, and that there is to be no significant future divine history. This would be a direct consequence of the neglect of the third person of the Trinity alleged by R. W. Jenson" (Gunton, *Becoming and Being*, 182).
47. Gunton, *Act and Being*, 141.

of sequence, albeit a divine atemporal sequence, so that "God is in himself Spirit, Father and Son: Future, Past and Present."[48] So God's love first originated in the love of the Father, then by order of succession received that love in the Son, lastly in the succession, that love was perfected in an eternal sharing in the person of the Holy Spirit—this eternal succession is a *becoming* from authentic love to perfected love.

C. The Holy Spirit as Giver of Particularity: Humanity and Creation

Gunton says, "It can be said that the doctrine of the Trinity is being used to suggest ways of allowing the eternal becoming of God—the eternally interanimating energies of the three—to provide the basis for the personal dynamics of the community."[49] In this statement, Gunton outlines his basic understanding of personhood for both the divine and human person. Unfortunately, Gunton does not explicitly state why the Holy Spirit deserves special focus over the doctrine of the Trinity for a proper understanding of personhood, so we must deduce that ourselves. When discussing personhood, Gunton does interact extensively with Zizioulas, John Macmurray and the Cappadocian fathers for support in advocating a relational account of personhood, so we will interact with their respective works for illumination into Gunton's logic. The difficulty arises in that Zizioulas, Macmurray and the Cappadocian fathers explain personhood in terms of relations, but this only implies multiplicity in construing the person—there is not an explicit need for a third person. For example, Gunton says that "communion is for Basil an ontological category. The *nature* of God is communion."[50] This is a direct reference to Zizioulas, who says "the being of God could be known only through personal relationships and personal love. Being means life, and life means *communion*."[51] Macmurray also states that "the Self is constituted by its relation to the Other; that is it has its being in its relationship; and that this relationship is necessarily personal."[52] These three sources indicate that Gunton's primary ontology is that personhood is conceived relationally, as either being-in-communion or otherness-in-relation; either way, this is a subject-other relationship—a third object or person is not necessary. Fortunately, Gunton does leave clues that aid in

48. Jenson, *God after God*, 191.
49. Gunton, *The Promise of Trinitarian Theology*, 81.
50. Ibid., 71.
51. Zizioulas, *Being as Communion*, 16.
52. Macmurray, *Persons in Relation*, 17.

determining how his Pneumatology overcomes the problems of conceiving personhood as a mere subject-other relationship; a relationship which leads to the Holy Spirit being conceived as nothing more than the "bond of love" between two parties. Therefore, we will attempt to flesh out Gunton's Pneumatology as an essential element to the ontology of the human person. Following the scheme presented by Richard of St. Victor, perfect love is defined as a love-in-communion, that is, "co-love." A love that is perfected is only "co-love" when it is freely shared by two agents (love in this context for Richard is a reciprocal activity between two agents). So it is the Holy Spirit who is the agent who allows the love between the Father and the Son to become perfected "co-love," by allowing them to freely share their love with the Holy Spirit. The Holy Spirit perfects their freedom and love-in-communion. Therefore, without a properly envisioned Pneumatology that includes freedom and perfection of communion, a theological account of personhood will be deficient. Not only must there be a proper account of perfection in Pneumatology, it must be ordered by the Holy Spirit's role in the divine life of God as the eschatological perfecting Spirit. So we must examine Gunton's works to see if we can determine how the Holy Spirit is conceived as bringing freedom and perfection to creation, and what happens if these aspects are missing from Pneumatology. First, we will examine how Gunton expresses the loss of relationality, and then his pneumatological solution to the problem.

For Gunton, without the personal agency of the Holy Spirit, creaturely freedom is lost. Gunton says that "we prefer to find freedom grounded in ourselves rather than lying in the gift of the creator."[53] Freedom is a divine gift but one that is pneumatically shaped; in other words, creation is given room to reach its God intended destiny, while the Spirit is working *eschatologically* to move creation to that destiny. For Gunton, when freedom is defined in terms of escaping from the oppressive other, or as an escape from heteronomy, an individualistic view of freedom develops; one which creates a system that separates an individual from the other—there is no trinitarianly given freedom to give and receive from the other. Gunton explains that Luther and Calvin expressed freedom as an inward transformation of either our moral or spiritual character, which for Gunton is not really freedom because it is non-relational. It is an over-spiritualized form of freedom. T. H. L. Parker, in his biography of Calvin, interprets Calvin's theology by saying that "liberty, however, is not physical but spiritual."[54] The concern for Gunton is that through Luther and Calvin—but ultimately

---

53. Gunton, *The Promise of Trinitarian Theology*, 118.
54. Parker, *John Calvin*, 71.

through Augustine—freedom is comprehended in very individualistic terms. Freedom was no longer understood as a relational concept, it could not be conceived in a community.[55]

When the Holy Spirit is not conceived as a personal divine agent of perfecting love, then freedom will be conceived in terms of Luther's freedom from the law or Calvin's freedom from sin.[56] Either way, inner transformation becomes the focus, and an emphasis on the past actions of Christ on the cross, with little concern for the freedom of our future selves, will rule the day. Since the Holy Spirit was conceived as the "bond of love" between the Father and the Son, instead of a divine agent of personal action of love, freedom was viewed primarily with reference to Christology. The victory Christ won gave believers victory over sin through justification, which was translated in terms of inner moral transformation. But simply viewing freedom in terms of inner transformation does little to affect our relationships with others and creation itself. Gunton says that Luther's

> conception of justification . . . led to the neglect of some of the features we have seen to be important. The meaning of the justice of God, so closely linked with justification, came to be too closely tied to individual sin and forgiveness, too loosely to the cosmic and social dimensions which have been a part of other developments of the subject.[57]

Alister McGrath explains that Luther abandoned the role of grace in justification, which led to the development of a forensic view of justification, one that places the stress of justification on the cross. McGrath says that "the origins of the concept of 'imputed righteousness,' so characteristic of Protestant theologies of justification after the year 1530, may therefore legitimately be considered to lie with Luther."[58] Later, McGrath states that

---

55. In *Institutes*, book 3, Calvin says, "Christian liberty seems to me to consist of three parts. First, the consciences of believers, while seeking the assurance of their justification before God, must rise above the law, and think no more of obtaining justification by it . . . Another point which depends on the former is, that consciences obey the law, not as if compelled by legal necessity; but being free from the yoke of the law itself, voluntarily obey the will of God . . . The third part of this liberty is that we are not bound before God to any observance of external things which are in themselves indifferent (διάφορα), but that we are now at full liberty either to use or omit them" (Calvin, *Institutes of the Christian Religion* 3.19).

56. Doyle states that, "with good reason, Luther's eschatology has been said to be mainly an eschatology of judgment, while Calvin's eschatology has been said to be mainly an eschatology of resurrection" (*Eschatology and the Shape of Christian Belief*, 160).

57. Gunton, *The Actuality of Atonement*, 101.

58. McGrath, *Iustitia Dei*, 229.

"Luther's reforming agenda brought about a significant lexical development within western Christianity, in which the phraseology of 'justification by faith' displaced that of 'salvation by grace.'"[59] For Gunton, this means that God's redeeming action is conceived as grounded in the past—in the eternal and timeless decree of the Father, and the cross of the Son—which gives the impression that all of the interesting activities of God have already taken place. This is not a harsh critique of Luther or Calvin, it is more in harmony with Gunton's earlier critique of Barth's Pneumatology which he perceives as having little to no room for a "significant future divine history."[60] Therefore, the doctrines of election and predestination will have no room for eschatology; eschatology is in danger of being another form of determinism in that everything is settled in eternity past between the Father and Christ.[61]

In this high Christology, eschatology becomes the enemy of freedom because the human creature is no longer free to be; Pelagianism is defeated but at the expense of liberty. Instead of eschatology being conceived as a now and not yet, eschatology becomes an other-worldly endeavor, meaning that we are waiting for our liberation from this existence. Our actions in this life have no bearing because there is no eschatologically driven work of the Spirit perfecting creation. Gunton complains that even in Barth, when election is conceived as a covenant between the Father and the Son, there is little room, if any, for the eschatological perfecting action of the Holy Spirit in our time and space. Concerning Barth's doctrine of election, Gunton says that "real eschatology is lost, or at least suggests only the playing out of that which has already been decided in advance in a way that endangers the freedom at once of the Spirit and of the creation."[62] In other words, the doctrines of election, predestination and eschatology have their basis in timeless decrees by a statically conceived God who only loves the other; that is, his Son. There is no movement towards a third, so that the love between the Father and Son is a timeless event that places tension between time and eternity. If the love between the Father and the Son is an atemporal event, and that is the form of perfect love, then perfect love

---

59. Ibid., 407.

60. Gunton says, "The orientation of Barth's theology to the past have given many critics the impression that everything has already happened in eternity, and that there is to be no significant future divine history" (*Becoming and Being,* 182).

61. Ferguson says that, "in manual of doctrine, the four last things were often identified as resurrection, judgement, heaven and hell. The task of eschatology was to elucidate these on the basis of information contained in scripture and tradition. In this way eschatology was the final piece of the jigsaw of Christian belief, and could be set out largely in isolation from the exposition of other doctrine" (Ferguson, "Eschatology," 226).

62. Gunton, *Christ and Creation,* 95.

is conceived of on the other side of eternity. Without the perfecting love of the Spirit, freedom is in jeopardy because eternity becomes *the* place where perfect love is present. Since creation exists in time, and Christ lived in time, eschatology cannot be conceived as an escape from time; if the creature cannot find its divine fulfillment in time, then the creature's freedom will be lost against the heteronomy of eternity. For Gunton, this forfeiture of freedom is overcome by the Holy Spirit as the eschatological perfector of creation. As we will see, a doctrine of the Trinity that gives room to the Holy Spirit's agency of eschatological perfection overcomes heteronomy and gives eschatological freedom to creation.

In order to link Pneumatology with freedom, Gunton turns to Coleridge. Coleridge addresses the problem of freedom by privileging the Trinity over pantheism. Raimonda Modiano comments that "For Coleridge the only correct answer to a theory of life was a transcendent deity, and the only alternative to pantheism was a system firmly grounded in the theistic doctrine of the trinity."[63] Coleridge was reacting against the pantheism of his day, especially Spinoza, who viewed God as simply the supreme cause who acted out of necessity. McFarland summarizes Spinoza's system as "we have no final control and no final choice;"[64] and "nor is there eventual hope through the intervention of a benevolent deity, for the God of Spinoza is mindless and soulless, vast and blank."[65] Spinoza's God does not act from freedom of the will but from a chain of necessity. Ultimately for Spinoza "there is . . . no hope in the future and no ultimate goal or meaning in life."[66] For Coleridge, any theology or philosophy that is not derived from the revelation of the Triune God is pantheistic. Gunton appropriates this idea and reorients it toward the notion of freedom. Gunton argues that Coleridge developed a view of philosophy towards dualistic categories of mechanistic or romantic pantheism. Within both schemes, the human person is nothing more than an "it" that is responding to some type of outside influence, and that "human freedom was abolished, the human moral agent turned into a cog in an impersonal machine or organism."[67] McFarland concludes that by accepting the doctrine of the Trinity, Coleridge "found, in the very terms of that acceptance, the guarantee of the joint reality of the One as One and the Many as Many."[68] Therefore, for both Coleridge and Gunton, human

---

63. Modiano, "'Naturphilsophilosophie,'" 59.

64. McFarland, *Coleridge and the Pantheist Tradition*, 69.

65. Ibid., 69–70.

66. Ibid., 70.

67. Gunton, *The Promise of Trinitarian Theology*, 23.

68. McFarland, *Coleridge and the Pantheist Tradition*, 229.

freedom can only be recovered by means of the doctrine of the Trinity; but for Gunton the Holy Spirit is essential to that freedom. As outlined above, for Richard of St. Victor it is the Holy Spirit who liberates and perfects the Father and the Son to be themselves through the divine *act* of perfecting "co-love." Therefore, the Trinity is necessary for freedom, and with the addition of Richard's method, the Holy Spirit liberates the Father and the Son to be their unique distinction by perfecting their distinctions in love. This way, the Holy Spirit is essential to the divine act of freedom; God liberates because the Holy Spirit perfects freedom.

The divine action of liberation, as witnessed in the economic life of God, must be the same divine action that is in the immanent life: God reveals as he is. The Holy Spirit liberates creation to be itself because God relates to creation out of a free love and not necessity. In this way, because the Spirit's action is that of perfecting in love, creation is free to relate to the Creator but as a creature. The perfect love between the Father and the Son, which is shared by the Holy Spirit, is now turned towards creation by the same action of the Triune God. The Holy Spirit prepared Christ a body so that Christ can share God's love with creation—an action of perfection by the Spirit. The Holy Spirit anointed Jesus Christ at his baptism to inaugurate Christ as the head of a new community—a community sharing in God's love. At the resurrection, the Holy Spirit created a new spiritual existence that demonstrated the Father's love, which was given to the Son, which through the action of the Spirit was also shared with creation. Creation is liberated from fulfilling some lack in the Creator because the Spirit is continually perfecting the love that was given from the Father through the incarnated Christ—God is complete in himself. Creation is not necessary for God to demonstrate love, God is co-love in his eternal being; creation is free to respond to God in an appropriate manner without becoming God to do so. Freedom is shaped by God's love, which means that freedom in creation is conceived as a gift from God that is ultimately *for* and *to* God. Freedom is not to be conceived as the freedom-to-be away from God or other creatures. The Father's two hands, the Son as redeemer and the Spirit as liberator, actualize freedom in creation so that creation is free to be in a relationship with God and with other creatures.

What this means is that the Holy Spirit liberates human individuals to become persons. By sharing in the "co-love" of the triune God, the human individual is drawn into relationships that are modeled after God's *being*: meaning that human relationships shape and constitute the human person by the Spirit in relation to God. Human freedom is a dynamic activity because the Holy Spirit is conceived as God's futurity. Human freedom is dynamic freedom because the Spirit is organizing and shaping creation within its creaturely existence that is oriented towards its final destiny. In order for the Holy Spirit to be viewed in eschatological terms, a proper Pneumatology must include the notion of *becoming*—creation is not static but dynamic. Just as there is a logical sequence in the triune Godhead that can be called divine time, there is also a temporal sequence in humanity's *becoming*—this way, freedom includes the idea that creation—especially the human creature—is conceived as open to the dynamic transforming action of the Holy Spirit that is moving creation towards its divine goal to be itself, that is, a new community-in-relation.

Gunton asks, "If the Holy Spirit is truly the creator of community wherever it is to be found, should it not be possible to say something about the way in which Christian freedom and political liberty may be supposed to bear upon each other?"[69] Gunton expects a "yes" to his rhetorical question, indicating that he expects the Spirit's liberation to have some bearing in the here and now. Freedom for Gunton is not merely an abstract or speculative doctrinal position indicating a piety of moral change, but a gift from God: "freedom is a mode of personal action."[70] Freedom is not freedom *from* but *for* the other; it is a freedom shaped by the triune God that is a personal freedom—freedom is the God-given ability to be a person-in-relation. God's freedom is inherent to who he is, but creaturely freedom is given from *by* the economic activity of God who restores the broken relationship with his creation. This personal relationship between the Creator and the creature, for Gunton, demands a Pneumatological approach, "for it is there, surely, that the relation between God's government and our freedom must come to expression."[71] It is the divine action of the Holy Spirit to perfect the relationship between the Father and Son, so in a temporally and analogous manner, the same action is seen in creation: the Holy Spirit liberates creation, and especially the human individual, towards the perfecting of the relationship with God. This takes place as the Holy Spirit creates community through the work and presence of the risen Christ. The Holy Spirit liberates humanity to reach its potential as authentic human being *in* and *because* of Jesus Christ. Just as Jesus exhibited an authentic humanity—which can be conceived of as an autonomy-in-relation—humanity is being shaped in the same way by the Spirit. Salvation does not generate an autonomous humanity that exists *apart* from others as an other-worldly promise; salvation takes place *within* our present situation as a reconstitution of proper relationality. The Spirit is building a community that should "serve as a witness to the life of the age to

---

69. Gunton, *The Promise of Trinitarian Theology*, 122.
70. *Act and Being*, 107.
71. Gunton, *Enlightenment and Alienation*, 103.

come, summoning all mankind to repentance and true community."[72] Just as the Father and the Son are perfected in their respective relations of origins due to the Holy Spirit shaping their love (which is simultaneously a sharing of their love), the Holy Spirit perfects creation by allowing God's internal love to be shared with it. So the community is a community of love that is also sharing God's triune love with each other, which should be a model of freedom, the freedom to love the other in a reciprocal and sharing relationship. Gunton laments that due to the stain of sin, the history of the church as a community has been less than desirable, and the history of the church is replete with examples of coercion and neglect of the community in favor of various institutional abuses.[73] But nevertheless, the church is a mere down payment of what the Spirit is perfecting for the *eschaton*: the church is constituted by the Holy Spirit to be a community defined by freedom as a grace of God in Christ.

To be a free human being is to be in a proper relationship, first with the Creator, then with other humans, and then with creation. Freedom requires community, which the Spirit gives as a non-coercion ability to relate to that which is other: "Freedom is never absolute, but always structured and ordered, either wrongly or rightly."[74] But what does this structure look like? To begin with, the Spirit liberates humanity from idolatry of self and the world, that is, a break from the law of works. The Spirit allows the Word to affect individuals so that they turn away from locating personhood within themselves by reaching out to God. Gunton understands the Spirit's work as a cosmological work because the Spirit is present wherever "there is unadulterated love between man and woman . . . [where] there are genuine forms of human community, and in so far as the creation is allowed in industry, agriculture, art and craft to praise its maker and to be directed to its perfection in him."[75] In this way, the Spirit is not only conceived from within the church community, but is that which is also located where there

---

72. Ibid., 106.

73. Gunton is primarily concerned with the lack of community between churches in the history of Christianity. He says that "the schism between East and West, which culminated in the eleventh century, centres on a divergence in the theology of the Spirit. Does the Spirit proceed from the Father or from the Father and the Son? Behind that apparently technical dispute there lies a history of progressive divergence between two Christian communities who are separated at least in part because they understand differently the person and work of the Spirit, and consequently the nature of the Church. The schism between East and West was succeeded . . . by the Reformation, a split within the fabric of Western Christendom itself" (*Theology through the Theologians: Selected Essays, 1972–1995*, 188).

74. *Act and Being*, 105.

75. *Christ and Creation*, 107–8.

are people freely loving others, as well as creation, in a way that gives praise to God in Christ. So where we find improved relationships, improved care and concern for creation, which is simultaneously cognitive of the Father's redemptive work in Christ, there the Spirit is eschatologically perfecting his creation. It is primarily through the church where freedom to be a person-in-relation is being expressed and enacted, but it is as a witness to the rest of the world. The Church of Christ becomes a new community, which is liberated by the Holy Spirit to resemble now what is going to be when perfected in the end. Gunton says, "the church is the place where we must locate our first account of the re-forming of the image of God. The image is re-formed and so realized in the process of human conformation to Christ by the action of the eschatological Spirit."[76] Therefore, a proper Pneumatology is necessary, so that freedom will not be conceived as an abstract unlimited or unrestrained ability to choose; freedom instead should be conceived as the ability to be this or that particular person in a true relationship. A proper Pneumatology is freedom but qualified as having a purpose and directedness, an *eschatological telos* towards perfection in relationship, first with the Trinity and then with other creatures.

Karl Barth says, "God's eternity is itself beginning, succession and end."[77] Robert Jenson, in his commentary on Barth, says, "God is in himself Spirit, Father and Son: Future, Past and Present."[78] Gunton borrows from Barth and Jenson and determines that a doctrine of God must include a futurity in the Godhead. Gunton criticizes Barth for not allowing the Holy Spirit to be *the* eschatological Spirit, but only as a way of speaking of the individual who has the Spirit. But even amidst that criticism, Gunton expresses that Barth does connect eschatology with the Spirit in reference to humanity, "for there is at least room for taking him to refer to real divine futurity, where the appropriate function of the Spirit is the anticipation in the present of that which belongs to the end of time, eschatological in the full meaning of the word."[79] Since the Holy Spirit is the divine person who completes the community of the trinity, thereby completing the divine temporal life of God, he is also the one who perfects eternal life. Without the Holy Spirit's action, there is too much weight placed on Christology; in that Christ's incarnation and resurrection—a past action—brings about a future action. George Hunsinger, commenting on Barth, says that, "in order for [Jesus Christ] to be the Lord of time, both his Resurrection and his Incarna-

---

76. Ibid., 115–16.
77. Barth, *Church Dogmatics*, II/1:611.
78. Jenson, *God after God*, 191.
79. Gunton, *Becoming and Being*, 164–65.

tion were necessary preconditions."[80] Gunton follows the same theological trajectory as Barth, while attempting to supplement Barth by including the work of the Holy Spirit in both the Incarnation and Resurrection as a necessary precondition. Gunton stresses the Holy Spirit in the Incarnation by noting that when the Spirit formed a body for the Son, the Spirit "enables this part of earth to be fully itself, to move to perfection rather than dissolution."[81] The Holy Spirit gives eternal life as the one who perfects the Father's will for his creation, so that perfection is theologically conceived as the opposite of dissolution, that is, eternal life. Jesus' resurrection has an ontological component in that the biblical account expresses a transformation of Jesus' mortal body to an immortal state. Jesus' body is "transformed into the conditions of the age to come."[82] What this means for Gunton is that the promised perfection to come and the perfecting work of the Holy Spirit are centered in Jesus' resurrected and transformed body which began at the Incarnation. In this way, Jesus Christ being fully human demonstrates the power of the Holy Spirit to take our past life, our present reality, and redeem them both thereby incorporating them into our future eternal existence. In other words, God's future is our perfection.

Gunton says that "the key to eschatology is then the way by which we consider the divine 'future' to come down to earth in the here and now of our world."[83] The Holy Spirit perfects creation by completing creation's temporal existence in its own future. What this means is that in the future, "eternity comes together with time. It is the place of eternity itself in time, the place of God in his relation to the world, the starting point of his action in the irruption of his future for his creatures, the source of the mighty workings of his Spirit."[84] Gunton finds that in the Holy Spirit creation is perfected towards a future, but a future that is open to eternity; Pannenberg says that "eternity is the undivided present of life in its totality."[85] Gunton evokes Pannenberg at this juncture in order to regard the future as the working or perfecting by God's Holy Spirit; a future that is moving towards a completeness *of* and *in* time—a type of created eternity. By this, creation's freedom is recovered in that determinism is overcome by the perfecting action of the Holy Spirit. In other words, eternity is not a timeless notion, but a perfection of life, a perfection of our past, present, and future. Instead

80. Hunsinger, "Jesus as the Lord of Time," 119.
81. Gunton, *Christ and Creation*, 52.
82. Ibid., 61.
83. Gunton, *The Triune Creator*, 220.
84. Pannenberg, *Systematic Theology*, 1:409.
85. Ibid., 2:92.

of the apparent interrelatedness where our past, present, and future are viewed in isolation—where eternity is viewed as a continual present—our past, present, and future are redeemed and now conceived as related in their completeness in the eternity of God. Again, Pannenberg says, "the futurity of God implies his eternity. But it is one thing to conceive eternity as timelessness or as the endless endurance of something that existed since the beginning of time, and quite another to think of it as the power of the future over every present."[86] In this way, the perfection of eternity by the Spirit is that he brings about the *future*, and not *the* future. Meaning that there is not a future that has already been established from eternity past—this is another form of determinism or fatalism. On the contrary, the Holy Spirit brings about the divinely ordered *future*, a future that is open and allows creation to develop itself; the creature is free to be—instead of being absolutely determined, the *future* is shaped towards eternity. Freedom is found in the perfection brought about by the Holy Spirit as the third member within the *taxis* of the Godhead. So perfection of creaturely eternity is a reflection of the perfection of the divine eternity of the Father, Son, and Holy Spirit. The coming of the Son in Jesus Christ is the coming of eternity to creation so that creation has a *future* that is ordered by the Father but perfected by the Holy Spirit; a future that culminates the life of creation's past, present, and future—theologically speaking, in eternity.

The Holy Spirit as the agent of perfection that incorporates both freedom and relation is the ultimate expression of Gunton's theology. There is a soteriological element in that the Holy Spirit perfects freedom and relationship; freedom is a liberation from the effects of sin that disrupts a proper relation with the Creator and other creatures. The imminent action of the Holy Spirit within the scheme of Richard of St. Victor is a perichoretic action between the three persons that becomes an open transcendental for Gunton. This is because the ontology of creation is conceived in terms of particulars who are distinctly what they are because of what they give and receive from each other. But this creaturely dynamic of mutual constitutiveness came into *being* and is actively directed to perfection by the free activity of the Father, Son, and Holy Spirit. This state of being and directedness toward perfection is distorted because of the fall—through sin and evil; and it is only through the Incarnation of the Son and the redeeming agency of the Holy Spirit that the created order is being redirected to its proper order. Gunton says that "the Spirit, by relating his people to the Father through the crucified and risen Jesus, moves towards perfection those first created

---

86. Pannenberg, *Basic Questions in Theology*, 2:244.

in the image and likeness of their maker."[87] This action is possible because the Holy Spirit perfects the relationship between God and the world by allowing them to maintain their otherness: "[t]he Holy Spirit represents God's otherness to Jesus: his allowing and enabling him to be himself, free and truly human."[88] Jesus as the Son of God is perfected because the Holy Spirit presents a divinely ordered *future* to Jesus, which allows him to be *that* particular human person in relation to God the Father. Jesus' future is not a determined one, but a *future* that is shaped by his relation with the Father through the agency of the Holy Spirit.[89] In this way, Jesus as the God-man presents himself to creation, as an other-in-relation with both God and creation. So when the Holy Spirit prepares Jesus a body, and raises Jesus from the dead, Jesus' *future* is being shaped by the Holy Spirit to be that free person in relation to both God and creation. In this way, "the Spirit sets the creation free to be itself, and so directs it as God's other to yet find its perfection in the fulfillment of its relation to God."[90] It is because of Jesus Christ that the relationship takes place, but creation is not overwhelmed by his divinity. This way, Gunton is avoiding both pantheism and deism

87. Gunton, *Christ and Creation*, 65.

88. Ibid., 90.

89. Freedom is an essential component to Gunton's metaphysics, especially in light of personhood. This leads us to the philosophical problem of the compatibility between God's foreknowledge and free will, especially in relation to biblical prophecy. Gunton is not overly troubled with this philosophical problem; it is more epistemological than a metaphysical problem of determinism and free will. Regarding the mediation of revelation, Gunton says, "whether it is through prophecy, or whether it is Christological or pneumatological, there are a variety of means through which we can gain Revelation" (*Revelation and Reason*, 76–77). Jenson says that "the old acts of God were but prophecies of his true reality in the future" (Jenson, *God after God*, 17). For Gunton, the Spirit liberates the God-man Jesus Christ to be the messiah of God; Jesus' future is shaped by the will of God through the agency of the Spirit, but it is an open and free future.

Craig says that, "in virtue of [God's] knowing all future-tense facts, as well as all present-and past-tense facts, God has literal foreknowledge of the future" (Craig, *Time and Eternity*, 243). Later Craig argues that prophecy by God does not deny freedom, because that would be to conflate *certainty* with *necessity*. So Craig says that "we can be certain, given God's foreknowledge, that x will not fail to happen, even though it is entirely possible that x fail to happen. X could fail to occur, but God knows that it will not. Therefore, we can be sure that it will happen–and happen contingently" (ibid., 258). Craig concludes that God's "foreknowledge is wholly compatible with contingency and, in particular, human freedom and it is best understood in terms of a conceptualist model of divine cognition, according to which God simply possesses essentially knowledge of all truth, including truths about future contingents" (ibid., 265). Therefore, Jesus' future was and is known by God as revealed in prophecy; it is a free future because the Holy Spirit liberated Jesus and therefore shaped his future to be guided by the Father's will.

90. Gunton, *Christ and Creation*, 90–91.

by developing a trinitarian understanding of reality. The agency of God in creation is maintained in the Father, and the providence of God over his creation is upheld in the relational action of the Son, and the eschatological perfection is maintained because of the relationship with the Holy Spirit. What this ultimately means is that several concepts coalesce into a conception of redemption that is perceived in eschatological relational freedom: the coming Kingdom of God is our final redemption from the fall. In other words, particularity for Gunton means the freedom to be the other, but always constituted by our relation with God and other humans and creation itself. God's divine sovereignty, providence, and soteriological actions finds their final expression in the Holy Spirit who perfects both freedom and relationship in the *eschaton*, that is, the divinely ordered *future*. Therefore, the Holy Spirit gives to each part of creation its particularity; the Spirit gives freedom and a new relation as a gift from God in Christ. Therefore, Gunton's Pneumatology encompasses the doctrine of God, Christology, soteriology, anthropology, and eschatology because the Holy Spirit is conceived as the divine agent who perfects particularity as beings-in-communion. The work of the Holy Spirit is as the third person of the Trinity who is the divine person that completes the "bond of love." The Holy Spirit's divine action then opens God towards his creation by perfecting the communion between God and his creatures. The Holy Spirit is the eschatological divine agent who perfects the Father's will through Christ by creating and restoring particularity which is ultimately expressed as beings-in-communion.

Chapter 3

A Pneumatological Christology

Introduction

AS WE SAW, GUNTON'S doctrine of God and Pneumatology are derived from his view of revelation which determines God's being from within his acts. God reveals himself as a being-in-communion, this way, "relationality" is an ontological reality that results in a conception of reality as being-in-communion. Communion as a category of *being* requires that the agency of the Holy Spirit is conceptualized as a personal other who perfects communion: this way, the Holy Spirit is the divine agent who perfects the divine communion of God as well as creation's communion with its Creator. Since Gunton's theology begins with the revelation *from* and *of* the triune God, it is of no surprise that he explicates the Incarnation as an act of the Father, Son, and Holy Spirit. Since God's act is his *being*, the Incarnation as a triune act also reveals God's *being* in creation. Gunton's Christology locates the role of the Holy Spirit concretely in the incarnation event rather than as an addendum to the Son's work. The Holy Spirit is involved in the incarnation from its temporal beginning, then through Christ's life, death, resurrection and glorification.

So first I will argue that Gunton's Christology remains faithful to the tradition, especially Chalcedon, while reformulating the incarnation so that it is an act of the Triune God. I will also argue that for Gunton, the Holy Spirit is an essential element in the incarnation event. I will do this by showing the reason why Gunton understands "Spirit Christology" to be a deficient doctrine. To this end, I will also argue that Gunton's Christology is better designated as a "Pneumatic Logos Christology," instead of a "Spirit Christology."

It is important that we first examine the two theologians who Gunton appropriated to develop his particular conception of Christology—in the persons of John Owen and Edward Irving. John Owen represents a "Spirit Christology" that limits the *Logos* to the assumption of human nature; the Spirit is central as the motivating power for the human nature. Edward Irving's Christology developed a tri-part view of the *hypostatic* union; the Holy Spirit joins with human nature, albeit in a different manner than the Son. Both theologians give something to Gunton that allows him to create his own particular Christology. By arguing that Gunton's Christology is a "Pneumatic *Logos* Christology," we will see that instead of the Spirit as the empowering presence, the Spirit is the agent who liberates the humanity of the Son so that it is free-to-be itself: the particularizing action of the Spirit—as presented in Pneumatology—is present in the incarnation. This way, Gunton's Christology is a systematic continuation of his Pneumatology because the Spirit who particularizes the Father and Son in the immanent life of God also particularizes the Son of God in the incarnation to be that Son who is constituted by his relation with the Father and the Spirit. The Spirit is a necessary agent who completes the communion of Father and Son—within the incarnation—with each other, and also the communion of the Son with creation. With this, we will now examine Gunton's rejection of an instrumentalist view of "Spirit Christology" in exchange of a relational model that stresses the divine action of the Spirit as revealed in the *act* of the Incarnation. Then we will look at Owen's and Irving's "Spirit Christology," and finally examine Gunton's Christology which borrows elements from these two theologians.

"Spirit Christology" against "Pneumatic Logos Christology"

The impetus for Gunton's Christology is to offer an antidote for a perceived deficient account of the Holy Spirit in the incarnation as expressed in much of Western theology. Gunton says, "The need is for an incarnational Christology which will yet do full justice to the historical particularity of Jesus and the detailed lineaments of his story. I want to suggest that the area where we should look is our understanding of the place of Pneumatology in Christology."[1] Steven M. Studebaker expresses Gunton's sentiments when he says, "perhaps most importantly, Spirit Christology brings Christology into a trinitarian focus. The incarnation is the result of the activity of the trinitarian God. The Son is incarnated, but the Father and Spirit are involved in the process that constitutes the incarnation of the Son in

---

1. *Theology through the Theologians: Selected Essays, 1972–1995*, 153.

Jesus Christ."[2] Instead of referring to Gunton's Christological model as a "Spirit Christology," it is more appropriate to refer to it as a "Pneumatic Logos Christology." A "Pneumatic Logos Christology" avoids the mistake of other Spirit Christologies, which can be viewed in adoptionistic, Apollinarianism, or even Nestorianistic terms. Gunton avoids using the term "Spirit Christology" because of the conceptual problems associated with viewing Christ as a man empowered by the Spirit to be the Son of God; that is, some form of adoptionist theology. Gunton criticizes Lampe's Spirit Christology because Lampe claims, "Spirit Christology cannot affirm that Jesus *is* 'substantively' God."[3] Lampe's Spirit Christology reduces Jesus to a (mere) man who was indwelled with the Holy Spirit in a unique way from birth. Christ's birth becomes directed and ordained by God, but the human nature retains its own *hypostasis* within itself, and not from outside.[4] On the other hand, James Dunn describes Spirit Christology as "an attempt to understand Jesus of Nazareth in terms of *inspiration* rather than of *incarnation*."[5] Dunn's definition of Spirit Christology as *inspiration* is more nuanced than this brief statement but still differs from Gunton's development. Gunton gives more prominence to the role of the Holy Spirit from *within* the act of *incarnation*, without displacing the appropriation of the incarnation to the Son. In other words, the eternal Son of God actually becomes a man in full cooperation with the Holy Spirit.

The primary drive for Gunton's Christology is the idea that the Holy Spirit is the liberating Spirit who brings about the incarnation in such a way that Jesus' humanity—his particular Jewishness—is able to be *that* unique bearer of God's redemption. This means that the humanity of Christ is not docetic, but is a real humanity because the divinity of Christ does not have to bear all the burden of the incarnation. Instead of conceiving the incarnation as two natures (divine and human) battling over dominance in the activities of Jesus Christ, the incarnation is conceived by Gunton as a perfect and free cooperation between the persons of the Son and the Holy Spirit by the will of the Father: "God the Spirit opens, frees, the humanity of the

---

2. Studebaker, "Integrating Pneumatology and Christology," 9.

3. Lampe, "The Holy Spirit," 124

4. Lampe even eliminates the pre-existent Son as taught in the tradition: "A Christology of this kind [i.e., Spirit-Christology] has the advantage of enabling us to dispense with certain mythical concepts, such as a pre-existent Son (for it is the possessing and inspiring Spirit that is the eternally pre-existing deity which operates humanly in Christ), a descent from heaven of a personal being who chooses to be born and become an infant, a divine being who may either exercise or voluntarily suspend his omniscience" (ibid.).

5. Dunn, *Christology in the Making*, 161.

Son so that it may be the vehicle of the Father's will in the world."⁶ In this way, the doctrine of the incarnation is shaped by the Father willing the Son, who in obedience and through the perfecting action of the Spirit, enters in person into the created order, which was made through him and which he continues to uphold. The Father's willing and the Son and Spirit acting as agents through which the Father completes his will does not take away from the equality of the three. It actually guarantees that full weight is given to all three divine persons in the divine economy. This action by God in the incarnation is not simply a conceptual model to explain Christ's relation to the world as God's ambassador, but it explains *that* reality; a reality of God's eternal existence as Father, Son, and Holy Spirit which is revealed in the incarnation. Gunton's Christology is shaped by his particular Pneumatology, which is expressed and shaped in particular by two voices: John Owen and Edward Irving. So a brief review of how Gunton appropriates their respective incarnational pneumatologies will shed further insight into Gunton's own Pneumatic Logos Christology.

A. Gunton and John Owen

It is no coincidence that Gunton chose John Owen as a theologian to gain insight, for John Owen was a Congregationalist, as was Gunton. Owen's Pneumatology did not necessarily develop from his ecclesial concerns, but primarily in opposition to the influence of Socinus and other anti-trinitarian figures. It was in reaction against those figures of his day that Owen developed a Christology with a strong dependence upon Pneumatology as a corrective to those heretical doctrines.⁷ Owen says, "I shall herein wholly avoid the curious inquiries, bold conjectures, and unwarrantably determinations of the schoolmen and some other."⁸ So in his usual approach, Gunton does not engage with the historical dimensions of Owen's thought; his concern is solely with Owen's presentation of the action of the Holy Spirit in the incarnation. Gunton states this as follows:

> What is interesting is that Owen's Christ is indeed the eternal Son become flesh, but also the chosen one whose life is *both*

---

6. Gunton, *Theology through the Theologians: Selected Essays, 1972–1995*, 116.

7. In a summary of Owen's writing, Spence says, "[I]n the following year Owen published his book *Vindiciae Evangelicae*, a reply to the arguments of both Biddle and the Racovian Catechism, considering carefully not only the ideas of the Englishman but also those of the leading European Socinians" (Spence, "The Significance of John Owen for Modern Christology," 178).

8. Owen, "A Declaration of the Glorious Mystery of the Person of Christ," 223.

predestined by God the Father *and* enabled and realised by the action of God the Holy Spirit. The Spirit is the one who, as Jesus' inseparable other, relates him to the Father and so enables his response which is both obedient and free.[9]

For Gunton, by placing limits on the direct operation of the eternal Word on Christ's human nature, Owen changes the focus of Christ's humanity away from a mere instrumental conception.[10] Therefore, it is necessary to view how Owen develops his Christology in a way that gives more weight to the Holy Spirit as well as the entire Trinity within the action of the incarnation. So it is to Owen we turn.

For Gunton, revelation shapes our rationality through the acts of Jesus Christ as the Son of the Father by the power of the Holy Spirit as witnessed in scripture. Owen begins his discourse on the natures of Christ along a similar trajectory: Owen says, "I shall therefore confine myself, in the explication of this mystery, unto the propositions of divine revelation, with the just and necessary expositions of them."[11] Owen summarizes the witness of scripture concerning Christ's two natures under four headings: the assumption of human nature; the union of the two natures; the mutual communication of the natures; and the predications about the person of Jesus Christ. For our purposes, it is his work on the idea that the Logos *only* assumed the human nature along with the associated implications that is of primary concern. Alan Spence puts it this way, "following the Socinian debate [Owen] went on, with a great deal of sensitivity, to develop a Christology that carefully incorporated the two different ways of understanding Christ, which we have described as incarnational and inspirational."[12] Spence develops a bifurcation of Owen's Christology whereby he attempts to hold in tension the early christologies of the Alexandrians and Antiochenes. Spence eventually concludes that the idea that the Logos *only* assumed human nature, which in turn defines "inspiration" as an action of the Holy Spirit on the human nature of Christ, is the crux of Owen's Christology.

---

9. Gunton, "Election and Ecclesiology," 222.

10. Gunton has in mind where Athanasius describes Christ's human nature as follows: "For He was not, as might be imagined, circumscribed in the body, nor, while present in the body, was He absent elsewhere; nor, while He moved the body" and "Now, the Word of God in His man's nature was not like that; for He was not bound to His body, but rather was Himself wielding it" (Athanasius of Alexandria, *On the Incarnation of the Word* 17.2.4).

11. Owen, "A Declaration of the Glorious Mystery of the Person of Christ," 224.

12. Spence, *Incarnation and Inspiration*, 16.

Regarding assumption, Owen says, "the first thing in the divine constitution of the person of Christ as God and man, is *assumption*."[13] Instead of an instrumental view of Christ's incarnation, for Owen, the only immediate act of the *Logos* on the human nature was to assume it into the *hypostatic* union with himself. Owen says, "the only singular immediate act of the person of the Son on the human nature was the assumption of it into subsistence with himself."[14] Christ's capacity to bring about the Father's will is accomplished through the action of the Holy Spirit as the *efficient* cause of the external action of the Triune God. Owen says, "as unto *original efficiency*, it was the act of the divine nature, and so, consequently, of the *Father, Son*, and *Spirit*."[15] But, "as unto the *formation of the human nature*, it was the peculiar act of the Spirit, Luke i. 35."[16] For Owen, the Son *assumed* human nature and the Spirit *formed* human nature, so that the incarnation is a triune event and the *person* of the Son *only* assumed, or took up human nature. This went against the traditional presentation of the union. For example, Francis Turretin says that the incarnation was "by assumption and sustentation."[17]; and Abraham Kuyper says that Christ needed the Holy Spirit to enable his "weakened nature, in increasing measure, to be his instrument in the working out of His holy design."[18] Both of these Reformed authors demonstrate that the *hypostatic* union is typically conceived in relation to the divine Word and the human nature; the Holy Spirit's role has been ambiguous. One of the reasons for the lack of attention to the role of the Holy Spirit in the incarnation is that the historical controversies focused on the two natures in the person of Jesus Christ (e.g., Arianism, etc.). So it is not surprising that theologians like Turretin and Kuyper did not develop the role of the Holy Spirit beyond the creation of the human nature and in moral terms of sanctification. Owen understands the role of the Son and Holy Spirit differently because he simply limits the role of the Son to *assumption* of the human nature: the divine nature of the second person does not act on the human nature beyond assuming it.

Since the Son *only assumed* human nature, it is logical to conclude that the Son did not form or create this particular human instantiation; it was created by the Holy Spirit: "the human nature of Christ being thus formed in the womb by a *creating act* of the Holy Spirit, was in the instant

---

13. Owen, "A Declaration of the Glorious Mystery of the Person of Christ," 224.
14. Owen, *Pneumatologia*, 262.
15. Owen, "A Declaration of the Glorious Mystery of the Person of Christ," 225.
16. Ibid.,
17. Turretin, *Institutes of Elenctic Theology* 13.6 (trans. Giger, 313).
18. Kuyper, *The Work of the Holy Spirit*, 92.

of its conception *sanctified*, and filled with grace according to the measure of its receptivity."[19] By using the phrase "according to the measure of its receptivity," Owen is establishing that sanctification is given in an appropriate measure that is commensurate with human growth. Spence says, "It is here that Owen's independence from the tradition is most apparent. He has taken firmly hold of the nettle which so many orthodox theologians were unwilling to grasp, that is, the scriptural witness to Jesus' lack of knowledge and growth in grace."[20] A critical claim is made by Owen: the divine nature of the eternal Son did not impose itself upon the human soul. Owen says, "His divine nature was not unto him in the place of a soul, nor did immediately operate the things which he performed, as some of old vainly imagined; but being a perfect man, his rational soul was in him the immediate principle of all his moral operations, even as ours are in us."[21] The point is that it was really the human nature of Christ that operated as a real human, and not as an instrument—the divine nature was not the motivating principle. The Son's humanity was a free humanity that was not dependent on the divine nature of the *Logos* for its action—it was the Holy Spirit, which *created* and *perfected* the human nature to be *that* particular human person. Again, Spence states that "the eternal Son does not immediately determine the humanity of Christ, the communication is 'voluntary' rather than 'natural' and is always through the Holy Spirit."[22] Owen says, "in their increase, enlargement, and exercise, there was required a progression in grace also; and this he had continually by the Holy Ghost: Luke ii. 40."[23] In a manner of speaking, the Holy Spirit afforded the human nature of Christ the means to have a proper relation to God, one of free obedience that increased in an appropriate amount depending on his particular stage in our time and space. Again, Owen says, "and this growth in grace and wisdom was the peculiar work of the Holy Spirit; for as the faculties of his mind were enlarged by degrees and strengthened, so the Holy Spirit filled them up with grace for actual obedience."[24] Even Jesus Christ's acts of obedience and sacrifice took place because the Spirit gave him the ability to freely act; in other words, the Spirit empowered Christ's human nature to be able to respond properly: "he dedicated himself to be an offering to God; and this

---

19. Owen, "A Declaration of the Glorious Mystery of the Person of Christ," 168.
20. Spence, *Incarnation and Inspiration*, 57.
21. Owen, "A Declaration of the Glorious Mystery of the Person of Christ," 169.
22. Spence, *Incarnation and Inspiration*, 115.
23. Owen, "A Declaration of the Glorious Mystery of the Person of Christ," 169.
24. Ibid., 170.

he did through the effectual operation of the eternal Spirit in him."[25] The divine nature of the Son was present in the incarnation for Owen, but the *Logos* voluntarily did not communicate any attributes to the human nature, thereby relying on the Holy Spirit. Owen says, "all other actings of God in the person of the Son towards the human nature, were voluntary, and did not necessarily ensue on this union. For there was no transfusion of the properties of one nature into the other; nor real physical communication of Divine essential excellencies to the humanity."[26] So regarding the work of the Holy Spirit on the human nature of Christ after his death, Owen says, "for here our preceding rule must be remembered, namely, that notwithstanding the union of the human nature of Christ with the divine person of the Son, yet the communications of God unto it, beyond subsistence, were *voluntary*."[27] What this ultimately means for Gunton is that the Son *voluntarily* withheld any imposition of his divine nature on the human nature, thereby relying on the operations of the Holy Spirit to empower his human nature. So for Owen, it was by the Spirit that Christ grew in wisdom, strength, and in his offices of prophet, priest and king.

Owen's model for the Holy Spirit's role in the incarnation becomes pivotal for Gunton, primarily due to his onto-relational scheme that developed from God's revelation as a Triune being. Gunton incorporates Owen's notion that the Son only *assumed* human nature into the language of *hypostasis*: the Son *assuming* human nature for Gunton is equated with the Son giving *hypostasis* to the human nature. Since personhood is defined relationally and not in individuated substantive terms, Gunton conceives the divine person of the Son as giving *hypostasis* to the human nature, while maintaining the divine nature of the *Logos*. This is because the *Logos*, the eternal Son, is the Son in relation to the Father and the Holy Spirit. This is in opposition to a non-relational model of personhood, where the Son's personhood is located in his divine nature in an isolated manner. Owen states that Jesus is called the Son "with respect only unto the Father and his eternal, ineffable generation, communicating being and subsistence unto him, as the fountain and original of the Trinity."[28] Since the eternal Son gives *hypostasis* to the human nature, the Holy Spirit's work is defined *within* the economic activities during the life of Jesus Christ; such as, conception in the womb of the virgin, Christ's baptism, temptations, public ministry, humiliation and exaltation. In viewing the Holy Spirit as

25. Ibid., 4, p. 177.
26. Owen, *The Holy Spirit*, 90.
27. Owen, A Discourse concerning the Holy Spirit 4, p. 180.
28. Ibid., 3, p. 165.

the *efficient* cause of Christ's capacity to do God's work, space is created for the freedom of Jesus' humanity to be itself; there is an emphasis on "his freedom, [particularity] and contingency: they are enabled by the (transcendent) Spirit rather than determined by the (immanent) word."[29] This move is essential because the freedom, particularity and contingency that the Spirit gives Christ's human nature is also at work in creation: the soteriological impact is that Jesus Christ, through the Spirit, is the head of the new creation. The new creation is perfected by the agency of the Holy Spirit who is shaping creation in conformity to the Word, Jesus Christ.

The Holy Spirit is the *efficient cause* of Christ's humanity which also brings about a restored relation between God and his creatures. In commenting on Owen's Pneumatology, Suzanne McDonald states,

> In turn, the Spirit's role in relation to us clearly corresponds to the notion of the Spirit as the *vinculum amoris* who both expresses and completes the mutual love of Father and Son in the Trinity. His person and work mean that he particularly is the one who conveys the love of God to humanity and enables the human response of love to God in return.[30]

For Owen, and for Gunton, the Holy Spirit provides a univocal function—albeit to a different degree—in the life of Jesus and the believers by establishing a proper relation with the Father. Spence comments that,

> Owen recognized that to affirm the humanity of Christ and to acknowledge his dependence on the Holy Spirit is to say much the same thing. The one implies the other. He argued that the humanity of Christ, because of its continuity with our own humanity, knew and experienced God as we do, that is, through the Holy Spirit. Having assumed human nature to himself, the eternal Son acted on that nature not directly but always through the mediation of his Spirit. The integrity of Christ's human self-consciousness, volition and understanding are thus protected. As man, Christ's knowledge, decisions and powers were never more than those of a human person open to the Holy Spirit. As the eternal Son of God, however, he has all the power, knowledge and wisdom of the one true God.[31]

But for Owen there is a different degree in the relationship between the Father and the Son and that between the Father and the rest of humanity;

---

29. Gunton, "The Church on Earth," 64.
30. McDonald, "The Pneumatology of the 'Lost' Image in John Owen," 327.
31. Spence, "The Significance of John Owen for Modern Christology," 182.

but in both relationships it is the Holy Spirit who brings it about.[32] The Holy Spirit, who empowers Christ from the moment of conception to be that particular incarnate Son of God, also empowers those from the domain and influence of sin who put their faith in Christ. Gunton does not identify (and neither does Owen) the redeeming action of God through the divinity of the Son alone: it is the perfecting eschatological action of the Holy Spirit that restores the communion between God and creation. Gunton says it best when he explains that,

> Only the Spirit can relate lost human beings to God the Father through Christ—election—yet the Spirit's otherness, modelled on the New Testament depiction of his relation to Jesus, generates an openness according to which the Spirit can determine a relation through an election which is yet uncompelled because it is the means of the realisation of the sinner's true being in Christ. The function of the otherness of the Spirit is thus to confirm and re-establish the true otherness of the creation in reconciled relation to God.[33]

Gunton's relational ontology is apparent here, for the Holy Spirit is the agent who sustains otherness-in-relation; that is, creation is enabled through Christ to reach its divinely intended destiny. The teleology of creation points towards an eschatological action by the Holy Spirit who brings creation towards perfection, which is defined as a proper relation with the Father through Christ.

So for Gunton and Owen, the perfection of creation is an act of God as Father, Son, and Spirit. The creative act of the Holy Spirit completes the inseparable and simultaneous act of the Triune God in the incarnation. The God-man Jesus Christ relied on the Holy Spirit to live a proper life towards God, just like any other human being. In a sense, the difference between the man Jesus Christ and other human beings is a matter of person and degree. Jesus Christ is unique because he is the second *person* of the Trinity; also, his relation with the Spirit is of an infinitely greater degree than with others. Owen's Pneumatology does not undermine Christ's human nature—it actually preserves it. Christ was really human, he thought and acted like a human, except for sin. As Jesus grew, the Holy Spirit empowered him with increasing degrees of grace and gifts in order to maintain Christ's human

32. Owen says, "As the *descending* of God towards us in love and grace issues or ends in the work of the Spirit in us and on us, so all our *ascending* towards him begins therein; and as the first instance of the proceeding of grace and love towards us from the Father is in and by the Son, so the first step that we take towards God, even the Father, is in and by the Son" (Owen, Pneumatologia, 319–20).

33. Gunton, "Election and Ecclesiology," 222.

nature, while also preserving Jesus through sanctification. It was a perfect sanctification that is commensurate with the growth of Christ's human nature so that when scripture speaks of Christ's growth in wisdom and knowledge, there is real growth because the Spirit is also perfecting the human nature's growth.[34] Carl Trueman says,

> Owen's careful delimitation of the Logos's role simply to that of giving hypostasis to the anhypostatic human nature is crucial: were there a direct communication of attributes between the natures and that simply by virtue of incarnation alone, then such a defense of Christ's true humanity and the dynamic of the gospel narrative would be impossible without resort to an heretical view of kenosis.[35]

It is apparent that for Gunton, Owen's Pneumatology is incarnational in that the economic activity of the Holy Spirit is defined on the basis of the incarnation event; the Spirit is not limited to the work of sanctification. The human nature of Christ is acted upon by the Holy Spirit while the Son is maintaining the hypostatic union of the two natures within his person.

At times it does seem that Gunton has a difficulty accounting for and maintaining the role of the Father in the incarnation, except volitionally. The Father wills the incarnation, but his two hands appear to do all the work. On the other hand, the divine nature of the Son seems to become extraneous and limited to effecting his own incarnation. Oliver Crisp criticizes Owen's account because the divine nature of the Son has too little work in the incarnation. The divine Logos appears too disconnected from his own humanity; the humanity of Christ can appear animated solely by the Holy Spirit in Owen's account. Crisp states,

> The principle cause for concern is that Owen's doctrine seems to generate a distinction between God the Son and his agency "in" or "through" his human nature at all moments after the first moment of the assumption of human nature in the very act of becoming incarnate. Thereafter, his divine nature does not act directly upon his human nature, but only mediately, via the agency of the Holy Spirit. But this seems theologically dubious.[36]

---

34. Spence says that Owen's concern (along with Edward Irving) "was that Christ's life should be seen as the dynamic overcoming of sinful temptation and real growth in grace, and thus be the prototype of the believer's life" (Spence, *Incarnation and Inspiration*, 53). Spence appropriates the term "inspiration" as an element of the *hypostatic* union as a means to explicate the distinctly human activities of Jesus, which includes growth, hunger, lack of knowledge and suffering.

35. Trueman, *John Owen*, 96.

36. Crisp, "John Owen on Spirit Christology," 15.

Crisp however does not give enough attention to Owen's concept of *assumption*: "that ineffable divine act . . . whereby the person of the Son of God assumed our nature, or took into a personal subsistence with himself."[37] Again, a*ssumption* is Owen's category aimed at limiting the activity of the divine nature of the Son to the taking up of human nature. Regarding *assumption*, Owen says that "this the Scripture expresseth sometimes *actively*, with respect unto the divine nature acting in the person of the Son, the nature assuming;"[38] Crisp's critique notwithstanding, Gunton appropriates Owen in order to demonstrate that the Holy Spirit is an active participant in the incarnation. Owen afforded Gunton the means to develop a trinitarian shaped view of the incarnation, and also was the impetus for developing and moving beyond the typical Spirit Christology. Owen's Christology does not change the ontology of the *hypostatic* union; the union is still conceived in terms of the divine nature of the Logos and a human nature. But Gunton is looking to radically recreate Chalcedonian Christology by locating the Spirit as an essential part of the *hypostatic* union. It seems to me that even though Gunton does not explicitly explain his Christology and interpretation of Owen this way, that this is the way to interpret Gunton. Owen is just a model for a Christology that incorporates the Holy Spirit, but he does not go far enough for Gunton. In order for Gunton to complete his Pneumatological Christology, he turns to Edward Irving for assistance.

B. Gunton and Edward Irving

The overarching question that thrusts Gunton's Pneumatological Christology is: "how can it be conceived that the Word became flesh without ceasing to be Word but equally, without depriving the historical person of Christ of real humanity?"[39] The incarnation is not simply an action of the eternal Son becoming man, it is an act of God; the revelation of the incarnation in some way must reveal the nature of the triune God. Gunton turns to Prestige, who in commenting on Cyril's kenosis Christology says,

> But the doctrine of human addition to Christ has to be balanced by the doctrine of divine kenosis or contraction, by which Christ made Himself on earth what might be called a miniature of His eternal self; and when the two doctrines are put together it becomes plain that the so-called addition was nothing but a

37. Owen, "A Declaration of the Glorious Mystery of the Person of Christ," 224.
38. Ibid.
39. Gunton, *Theology through the Theologians: Selected Essays, 1972–1995*, 154.

repetition, on a smaller scale, and in a limited sphere, of what Christ already was eternally.[40]

In other words, in the incarnation the Son must retain all of his divine attributes, while gaining all the attributes of a human nature without it being overwhelmed by the divine nature. The incarnation is an actual expression of God's very nature; it is not simply an "alien" external miracle performed by God upon creation. The incarnation must incorporate a robust sense of a real human nature in Christ without that humanity being understood as a passive instrument wielded about by the Word. We saw earlier that John Owen's particular Spirit Christology placed an emphasis upon the Holy Spirit's influence on Christ's human nature. The problem for Gunton is that Owen's view of the incarnation was primarily moral and not ontological; and therefore not fully Trinitarian. Since in Owen's scheme, the *action* of the Holy Spirit as the perfector of both ethics (sanctification) and ontology (*being*) was not sufficiently accounted for, Gunton discovered an ally in Edward Irving, in whom he believes he finds a theologian whose writings do pneumatological justice to the real divinity and full humanity in the incarnation.

First, Gunton interprets Irving's theology as having a very robust supralapsarian character, meaning that the incarnation finds its basis in the being of God, and not simply in divine decrees alone. The incarnation is based on God's grace and not humanity's fall. Irving says, "accordingly, it is written concerning this mystery of the incarnation, in various parts of Scripture, that it came not within the coasts of time, but had its origin before the foundation of the world."[41] Irving does not neglect the Fall as a source for the necessity of the incarnation; for he uses Aristotelian causal language to explicate the reason that the incarnation took the shape that it did. For Irving, the fall of Adam was the "immediate" and "formal" cause of the incarnation, but the eternal "efficient" cause of the incarnation is found within the depths of God (cf. John 17:24; I Peter 1:18–20). There is a sense within Irving's thought that the Father has eternally loved the Son with a view towards all of the Son's economic offices; this way the economy of salvation reveals the immanent Godhead for Irving. Biblical passages such as 1 Peter 1:20 reveal that mankind's redemption is to be found "in the eternal counsel of God."[42] The incarnation is simply the manifestation of God's eternal purpose and grace (cf. 2 Tim. 1:9); it is about the persons of the Father, Son, and Holy Spirit instead of natures. Irving states,

---

40. Prestige, *Fathers and Heretics*, 163.
41. Irving, *The Collected Writings of Edward Irving*, 11.
42. Ibid., 12.

that it is a great purpose of the Divine will which God was minded from all eternity to make known unto his creatures, for their greater information, delight, and blessedness; to make known, I say, to all His intelligent creatures, the grace and mercy, the forgiveness and love which he beareth towards those who love the honour of his Son, and believe in the word of his testimony.[43]

It is the love between the persons of the Father and the Son that is the source of the incarnation for Irving. Since Irving expresses the incarnation as an event that originated in the will of the Father and the love between the Father and the Son, Gunton interprets this as privileging the persons over the natures—meaning that the incarnation is about the personal and not so much about the two natures. Gunton says that "natures are not hypostases, and so do not have attributes; in a sense, they are attributes, ways of speaking of the fact that everything that Jesus does is both fully divine and fully human action."[44] So far, for Irving, the incarnation originates within the eternal life of the Godhead, and simply manifests God's grace and love to his creatures in the incarnation. At this point, Gunton is attracted to Irving due to his ability to overcome the doctrine of *kenosis*, which he takes to be an attempt to recover the humanity of Christ but at the expense of his full divinity.[45] Gunton is also attracted to Irving because the *first* cause of the incarnation is within God's very being, so that the incarnation reveals something proper to God's self.

Irving's theology follows Augustine in emphasizing the will of man as the seat of human sin. For Irving says, "this is the redemption, this is the at-one-ment, which was wrought in Christ, to redeem the will of a creature from the oppression of sin, and bring it to be at one with the will of the Creator."[46] Because he connects sin with the will of man, Irving places a strong emphasis on the humanity of Christ as a real fallen humanity: the *Logos* assumed to himself a real fallen human nature because sin is located in the will, and not as an essential property of human nature itself.

---

43. Ibid.

44. Gunton, *Act and Being*, 149–50.

45. Gunton says that, in Irving's theology, "*kenosis* or self-emptying, [is an] expression of the inner dynamic of the Trinity, not as the sloughing off of certain attributes." (*Theology through the Theologians: Selected Essays, 1972–1995*, 156). Elsewhere Gunton explains that "a solution was attempted by a new use of the concept of kenosis . . . At the incarnation, [the eternal Son] emptied himself in the sense that he abandoned for a time some of the attributes of divinity." (*Christ and Creation*, 83). For Gunton, the doctrine of *kenosis* informs us about the divine action of the triune persons, instead of attempting to reconcile the divine nature of Christ with human actions.

46. Irving, *The Collected Writings of Edward Irving*, 5. Augustine says, "The will is the cause of sin" (Augustine, *On the Free Choice of the Will*, 106).

Without entering into a defense of Irving's view of Christ's human nature, the pertinent position is that Christ was conceived by the Holy Spirit as a true human composed of body and soul, in the same manner as with other humans. The difference is that the Holy Spirit remained with him and sanctified him, "so that he was in very deed a holy thing from the beginning of his creature being."[47] For Irving, it is essential that Christ had a fallen human nature because this gives the work of the Holy Spirit within the incarnation significance.[48]

---

47. Irving, *The Collected Writings of Edward Irving*, 121.

48. This idea of Irving's was not well received by his contemporaries, and for that matter, was considered controversial even up to the early twentieth century. One of Irving's biographers, Mrs. Oliphant, explains that Irving crafted a letter in response to criticisms by Marcus Dods (Oliphant, *The Life of Edward Irving*, 113). In one of his works, Dods says that some taught that Christ took on a fallen nature, and he compared those who taught that to Manichaeism: "[A]nd they who teach that our Lord took a fallen nature must be laboring under some strange delusion if they deny that they are teaching the very doctrine upon which Manichaeism is built, as clearly as ever Manichaeus taught it" (Dods, *On the Incarnation of the Eternal Word*, 376). Over forty years subsequent to Dods, Bruce also found Irving's doctrine of fallen nature incorrect, and also resulted in problems with Irving's explication of the temptations (Bruce, *The Humiliation of Christ*, 266–82). In the early part of the twentieth century, Mackintosh described Irving in both complementary and acerbic tones. Mackintosh lauded Irving for his high Christology, but stated that his "life was one of the greatest and saddest of the century" (Mackintosh, *The Doctrine of the Person of Jesus Christ*, 276). The issue for Mackintosh is that Irving's position of the fallen nature of Christ confuses the idea of "corrupt" with "corruptible"; the Holy Spirit sanctified Christ's flesh to be incapable of sin. Mackintosh understands Irving's theology as defining Christ as being capable of sin, but not sinning. Mackintosh says that "it is after all only a loose idea of sinlessness which takes it as compatible with the existence in Christ of a potential fault and strong efficacious germ of evil" (ibid., 278). Baillie (1948) was also critical of Irving's position, stating that the belief that Christ's humanity was fallen had always been considered heretical. The flaw in Baillie's position is that his "knowledge of Irving appears to have been second-hand (*via* Bruce): obviously Irving was not then, as he is now, required reading in the Scottish universities" (MacLeod, "The Doctrine of the Incarnation," 43). On the other hand, Barth agrees with Irving's assessment of Christ's human nature. Barth explains that "there must be no weakening or obscuring of the saving truth that the nature which God assumed in Christ is identical with our nature as we see it in the light of the Fall" (Barth, *The Church Dogmatics*, I/2:153). In the same discussion, Barth says "the same doctrine was delivered about 1827 by the Scottish theologian Edward Irving and it led to his excommunication" (ibid., 154). So Irving's position on the fallen nature of Christ's humanity is not without its critics and recent supporters (cf. T. F. Torrance, Thomas Weinandy, etc.). We will end our discussion with a quote from Weinandy: "Irving believed that only if Jesus confronted this reality in his own frail humanity could he heal and transform our depraved humanity. Only through the assuming of sinful flesh could he, in reality, restore us to God" (Weinandy, *In the Likeness of Sinful Flesh*, 61).

When Irving fully develops the significance of the Holy Spirit he does so by restructuring the traditional view of the *hypostatic* union so that the composition of the God-man Jesus Christ is that of a fallen human nature and soul, which was assumed by the person of the Son and joined with the Divine nature in the person of the Holy Spirit. The Holy Spirit is the perfecting agent of what took place *within* and *with* the human nature of Christ, forming his body out of fallen humanity; otherwise it would not be a real humanity.[49] At this stage, Irving and Owen have a very similar Pneumatology in that the Holy Spirit is the agent who is continually acting upon the human nature of Christ in such a way that the Son's divine nature is not wielding the human nature in an instrumental manner. But, in keeping with the Chalcedon formula, there are only two natures in the God-man, the human and the divine. The human nature of Christ is created from within fallen creation, so that Christ shares the same fallen nature as all of humanity; but the sanctifying work of the Holy Spirit united Jesus' will with the Father's will, keeping Jesus from sin. The person of the *Logos* has the incarnational role of self-emptying and eternal obedience to the Father, while the Holy Spirit upholds the human nature. By conceiving of sin as being located in a defective will, Irving has the conceptual space to perceive a fallen human nature in Jesus, yet to speak of Jesus as sinless. Therefore, Jesus' humanity is a full human nature because it is the same human nature as we have, except for a defective human will. Irving's incarnational Christology is in line with Gunton's requirements that the incarnation is conceived as an expression of God's being while maintaining a real human nature. In other words, within the *hypostatic* union, Irving constructs a Christology that is faithful to Chalcedon: there is a full divine nature and a full human nature. So far, this is nothing especially unusual; but as we will see, Irving's approach is unusual.

At this stage, Irving's Christology takes an ontological turn that is unexpected, but explains Gunton's interest in it as a resource for his own Christology. Irving reshapes Chalcedon Christology so that the Holy Spirit becomes the source of the divine nature within the incarnation. It should be remembered that for Irving, Christ was conceived by the Holy Spirit as a true human composed of body and soul, in the same manner as with other humans. The difference is that the Holy Spirit remained with him and sanctified him, so that he was from conception a holy thing from within his creaturely being. To quote Irving at length:

---

49. Irving says, "[S]o that the great operative cause in the redemption of the creature is the Holy Spirit taking the possession of it, and sanctifying or separating it from the wicked mass" (Irving, *The Collected Writings of Edward Irving*, 428).

> Yet do I not hesitate to assert, that this is the idea of the person of Christ generally set forth: and the effect has been to withdraw from the eye of the Church the work of the Holy Spirit in the incarnation, which is as truly the great demonstration of the Spirit's power and manner of working, as the incarnation itself is of the Father's goodness, and the Son's surpassing love. This comes from the omission of the third part in the composition of Christ, which is, the substance of the Godhead in the person of the Holy Ghost: to whose Divine presence and power it is that the creation of the body in the womb of the virgin is given, the mighty works which Christ did ascribed, and the spotlessness of His sacrifice attributed, in the Holy Scripture.[50]

Irving was commenting on the idea that the incarnation is a union of the Son alone, "which directly leadeth unto an inmixing and confusing of the Divine with the human nature, that pestilent heresy of Eutyches."[51] What Irving is saying is that the church has somehow neglected the ontological location of the Holy Spirit in the incarnation, the "third" part in the composition of Christ. There is a type of divine composite within the God-man Jesus Christ: a fallen human nature and soul is assumed by the eternal Son and joined by the Divine nature in the person of the Holy Spirit. But, in a sense, there is in fact a threefold composition within the person of Jesus Christ; the Son, the human nature and the Holy Spirit. Irving explains:

> It was not with Christ, in this respect, as it was with Jeremiah and the Baptist, who were filled with the Holy Ghost from the mother's womb: he was not merely filled with the Holy Ghost, but the Holy Ghost was the author of His bodily life, the quickener of that substance which he took from fallen humanity: or, to speak more correctly, the Holy Ghost uniting himself for ever to the human soul of Jesus, in virtue and in consequence of the Second Person of the Trinity having united himself thereto, this threefold spiritual substance, the only-begotten Son, the human soul, and the Holy Spirit—(or rather twofold, one of the parts being twofold in itself; for we may not mingle the divine nature with the human nature, nor may we mingle the personality of the Holy Ghost with the personality of the Son)—the Eternal Son, therefore, humbling Himself to the human soul, and the human soul taken possession of by the Holy Ghost, this spiritual substance (of two natures only, though of three parts) did animate and give life to the flesh of the Lord Jesus; which was

50. Ibid., 124.
51. Ibid., 123.

> flesh in the fallen state, and liable to all the temptations to which flesh is liable: but the soul of Christ, thus anointed with the Holy Ghost, did ever resist and reject the suggestions of evil . . . I believe it to be necessary unto salvation that a man should believe that Christ's soul was so held in possession by the Holy Ghost.[52]

So in essence, the incarnation involves the Son taking upon himself human nature, both material and immaterial; with the Holy Spirit also uniting himself with the immaterial human soul of the God-man. Graham McFarlane explains that Irving approaches the incarnation from the standpoint of "who" and "how": who is the agent of the incarnation and how is the union possible? Traditionally, the "who" question, in regards to the incarnation, has been associated with the Son alone—the Son unites himself to human nature. McFarlane says that "for Irving, this is not enough. Rather, the answer must refer both to the Son and the Spirit."[53] Irving is attempting to secure a place for the Trinity within the saving action of the incarnation; so he must demonstrate that the Son reveals the Father and the Spirit. In answer to the "who" part of the question Irving relies on the Chalcedon formula and declares that Christ is one person with two natures. McFarlane explains that when Irving reiterates the Chalcedon formula that "it is a question about being. Thus he gives an ontological answer: it is the divine Son."[54] But,

> when Irving considers the identity of the agent of incarnation from a soteriological perspective, he appears to make a considerable shift in emphasis, but due to the fact that his main concern is with the place of the divine in incarnation, this second consideration is less obvious. However, it is only within this context that the Spirit's relation to Christ makes sense, for it is a context within which he wishes to stress the full humanity of the one who brings salvation.[55]

There are two dimensions in Irving's Christology—ontology and soteriology. Irving uses soteriology to locate the entire Trinity, for it is God who saves; the entire Godhead must be involved in salvation.

Once Irving engages in a soteriological shift, McFarlane explains that Irving is now addressing the question of "how": how will the human nature, in a fallen state, unite with the divine action of the Triune God? For

---

52. Ibid., 126.
53. McFarlane, *Christ and the Spirit*, 148.
54. Ibid., 151.
55. Ibid.

McFarlane, once we understand the "who," and then realize that Irving is looking for the "how," only then can we begin to understand Irving's explanation of the Spirit in the incarnation. McFarlane says that "Irving's solution is to identify the human soul of Christ as a theological means, with which he joins an inspirational dimension to his thoroughgoing incarnational Christology."[56] The Christological debates wrestled with the human rational soul of Christ, and eventually declared Apollinarism, Eutychianism, and Arianism as heresies. Irving found that the rational soul is the place where the Holy Spirit mediates the reconciliation between divinity and humanity. The problem is not the state of Christ's human soul, but the function of that soul; a function with which the church fathers were not in complete agreement. For example, Aquinas argues that assumption takes place in the subsistence and not in the soul. He states that

> our word is united to our speech, by means of breathing [spiritus], not as a formal medium, but as a moving medium. For from the word conceived within, the breathing proceeds, from which the speech is formed. And similarly from the eternal Word proceeds the Holy Spirit, who formed the body of Christ, as will be shown. *But it does not follow from this that the grace of the Holy Spirit is the formal medium in the aforesaid union.*[57]

In other words, the grace of the Holy Spirit, which is in the soul, is not where the assumption takes place. But for Irving, the soul is the medium for both the ontological and the soteriological aspects of the incarnation. In light of Irving's lengthy quote above,[58] McFarlane states that "the most important [item is] the place Irving attributes to the soul. It is the central location of incarnation."[59] Irving's incarnation ontology is a two-nature but three-part construction, with the third part being the Holy Spirit. McFarlane explains that "the Son unites himself to a human soul which is assumed, in turn, by the Spirit."[60] In other words, Irving's construction of the incarnation gives the role of assuming the rational soul to the Holy Spirit, thereby completing his tri-part view of the incarnation. David Dorries, who comments on Irving's incarnational Christology, says that "although the substance of Christ's humanity was no different than the nature common to man, it was inhabited and possessed by the Spirit from the moment of conception."[61]

56. Ibid., 157.
57. Thomas, *Summa Theologica* 3.q6.a6; emphasis added.
58. See p. 82n52.
59. McFarlane, *Christ and the Spirit*, 159.
60. Ibid.
61. Dorries, *Edward Irving's Incarnational Christology*, 132.

The Holy Spirit takes possession of the human soul of Christ, but it is Christ in his humanity who wields the Spirit; the Son assumes human nature, but the Spirit empowers the Son's humanity, via the soul, to be obedient to the Father's will. This way, the Son relates to the Father's will through the Spirit so that the triune action of God is always present in the incarnation. Irving is able to maintain the Chalcedon formula of two natures joined in the one person of Jesus Christ. The unique perspective of Irving is that the divine nature in the *hypostatic union* is provided by the Holy Spirit and not the eternal Son. Gunton asks, "is Irving's christology in that sense kenotic? The answer is, surely not."[62] Later, Gunton says, "[Irving's] christology is sometimes referred to as a 'Spirit christology,' but that is precisely what it is not."[63] Gunton is well aware of Irving's Christological ontology because he quotes directly from Irving that "the soul of Christ, [was] anointed with the Holy Ghost."[64] The point being that Gunton is implicitly adopting Irving's Christology, which proposes that instead of the Son's divinity doing all the work in the incarnation, it is the Word who provides *personhood* and *union* and the Holy Spirit is the one who provides *the* Divine nature upholding *that* particular humanity.

In light of Irving's Incarnational Christology, Gunton believes that the tradition should reconsider the relation between the Word and the Spirit in the incarnation, for too much stress has been placed on the divinity of Son at the expense of the humanity, which has led the Western tradition towards a "tendency to premature universalising."[65] Gunton explains that "the form that the universalising has taken has been docetic in direction, producing a tendency to conceive the motive force, so to speak, of Jesus' life as being the eternal Word."[66] So for Gunton it is a mistake to assume that the divine nature of the Son is that which gives life to, or empowers, the human nature of Jesus Christ. Gunton says, "in view of the fact that the ecclesiology of John Owen will concern us later, it is not inappropriate to note here that his christology, in this respect anticipating by a century and a half that of Edward Irving, attempts precisely that reordering."[67] That is, the same reordering of the relationship between the Word and Spirit in the incarnation that Irving developed. The anticipation by Owen and Irving's reordering is precisely what Gunton appreciates in these two theologians. Gunton then

---

62. Gunton, *Theology through the Theologians: Selected Essays, 1972–1995*, 164.
63. Ibid., 165.
64. Ibid., 162.
65. Gunton, *The Promise of Trinitarian Theology*, 68.
66. Ibid.
67. Ibid., 68–69.

states that Owen limited the direct operation of the *Logos* on Jesus' human nature in a direct contradiction of Athanasius' instrumentalist view. Gunton repeats Owen's view that the *Logos*' divinity is that agent that accomplished the *assumption* of human nature, which means that "the humanity remains authentically human and it not subverted by the immanently operating Word."[68] The *hypostatic union* is not so much a transference of properties but the *assumption* by the *Logos* of human nature which was prepared by the Holy Spirit. To further stress this point, Gunton says, "such a conception does much to create space for a conception of the humanity of Jesus which gives due emphasis to his freedom, particularity and contingency: they are *enabled* by the (transcendent) Spirit rather than *determined* by the (immanent) Word."[69] It is clear that Gunton has adopted Irving's Christology from the following quotation:

> The cantus firmus of Irving's christology, and, more than that, the intellectual and ontological basis of it, is a trinitarian conception of God, and indeed one owing more to the East than the West. It was his unerring grasp on the distinctive *hypostasis* of the eternal Son in relation to those of the Father and Spirit that enabled Irving to risk the daring christology for which he was condemned, but which now has so much to teach us.[70]

Gunton is not only impressed with Irving, but he takes Irving's Christology into his own thought. Gunton says, "if there is too strong an *identification* of the incarnate with what, however unsatisfactorily, we call the pre-incarnate Word . . . once again the "space" of Jesus' humanity is in danger of being invaded."[71] Gunton resolves this danger precisely by way of the claim that "the human life of the Son is not, so to speak, pre-programmed from the start—as much early docetic Christology sometimes suggests[72]—but is maintained in holiness by virtue of Jesus' free response to

---

68. Ibid., 69.
69. Ibid.
70. Ibid., 98.
71. Gunton, *Father, Son, and Holy Spirit*, 98.
72. Gunton classifies Apollinarianism and Eutychianism, and any other forms of monophysitism as being docetic because of the weak view of the humanity of Christ. But more recently, Gunton finds that Schleiermacher's Christology is docetic, but also unique; in that he attacks dualism and in some sense employs it for his own purposes. Schleiermacher attacks the "two-nature doctrine" of Christ because to use the word "nature" is no longer appropriate for it has undergone many changes. So for Gunton, Schleiermacher's reasons are dualistic in the sense that there is one reality for humans and one reality for God in the strongest sense–they cannot even share the same predicates. Gunton says "without doubt we encounter here a modern form of the . . . dualism

the guidance of the Spirit."[73] Gunton insists that Jesus' humanity is not being overly influenced by the divine nature of the *Logos*, but is being liberated by the divine nature of the Holy Spirit. Irving says that the "mere apprehension of [the human nature] by the Son doth not make it holy. Such a union leads directly to the apotheosis or deification of the creature, and this again does away with the mystery of a Trinity in the Godhead."[74] For Irving, the problem is that the tradition has viewed the Word as acting upon the flesh to make it holy, but "the effect has been to withdraw from the eye of the Church the work of the Holy Spirit in the incarnation, which is as truly the great demonstration of the Spirit's power and manner of working, as the incarnation itself is of the Father's goodness, and the Son's surpassing love."[75] Since the Spirit's power, in respect to the incarnation, is seen in the creation of a body for the Son, it follows that the Spirit's work is also to perfect that same body—the Spirit's sanctifies in order to complete the Trinitarian act of redemption by liberating the creature. The language of "liberation" is Gunton's language, and not Irving's; it signifies the liberation from sin so that the creature can be in a proper relationship with the Triune God. The humanity of the Son is a real humanity because the divine nature of the Logos *assumed* it as his own and the Holy Spirit acts to liberate this same human nature from the effects of sin, thereby allowing the Son's human nature to be what God the Father intended. So what we have in Irving's Christology is a means to express the Spirit as the divine nature acting in the Incarnation while allowing the person of the eternal Son to provide the personhood to the *anhypostatic* human nature: the Spirit is an active presence throughout the entire incarnation event.

---

that has so plagued Western theology." Gunton also critiques Pannenberg for a docetic Christology, but for slightly different reasons. Pannenberg states that "Jesus' unity with God is not to be conceived as a unification of two substances, but as this man Jesus is God" (Pannenberg, *Jesus-God and Man*, 283). In the case of Schleiermacher and Pannenberg, Gunton coins their Christology as docetic simply because too much weight is placed on the humanity; there is movement to universalize Christ's humanity. For Schleiermacher, it is Christ's "God-consciousness," and in Pannenberg, Christ is the divinized man; either way, the direction is not from the eternal second person to the humanity. Gunton says that when too much weight is placed on the humanity that there "is no guarantee of freedom from docetism. The humanity of Jesus can be etherealized and disappear from view more easily by this method than by one beginning more straightforwardly in the transcendent. Because it is eternalized rather than conceived as coming from the eternal, the humanity tends to be lose in a process in which too much weight is loaded upon it" (Gunton, *Yesterday and Today*, 29).

73. Gunton, *Father, Son, and Holy Spirit*, 193.
74. Irving, *The Collected Writings of Edward Irving*, 124.
75. Ibid.

C. Gunton and Chalcedon

Owen and Irving developed a "Spirit Christology" that places more stress on the Holy Spirit within the incarnation, albeit for differing reasons. Gunton is not concerned with their motivations, but with the final configuration of the Spirit in relation to the Son and human nature. Gunton adopts their Spirit Christology into his own project as a way of assuring that the incarnation is a trinitarian event by emphasizing the pneumatological dimension. Before we examine Gunton's slight modification of Chalcedonian Christology, it is necessary to establish the way that he uses the terms "substance," "nature," and "person."

First, we must recognize that Gunton views the modern world as rejecting Aristotelian substance metaphysics. For Gunton, Locke's empiricism, Berkeley's idealism, Spinoza's pantheism and A. J. Ayer's logical positivism, indicate a move away from *substance* in metaphysics as the primary category of *being*.[76] In regards to Ayer, Gunton states, "a modern philosopher like Ayer rejects the whole conception of philosophy; it is a waste of time to seek for entities that we cannot see, hear, taste, touch, or smell. *Substance* is one of these."[77] Gunton says that "this progressive weakening of the concept of substance has necessarily had its consequences for the way in which man thinks about the world."[78] In the physical sciences, Gunton refers to figures such as Michael Faraday and John Polkinhorne as examples of a relational approach to reality that also undermines "substance" as the basis of reality. Even in the realm of psychology, John Macmurray develops a relational model of the person, which Gunton interprets as a move away from individual substances being the primary determinates for personhood. Gunton is oversimplifying the situation, but this does demonstrate that Gunton has rejected substance metaphysics for a more relational approach. So from empiricism to idealism, Gunton views the modern world as rejecting classical Aristotelian substance metaphysics—especially in light of quantum physics—for more relational types of enterprises. Bertrand Russell says that "Hume banished the conception of *substance* from psychology, as Berkeley had banished it from physics."[79] All this culminates in Gunton's appreciation

---

76. Gunton has in mind that philosophers like Locke, Berkeley, Hume, and Kant did not necessarily deny "substances"; but as *idealists, empiricists, immaterialists,* and/or *skeptics*, they denied the actual existence and explained "substance" as being an idea in the mind.

77. Gunton, *Becoming and Being*, 19; italics added.

78. Ibid.

79. Russell, *A History of Western Philosophy*, 662.

for Hartshorne and Barth as key figures who represent the theological rejection of "substance" as the primary category for being.

Instead of "substance" language, Gunton utilizes "events" or "acts" as better explanations of our reality, especially in light of God's acts which reveal something about God and our reality in relationship to God, our Creator. In Gunton's early dissertation, he used Hartshorne to demonstrate that contemporary theology is moving away from substance metaphysics. Since Gunton is aware that A. N. Whitehead is the philosophical predecessor to Hartshorne, we will examine Whitehead's metaphysics.[80] In commenting on Whitehead's philosophy, John Cobb, Jr. says "the apparently substantial things that so profoundly shape our sense of reality are more accurately described as stable patterns of activity than as substances."[81] For Gunton, events or actions are just as basic to reality as "substance"; and they are better explanations of reality. In explicating Whitehead, C. Robert Mesle says, "process philosophers recognize the importance of the language of being, but find deeper wisdom and greater clarity in a vision of the world as becoming, as relational process."[82] Gunton argues that "process philosophers like Hartshorne wish to replace the notion of substance with an alternative metaphysical category, and one more in line with the way modern men look at the universe."[83] Whitehead establishes the foundation for process theologians like Hartshorne, and gives them the tools to move away from static conception of *being* as the fundamental basis for reality. As a disciple of Whitehead, Hartshorne replaces "substance" by elevating "becoming" to an ontological category over "being"; events-in-relation are conceived as a better representation of reality.[84] Gunton concludes that modern theologians have no philosophical grounding for giving priority to "substance" and notions of static "being" over "becoming"; events or acts are not simply occasions to describe the actions of individual entities, they are what constitutes reality. Reality is conceived as a complex existence of interrelated occurrences taking place within our space-time arena. So Hartshorne represents a rejection by theology of "classical theism," which for Gunton is

---

80. See Gunton, *Becoming and Being*, 85.
81. Cobb, "Alfred North Whitehead," 171.
82. Mesle, *Process-Relational Philosophy*, 50.
83. Gunton, *Becoming and Being*, 19.
84. Frankenberry states, "[B]ut if Hartshorne's method is in the service of exploring the universal and inescapable features of experience as such, it is experience conceived as *becoming* that is his focus. The hinge on which each of his major arguments turns is the important priority of becoming over being in experience, a radical inversion of the metaphysical ultimacy traditionally accorded to 'being'" (Frankenberry, "Hartshorne's Method in Metaphysic," 292).

another term for theology that is based in Aristotelian substance metaphysics. Hartshorne's doctrine of God serves as a transitional step between the "classical" one and Barth's proposal. Gunton understands that the material content of Barth's revelation hinges on the notion of *becoming*. For Gunton, Barth does not develop the idea of *becoming* in a philosophical vacuum, but through revelation. Gunton states that God's *becoming* is God becoming his self-revelation in Christ; this *is* his nature and not contradictory to it.[85] The point for Gunton is that Barth is not conceiving God's nature through philosophical speculation but in the self-revelation of God in Christ; it is God who *becomes* Jesus Christ. Eberhard Jüngel says, "God is none other than the one who he is in his revelation. He is thus in this being of his already *ours* in advance, and therefore the statement is true: God's being is *in becoming*."[86] So, Barth says, "we have already had to resist the threatened absorption of the doctrine of God into a doctrine of being: and we shall have to do this again . . . God is not swallowed up in the relation and attitude of Himself to the world and us as actualised in His revelation."[87] The point to note here is that Barth is attempting to prevent a collapse of the doctrine of God into an *a priori* philosophy of *being*, which would overshadow the actualization of God's *being* in his revelation *pro nobis*. Gunton praises Barth's method of constructing a doctrine of God based on God's *acts*, that is, God's revelatory events. Finally, Gunton says,

> in sum God's being is known in and through his action, his triune act. God's action is triune in the sense that it is the action of Father, Son and Spirit, whose *opera ad extra* are inseparable from one another, though they are distributed, so to speak, between the three persons: the Father being the originating source of action, which he performs through the Son's involvement in the created world and the Spirit's perfecting of created things in anticipation of and on the Last Day.[88]

Therefore, Whitehead, Hartshorne, and Barth demonstrate that theology for Gunton has shifted away from static *being* as the underlying substance of reality to *becoming*. For Gunton, *becoming* is a metaphor which

---

85. Barth says, "The God who reveals Himself here can reveal Himself. The very fact of revelation tells us that it is proper to Him to distinguish Himself from Himself, i.e., to be God in Himself and in concealment, and yet at the same time to be God a second time in a very different way, namely, in manifestation, i.e., in the form of something He Himself is not" (Barth, *Church Dogmatics*, I/1:316).

86. Jüngel, *God's Being Is in Becoming*, 78.

87. Barth, *Church Dogmatics*, II/1:260.

88. Gunton, *Act and Being*, 113.

connotes that events in relation to other events and subjects are the basic components of reality. So when Gunton defines "personhood," "nature," and "substance," he does so with an ontological assumption that *acts* and *events* have become the fundamental way to explicate reality.

So first, we recall that Gunton defines "personhood" relationally. But based on the previous discussion, we now understand that this is also due to his commitment to an ontology that privileges *becoming* over substance. Second, "nature" for Gunton is not a thing that does something; it does not have attributes. Gunton says, "natures are not hypostases, and so do not have attributes; in a sense, they are attributes, ways of speaking of the fact that everything that Jesus does is both fully divine and fully human action."[89] In a footnote, Gunton says, "natures do not do things, but express the whatness, *quidditas* of entities."[90] The "whatness" for Gunton is the *action* that is experienced or revealed in a particular entity that defines the nature. This is not much different than Aristotle's definition of nature as a principle of activity.[91] Third, "substance" for Gunton is not that which is the fundamental and unchanging part of a thing; that irreducible something which serves as a place for the accidents to inhere. Gunton says, "we may use the word substance of the particular things of our experience without having to suppose any of the hidden essences of mythology, of something different below the surface."[92] For Gunton, "substance" simply refers to particular entities, those things, people or creatures of our everyday experience. It is the notion of "experience" that draws "substance" into the realm of relationality.[93] When we experience an other, we experience its substance in its particularity: "things are important as things, in all their concrete substantiality."[94] "Substance" is given to the creatures as a gift of God; substance requires relationality, and relationality requires substance. As we can see, Gunton's understanding of the terms "personhood," "nature," and "substance" rely on his elevating *becoming* as a primary category of reality. Obviously, "nature"

---

89. Ibid., 149–50.

90. Ibid., 150.

91. "The discussion should have established that primary nature, in the fundamental account, is the substance of those things with a principle of process within themselves qua themselves. Matter is then said to be nature by dint of its being receptive of the above, and it is because they are processes from it that productions and growth are said to be natural. And it is such nature that is the principle of process for things having natural being, in some way dwelling in such things either potentially or actually" (Aristotle, *Metaphysics*, book Delta, 1015a).

92. Gunton, *The One, the Three, and the Many*.

93. See discussion on ibid., 35n78.

94. Ibid., 204.

and "substance" are not synonymous terms; the former refers to events and the latter refers to particularity. So for Gunton to be a "person" is determined by relation(s) with other person(s); and "nature" is defined as the event or activity of the entity in question. Now that we have a basic understanding of Gunton's terms, we can investigate how Gunton uses the terms "person" and "nature" to develop his Pneumatic Logos Christology.

Gunton appropriates the Spirit Christology of Owen and Irving in order to meet his particular anthropological requirements of autonomy and freedom. As previously cited, for Edward Irving the incarnation is a union of the *person* of the *Logos* and the Holy Spirit to the human nature[95]: it is the *person* of the *Logos* who assumed and *hypostasized* human nature but it is the Holy Spirit who united with the human soul and empowered it towards obedience to the Father's will. In essence, Irving has created a scheme where the Holy Spirit can be conceived as being incarnated instead of the Son. Gunton and Irving never interpreted the incarnation is this manner, but it is difficult to understand how neither of them came to this conclusion, except that Irving has always held to the Chalcedon tradition in his writings. Nevertheless, Irving has devised a scheme which places the Holy Spirit squarely in the middle of the incarnation by uniting the Spirit with the soul of the human nature.[96] Therefore, we must unpack how Gunton makes use of Irving's scheme while avoiding a situation where the Holy Spirit can be perceived as being incarnated; while also meeting the requirements of autonomy and freedom; and while remaining faithful to the Chalcedon Creed. Our aim is to flesh out Gunton's Christology while taking into consideration the Christology of Owen and Irving.

First, Gunton is reacting against those who wish to abandon the creed,[97] those who are critical of the creed,[98] and those who, in their own

---

95. To be fair, Irving does say a "threefold spiritual substance" that is really "twofold, [with] one of the parts being twofold in itself" (Irving, *The Collected Writings of Edward Irving*, 126).

96. Irving stresses this point further: "And from this time forth beginneth the procession of the Holy Ghost from the Father and the Son, through the man-soul of Jesus" (ibid., 145).

97. For example, Baillie says, the Chalcedon creed "has been sharply criticized in the modern world, as making an unnatural dualism in the Christ whom we know from the Gospel story, and the criticism in not unjust. We should not naturally express the truth in those terms to-day" (Baillie, *God Was in Christ*, 152). Also, Mariña, in commenting on Schleiermacher says "that Schleiermacher ultimately rejects the language of two 'natures' coexisting in one person" (Mariña, "Christology and Anthropology," 153).

98. For example, after a survey of the criticism of the Chalcedon creed, Braaten states that "there is truth in each of the types of criticism we have summarized . . . The issue today is not *whether* the classical christology is to be criticized, but *why?*" (Braaten, "Classical Christology and Its Subsequent Criticism," 513).

way, are faithful to the creed.[99] Gunton realizes that he cannot simply restate Chalcedon; he must establish its necessity by demonstrating its trinitarian structure, and its ability to bring freedom from bondage to humanity. To this end, Gunton derives his particular Christology from the divine economic *actions* of the Father, Son, and Holy Spirit within the incarnation event as opposed to philosophical speculations regarding natures and substances. Second, Gunton recognizes that Irving's Spirit Christology stresses the pneumatological dimensions by uniting the Holy Spirit to the human soul of Christ. The problem is that Irving has potentially constructed the incarnation as either two divine natures (which is impossible) or two divine persons (which is against the creed) in the incarnation. Gunton overcomes this problem by making use of his ontology of *becoming* that defines "personhood" relationally and "nature" in terms of event or action. Gunton says that "the Father's action . . . is love in action."[100] Gunton says that grace is the form of action of the Son: "In the face of sin and evil, grace takes the form of incarnational engagement with that which opposes God's love."[101] Regarding the Holy Spirit, Gunton says that "the Spirit's action is perfecting, eschatological action, realizing by anticipation that right relation between God and the creature and within created existence which is promised for the world to come."[102] Gunton also recognizes Basil of Caesarea's famous axiom that the Father is the original cause; the Son is the creative cause; and the Spirit is the perfecting cause. So this means that the nature of the Father is as the originating cause of love; the Son's nature is as the creative cause that reveals the Father's love; and the Spirit's nature is as the perfecting cause of love. By distinguishing the natures, Gunton feels he has the freedom to hold to one divine nature, but in three distinct modes of actions. To summarize: Irving's Christology is comprised of the Logos and the Holy Spirit; Gunton defines "personhood" relationally; and the "natures" of the divine persons are one divine nature, but expressed in three distinct modes of actions as appropriated to the respective trinitarian person—originating, creative, and perfecting.

It is important for Gunton that "personhood" and "nature" are not associated too closely as to become synonymous terms: simply stated, "person" describes the relation and "nature" describes some type of event or action. Gunton appropriates Irving's Christology, but modifies it so that there

99. In keeping with the Reformed tradition regarding the Chalcedon creed, Brunner says, "I believe that I am presenting the meaning of the Reformed doctrine" (Brunner, *The Mediator*, 343n1).

100. Gunton, *Act and Being*, 140.

101. Ibid., 141.

102. Ibid.

is not a possibility of two divine persons or two divine natures within the *hypostatic* union. Since "personhood" is defined in terms of relation, Gunton can say that the person of the Son united with human nature. As stated earlier, personhood and nature are not synonymous terms, and they are defined differently—the former in terms of relation, and the latter in terms of action. The nature of the Son is as the creative cause, so his divine action is to create the union by assuming human nature. So this establishes the personhood of the union in the person of the Son; and establishes that the divine nature of the Son is also involved in the incarnation; albeit not in an active manner. The nature of the Holy Spirit is as the perfecting cause; that is, the eschatological agent of liberation. So the Holy Spirit's divine nature in the incarnation acts upon the human nature to liberate and perfect it for the Son's and Father's work. This means that the Spirit is the divine nature in the incarnation because the humanity of Christ is liberated by the perfecting and liberating work of the Spirit. If the Son's divine nature worked on the human nature beyond creating the union, it would be the Son's divine nature that created the motivating will to obey the Father's will. Gunton understands this as the divine nature overwhelming the human nature, and in a manner of speaking, forcing the human nature into submission. But if the Holy Spirit's nature is defined as an act of liberation and as the divine nature in the incarnation, then the Spirit works to liberate the human nature from bondage to sin towards an openness to the Father's will. Within the incarnation, the Son and the Spirit complete the Father's will because the Son *assumes* and the Spirit liberates. Gunton's Pneumatology affords a more decisive role for the Spirit in the incarnation that ultimately completes the trinitarian picture of the incarnation.

Gunton's vision of the incarnation is a modification to the tradition's view of the Chalcedon creed. The way the creed is typically presented is as two natures united in one person: the divine nature of the *Logos* and the *anhypostasized* human nature. The Reformed tradition tends to stress that is was the *person* of the Son who assumed human nature, where the Lutheran tradition tends to focus on the divine nature of the eternal Son. Either way, the incarnation is presented as a union of the divine nature of the eternal Word with the human nature. The following diagrams pictorially represent the traditional view of Chalcedon:

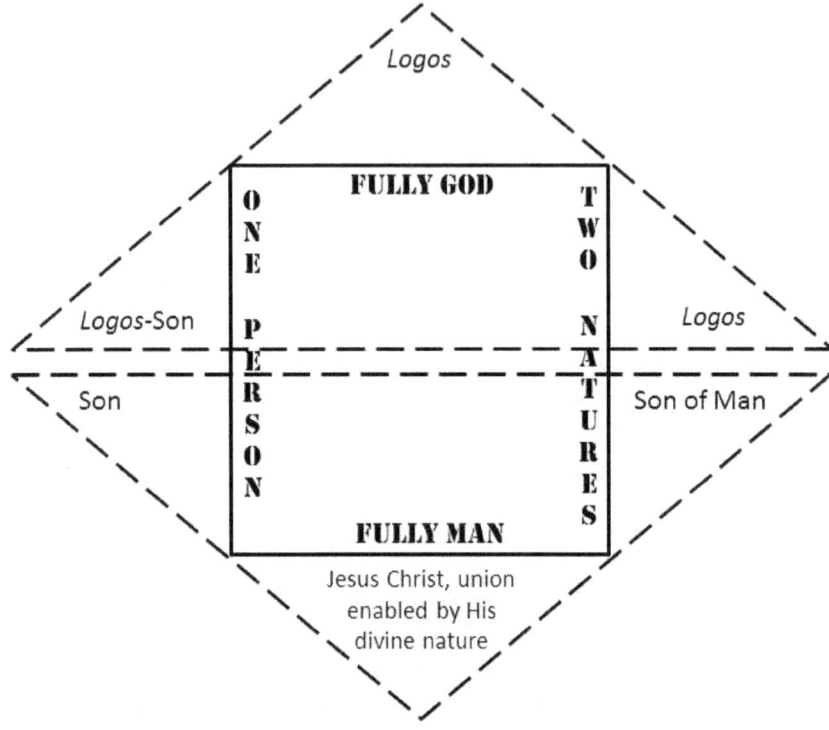

Figure 1: Traditional View of Hypostatic Union

In this view, the ontology of the incarnation is configured as a *Logos*-man event; there is little if any involvement from the Father and the Spirit. This explains why the controversies after Chalcedon centered on the incompatibility of Jesus' two natures with various explanations from communication of attributes to *kenotic* theologies. Oliver Crisp explains that classical Christology focused on the two natures of Christ as *the* motive power in the union; the Spirit had little to no involvement after the initial formation of the human body. In reference to the miracles performed by Christ, Crisp states that

> I take it that on a classical Christology, this is exactly what the divine nature of Christ enables his human nature to do, via nature-perichoresis. It could be argued that it is the Holy Spirit that enables the human nature of Christ to perform miracles, rather than Christ's divine nature, if, say, the divine nature of Christ is not thought to act in and through the human nature of Christ in this way during the incarnation. But I take it that this is not a conventional view of the means by which Christ was able to perform miracle. A conventional view would claim

that Christ was able to perform miracles in virtue of the action of his divine nature in and through his human nature in the hypostatic union.[103]

Crisp's quote gives us insight into the way that Gunton understands the classic view of Christology, that the divine nature of the Son acts in and through the human nature, which in turn views the incarnation as an event that is concentrated on the dual natures of the Son of God. But Gunton's modification of the creed stresses that "nature" represents events or actions, and not necessarily the essence of a thing. So his account of Chalcedon can be represented pictorially with the following diagram:

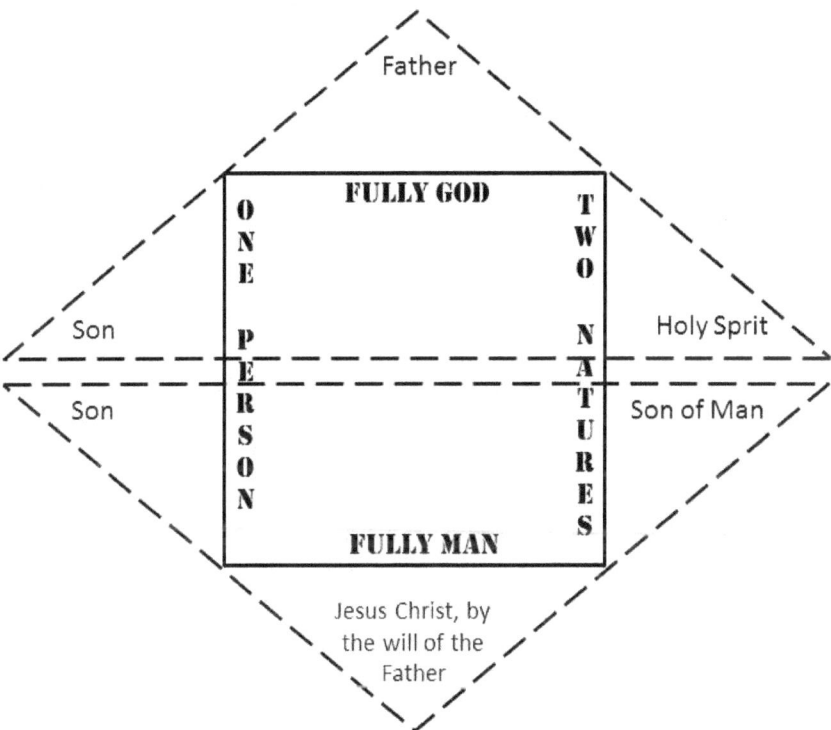

Figure 2: Gunton's Pneumatological Christology

Since "personhood" is constituted by relations and not natures, Gunton does not have to adhere to a one-to-one correspondence between the two. So the *person* of the Son assumed human nature; and the "nature" of the Holy Spirit provides the divine action within the incarnation. The *person* of the Son

103. Crisp, "Problems with Perichoresis," 134.

is the *hypostasis* in the incarnation, but the Spirit is the divine nature because he provides the divine action of perfecting, which can be defined as sanctifying. Since the Father is the originating cause and source of the Godhead, the Father's nature (divine action) provides the "fully God" requirement; the Son's nature provides personality (or *hypostasis*); and the Spirit's nature provides the divine nature of *koinonia*—the divine action of perfecting the relationship between the Son and the Father. Therefore, the incarnation is a trinitarian event from the beginning, one that continues throughout Christ's earthly life and then with the resurrection. The primary difference for Gunton is that the Holy Spirit is the divine nature in the incarnation, but only because "nature" for Gunton is construed in terms of action.

So for Gunton, this means that in the incarnation the person of the Holy Spirit provides the perfecting action of creating, sustaining, and sanctifying a body for the person Jesus Christ. In this sense, sanctification is the Holy Spirit's divine action of perfecting and liberation—the human nature of Christ is liberated from the effects of sin. Otherwise, the divine nature of the Son would overwhelm the human nature, thereby creating the Appollinarian problem all over again; as seen when some read the scriptures as ascribing divergent activities in the Bible to either the humanity or the divinity of the Son. For Gunton, the activity of Jesus Christ is the unified work of the *person* and not the natures independent of the person. If the Holy Spirit is considered the divine agent who works *in* and *with* the human nature of Christ, then instead of describing incarnational activities from one of the two natures of the Son, they can be described as the activity of the person of the Son who works by the power of the Holy Spirit to the glory of the Father.

Gunton's trinitarian conception is maintained because the incarnation originates in the will of the Father; it is this will that the Son continually honors and obeys as the man Jesus Christ. There is no need to argue about the *communicatio idiomatum*[104] or the validity of the doctrine of kenosis,[105] because the Son did not lose any attributes but rather gained a new nature

---

104. Gunton says "that almost any doctrine of the *communicatio* leads into apparently insuperable difficulties, as the history of the so-called kenotic Christology only too well witnesses. However, if the attributes of the Son are first of all derived from his incarnate condition–from the act of becoming man and living a human life–then we shall be concerned not primarily with omnipotence etc., but with the eternal Son's capacity to become man without loss of his divinity" (Gunton, *Act and Being*, 151).

105. Here is the question that Gunton asks in its entirety: "Is Irving's Christology in that sense kenotic? The answer is, surely not. He is not writing as he does in order to find some way out of the supposed incompatibility of eternal Son and human Jesus, but speaking of the human life as the outcome of the Son's self-giving. In that respect, the incarnation is the *expression* of the Son's eternal reality and not an exception to it, as kenotic theories . . . tend to teach" (*Theology through the Theologians: Selected Essays, 1972–1995*, 164).

that exists in time and space as a true man who relies on the Holy Spirit to maintain a relationship with the Father. In this way, the focus of the incarnation is that Christ's human soul was taken possession of by the Holy Spirit due to the eternal Son's union with the human nature. The Son's role in the incarnation is a continual self-emptying of his divinity *into* the human nature to maintain the union, or the *assumption*; the human nature is allowed to be human "by coming into harmony with the former [i.e., the divine nature] through the mighty power of the Holy Ghost."[106] So the Holy Spirit's divine nature (or action) allows the human nature the freedom to be *that* messiah of God. In other words, there are two natures, the human, which was formed by the second nature which is the divinity of the Holy Spirit. But the Word gives personhood to the two natures as the expression of the eternal Son of the Father: the Chalcedon configuration is maintained and upheld, albeit, modified.[107] This way, the divine omnipotence is defined

---

106. Irving, *The Collected Writings of Edward Irving*, 134.

107. In my opinion, this is an area of Gunton's theology that many commentators have overlooked due to the lack of interest in Irving as a representative of Reformed theology. For example, Green has one reference to Edward Irving, where he states, "[T]here is one particular aspect of Gunton's Christology which should be briefly noted. Gunton appears to affirm Edward Irving's contention that in the incarnation the Son took on not a sinless humanity or flesh, but took on truly sinful and fallen humanity, or flesh" (Green, *Colin Gunton and the Failure of Augustine*, 53). Green understands Irving's Christology from a moral perspective; the Holy Spirit "sustains and perseveres the incarnate Christ" (ibid.), so that Christ is conceived of having a fallen human nature, but without sin. Green finally says, "[I]n the end, Gunton wishes to affirm a generally traditional Christology" (ibid.).

In the book, *The Theology of Colin Gunton* (Harvey, ed., *The Theology of Colin Gunton*), which is a compilation of essays, various authors mention Edward Irving. Unfortunately, none of the authors attempts to engage Irving's writings. For example, John Webster, Justyn Terry, and Lincoln Harvey all mention Irving, but just in passing or in light of another theological interest, such as atonement or sin. Stephen Holmes discusses Irving beyond a passing comment, but not much, and only as a means for Gunton to develop a concept of mediation. Both Alan Spence (who states that Gunton's Christological conceptions "places [him] at a considerable distance from the perspectives of . . . the Chalcedonians" (Spence, "The Person as Willing Agent"), and Paul Cumin, who says that Gunton's particular approach to Spirit Christology "is a remarkable claim" (Cumin, "The Taste of Cake," in ibid.) recognizes the importance of Irving to Gunton's christological developments, and the need to stress the humanity of Jesus. The problem for both is that eventually they perceive Gunton as simply attempting to explain Christology using the same framework of traditional *Logos*-humanity categories. The Spirit for them is an addition to the incarnation that provides empowering action, and not as an essential element to the incarnation event.

This is not to say that had all the above other committed to a closer reading of Irving that they would have reached the same conclusion that I have in this paper; because they had various reasons for writing. But it seems that in order to fully understand Gunton's conception of the incarnation, that a closer reading of Edward Irving is necessary in order to better integrate Gunton's incarnation theology with his other doctrines and philosophies.

as the Son's ability to pour out himself into the human nature and rely on his communion with the Holy Spirit to maintain his relation to his Father. Gunton feels that he is faithful to both the tradition and to the biblical narrative by taking this approach. God is defined from within the incarnational act instead of from speculative *a priori* philosophical notions. In this way, the humanity of Jesus Christ is essential to our understanding of God's divine nature and God's action of redemption. When Jesus acts, he acts as one who is sent from the Father, who is empowered by the Holy Spirit; that is the only way he can act. Jesus' actions reveal his relationship with the Father and the Spirit, thereby revealing the Father's action of originating love, and the Spirit's action of perfecting love, while revealing the Son's action of creative love. For Gunton, by stressing the pneumatological dimension of the incarnation, God's triune nature is revealed in the incarnation so that God's love as Father, Son, and Spirit is revealed in creation, redemption, and at the *eschaton*. This way, Gunton's Christology is not simply a Spirit-Christology, but a Pneumatic *Logos* Christology that is an expression of the divine life of the triune God.

Chapter 4

Ecclesiology: The Church as Pneumatic Community

Introduction

GUNTON'S RELIANCE ON ONTO-RELATIONALITY has shaped his doctrine of God, Pneumatology, and Christology—all doctrines are in some way related to God's being-in-communion. As we just examined, Gunton's Christology is conceived as a trinitarian event which embraces humanity through the liberating action of the Holy Spirit. Jesus assumed a fallen human nature, but he was sinless due to the perfecting action of the Holy Spirit. What this means for Gunton is that the same action of the Spirit in the life of the Son is present in the church. The Church is being perfected by the Spirit towards a proper relationship with the risen Christ to the glory of the Father. The Church is communal because it is constituted by the Spirit: the Spirit perfects communion in the Godhead, in the life of Christ, and now in the Church.

In explicating Gunton's ecclesiology as a Spirit-constituted community, we will first examine the manner in which Gunton defines the problem. For Gunton, the problem with the West's ecclesiology is that it was not developed with a proper account of the Spirit. Ecclesiology developed within the context of a strong Christology, which led the search for a perfect church because the perfect Christ was the basis for the church. In seeking a perfect church, the platonic idea of the universal as more real than the particular was incorporated in the idea of the invisible church as that which is more real than the visible church. So in order to overcome the pneumatological weakness, Gunton purports that the Spirit should be conceived as the giver of community; instead of stressing Christology, ecclesiology must incorporate a stronger pneumatology as well.

In order to develop the makeup of the Church as constituted-in-relations, first, we will follow Gunton's argument that the Church's unity is not based in the clergy. It is not the hierarchy of the church that is the location of the unity, or the real church, but the reciprocal nature of the entire community. Gunton supports this assertion by commenting on Tertullian and Novatian as early theologians who wrote against the clergy during a time when the clergy was considered the church. Next, we will discuss Gunton's use of Yoder to connect Christology with ecclesiology. By engaging with Yoder, Gunton stresses that the humanity of Christ is instrumental in understanding the creaturely reality of the Church; Christ's humanity can overcome invisible/visible dichotomy of the church. Then, we will examine John Zizioulas and John Owen who develop an account of ecclesiology that constitutes the church in free relations as a work of the Holy Spirit. Lastly, we conclude with Gunton's ultimate expression of the church as the eschatological visible work of the Spirit. For Gunton, the visibility of the church in the here-and-now is an expression of the new community to come. The Spirit is the down payment of things to come; he is creating a sample of the new community now, which will be perfected in the end. Ultimately, the Church is an expression of God's triune being and is a reality now—the church is not an invisible church, but an eschatological reality that will be completed in the end. So now, we will look at how Gunton defines the pneumatological defects in ecclesiology.

A. The Church as the One over the Many

Gunton understand the history of philosophy throughout the West as a recapitulation of the problem between the one and the many. He also understands the problem of the "one and the many" as having an impact on Western theology in the area of ecclesiology. The history of the doctrine of the Church is interpreted as a privileging of the one over the many; that is, the universal nature of the church is stressed over the particularity. Gunton interprets the Western tradition's invisible/visible church dichotomy as a privileging of the universal over against the particular. The particular members in the local church are not consider as the real church; the real church is that which is invisible to human beings but visible to God. Jenson says that "the concept of the invisible church has occasioned little but trouble through theological history."[1] For Gunton, the idea of the invisible church is simply the same error as found in platonic views on God—the error of searching for an underlying real substance. Instead of searching for the real

1. Jenson, *Systematic Theology*, 174.

church, Gunton is concerned with the constitution of the visible church. This establishes that instead of investigating the polity of the church, Gunton is more concerned with the "being of the church," that is, what makes the church the church. Gunton says that "there is a case for saying that the question of the being of the church is one of the most neglected topics of theology."[2] Gunton's ecclesiology is built upon his idea of *open transcendentals*, by which he attempts to define our reality based on the revelation of God as a triune being-in-communion. Gunton states, "The case to be argued . . . is that the manifest inadequacy of the theology of the church derives from the fact that it has never seriously and consistently been rooted in a conception of the being of God as triune."[3] That is, it is the question of *being* which is critical in establishing what it is for the church to be the church. Elsewhere Gunton says that "personal beings are social beings, so that of both God and man it must be said that they have their being in their personal relatedness: their free relation-in-otherness."[4] Thus, Gunton asserts that ecclesiology in Western theology did not develop with enough consideration to the being of God as triune, but it incorporated ideologies from outside of the revelation in scripture that focused more on the invisible nature of the church and clerical structures.

Regarding the development of ecclesiology, Gunton says that "here, if anywhere, the thesis associated with the name of Harnack, that the implications of the gospel came to be overlaid with an ideology foreign to them, is more than amply confirmed."[5] In other words, per Harnack, instead of the ecclesiology being defined solely by the Gospels, something outside of the Gospel record influenced its development. Harnack comments that early on in the East "the church was really, therefore, nothing but the sum of all individual believers in heaven and upon earth."[6] Again, Harnack comments that "the contradictory notions of the Church, for so they appear to us, in Irenaeus and Clement and still more in Tertullian and Origen, need not astonish anyone who bears in mind that none of these Fathers made the Church the subject of a theological theory."[7] According to Harnack, what did develop is a view of the church as a hierarchy, or one that espoused the clergy as the point of unity. What is important in our conversation with Gunton is that he views this conception of the church to actually have derived from a preexisting

---

2. Gunton, *The Promise of Trinitarian Theology*, 56.
3. Ibid.
4. Gunton, *The One, the Three, and the Many*, 229.
5. "The Church on Earth," 50.
6. Harnack, *History of Dogma*, 3:235.
7. Ibid., 2:83.

ideology instead of from revelation of the Triune God. Gunton says that "the development in the West is both more explicit and more dismal, for the theology of the church appears to have derived in large measure by analogy from the conception of an earthly empire."[8] Gunton is primarily referring to Cyprian, who stressed the unity of the church (Cyprian was motivated by political expediency more than theological developments).[9] Cyprian states that "the episcopate is one, each part of which is held by each one for the whole."[10] When Gunton reads this statement, as referenced by Harnack, he interprets this as locating the unity of the church in the universal authority of the clerics or Christian doctrine: the individual members of the church are not essential for the unity of the Christian community in this scheme.

In the East and the West, Gunton finds a development of the church that is not concerned with the *"being"* of the church, but with the development of soteriological and Christological dogmas apart from ecclesiological considerations. Harnack says that "even in John of Damascus, who in his great work on dogma has given no place at all to the Church."[11] Gunton says that "the real Church—represented by the clergy?—is the invisible Church, those known only to God, the elect. It is ironical, but not surprising, that such a conception, too, required increasing stress on the institutional and clerical organization of the body."[12] Gunton concludes "that the conception of God as a triune community made no substantive contribution to the doctrine of the Church."[13] Simply stated, for Gunton, the early fathers developed the doctrine of the church without proper engagement with the doctrine of God; the *being* of God as triune did not influence their ecclesiology.

Gunton says that "the official recognition of the church meant that it was no longer certain whether it was a community of believers at all, so that it appeared rather to be a mixed community of the saved and the lost."[14] What this means is that (Neo)Platonic thought was the impetus for creating a dualism between the physical and immaterial—which is the real—church. This is simply another form of Gunton's complaint that there is a tendency in theology to stress the universal over the particular; that is,

8. Gunton, *The Promise of Trinitarian Theology*, 58.

9. Ibid., 59. Gunton recognizes that Cyprian was motivated by other controversies and was not concerned with developing a proper ecclesiology. Later, Gunton responds that "Harnack's comment is justified, in that the letters breathe a spirit of authoritarian commitment to the unity of the church above all else" (ibid.).

10. Cyprian of Carthage, *On the Unity of the Church* (ANF 5:423).

11. Harnack, *History of Dogma*, 3:235.

12. Gunton, "The Church on Earth," 52.

13. Ibid.,

14. Gunton, *The Promise of Trinitarian Theology*, 59.

the immaterial over the physical. Just as theologians have been preoccupied with the substance behind the three persons in the Godhead, ecclesiology has been preoccupied with the substance—the real invisible church—behind the visible community. Gunton refers to this tendency as "the platonising distinction between the visible and invisible church."[15] There must be a reconciliation in ecclesiology between the "one and the many"—the ontology of the church is at stake.

Gunton's concern is clear when he criticizes Eastern and Western ecclesiologies as not shaping the ontology of the church in light of the Trinity. The categories of relation, freedom, and unity-in-communion have very little consequences for what it means for the church to be the church. In other words, ecclesiologies that rely on hierarchies of the clergy, or models based on strict discipline defined by laws that maintain the unity, in Gunton's estimation are not based on the Trinity. Ultimately, hierarchical models indicate a weak Pneumatology because hierarchal models locate the unity in the clergy at the expense of the laity. Since the Holy Spirit is the eschatological Spirit—which means liberation and communion—the *being* of the church must take into account the Spirit's work as perfecting the church as a free community constituted by relations. The Spirit liberated Christ's humanity to be free to be the Son of God in relation to the Father, and the Son of Man in relation to humanity. It should be recognized that the same divine action of the Holy Spirit works on the particular human nature of individuals in the church and the larger church as a whole. Gunton asks, "[m]ay it not at least be suggested in a world where neoplatonism was influential, the urge to think in terms of degrees of reality, of a hierarchically structure world, was compelling in the absence of a drive to think otherwise?" For Gunton the means to overcome the tendency to stress the unity over the particular is to develop an ontology that gives a proper account to the person of the Holy Spirit as the agent of liberation, freedom, and perfection. As we will see, Gunton shapes his ecclesiology pneumatologically through the categories of eschatology, Christology, and persons-in-relation.

B. The Church and the Eschatological Spirit of Community

Gunton has determined that the church has developed a concept of unity apart from the unity of the triune persons; that is, a unity based on other philosophical, theological and sociological pressures, which resulted in an invisible-visible dichotomy and/or authoritarian community. Gunton's

15. Ibid.

predilection for the patristic fathers caused him to search their works for a counter-pattern of unity that is more in line with the concept of *being* based on the revelation of the three triune persons-in-communion. In other words, Gunton sought a model in the early days of the church that allows for a Pneumatology that shapes unity as that which is given and received by persons-in-relation. Gunton engages with the doctrines of Tertullian and Novatian, for in them he finds an incipient ecclesiology that stresses the unity of all members over an oligarchy of bishops.

So, we will now turn to Tertullian. Tertullian states that "inasmuch as, wherever there are three, (that is, the Father, the Son, and the Holy Spirit,) there is the Church, which is a body of three."[16] The point for Tertullian is that the church is located where three believers are present; as opposed to equating the church's presence in the offices of three bishops. Gunton perceives Tertullian's construal of Church unity as a function of the agency of the Holy Spirit. For Gunton, Tertullian serves as an authority who corresponds the work of the Spirit with constituting the church as a communion. Gunton overlooks parts of Tertullian's teachings considered heretical; for example, he states that "there is much wisdom to be found in the history of those who have been called heretics because their teaching and behavior endangered not so much the creed as the seamless unity of the institution."[17] Gunton is interested in the way Tertullian disrupted the hierarchal tendencies of his time that located the unity of the church within the higher class of the clergy.[18] So where Tertullian's polemic is against the question of granting forgiveness to those in the church who are guilty of adultery or fornication, Gunton interprets this as a concern "in large measure [of] the abuses consequent upon the arrogation of the power of the keys to the clergy."[19] This is overly simplistic; for Tertullian was primarily concerned with diffusing the bishops' authority so that their authority to forgive adultery and fornication will be annulled—he was not concerned with the bishops' authority in the abstract. Tertullian is arguing for a stronger sense of Christian morality, which he felt was being undermined by the bishops. He is not arguing against the bishops because he is solely interested in church polity, but their authority to forgive certain sins. But due to Gunton's desire to overturn the clerical hierarchy and find unity in all members, he cannot read Tertullian as arguing for greater Christian morality; for Gunton, Tertullian is remov-

---

16. Tertullian, *On Baptism* 6 (ANF 3:672).
17. Gunton, *The Promise of Trinitarian Theology*, 61.
18. Consistent with Gunton's method of using history, he downplays the controversy between Tertullian and the church leaders.
19. Gunton, *The Promise of Trinitarian Theology*, 61.

ing the authority of the bishops as the highest place of authority and unity, therefore, the *being* of the church is located, by Tertullian, in the particularity of the individual believers, but only as they are related to God in Christ and to each other.

Tertullian's ecclesiology is intimately connected to his individualistic understanding of the Holy Spirit over against an institutional understanding; as a result, the individual is elevated as the bearer of the Spirit. For Tertullian, all individual believers constitute the body of the church, because each member is indwelled with the Spirit—the Spirit is not limited to the order of bishops.[20] One author translates Tertullian's *De Pudicitia* (*On Modesty*) as follows:

> For the very Church itself is, properly and principally, the Spirit himself, in whom is the Trinity of the One Divinity—Father, Son, and Holy Spirit. (The Spirit) combines that Church which the LORD has made to consist in "three." And thus, from that time forward, every number (of persons) who may have combined together into this faith is accounted "a Church," from the Author and Consecrator (of the Church).[21]

Gunton interprets Tertullian's Latin phrase, *Illam ecclesiam congregat quam Dominus in tribus posuit*, in the above quotation, as "[The Spirit] gathers (congregat) that church which the Lord has made to consist in 'three.'"[22] At this point, Gunton is emphasizing that it is the agency of the Spirit to "gather" instead of the weaker "combining" of Thelwall's translation. Gunton says that the "point is clear in drawing links between three terms: the Trinity, the community of faith and its free act of congregating."[23] Gunton appropriates Tertullian at this stage in a way that opens the doctrine of the church to a more systematic account; probably even more than Tertullian himself realized. The unity of the church is grounded in the persons of the Father, Son, and Spirit; and the unity is realized by the agency of the Holy

---

20. Tertullian's stress on the individual is seen in the following: "Over the waters of baptism, recognising as it were His primeval seat, He reposes: (He who) glided down on the Lord "in the shape of a dove," in order that the nature of the Holy Spirit might be declared by means of the creature (the emblem) of simplicity and innocence, because even in her bodily structure the dove is without literal gall . . . so by the self-same law of heavenly effect, to earth–that is, to our flesh–as it emerges from the font, after its old sins, flies the *dove* of the Holy Spirit, bringing us the peace of God, sent out from the heavens, where is the Church, the typified ark" (Tertullian, *On Baptism* 8 [ANF 3:673]).

21. *On Modesty* 21.16–17 (ANF 4:99–100).

22. Gunton, *The Promise of Trinitarian Theology*, 61–62; brackets and parentheses in original.

23. Ibid., 62.

Spirit who causes a free act within the individual believers towards new relations in the church of Christ. It is interesting that Gunton overlooks Tertullian's phrase that the "Church itself is, properly and principally, the Spirit Himself." Tertullian's motive for equating the Church with the Spirit probably has its roots in Tertullian's Montanist background, which espoused the belief that Spirit-inspired individuals have the same authority as the clergy.[24] Nevertheless, this indicates that Gunton overlooks Tertullian's motivations, because Tertullian's outcome is a church that is constituted by the individual believers as a community, and not only by the clergy. Finally, to stress Gunton's point for using Tertullian, Tertullian concludes by saying that "but (it will be) the Church of the Spirit, by means of a spiritual man; not the Church which consists of a number of bishops."[25] So it is not a hierarchy of bishops or an invisible real church that constitutes the church, but the individuals who are united by the agency of the Holy Spirit in Christ.

Gunton strengthens his case that some of the early "heretics" were useful by turning his attention to Novatian by way of Harnack. Unfortunately, very few works of Novatian survived, so most of our information comes through secondary sources. Gunton says that Novatian "has a different ecclesiology from his opponents because he has a different soteriology and eschatology."[26] It is not so much Novatian, but Harnack's interpretation of him that is driving Gunton's interpretation and appropriation of Novatian. Harnack explains that at the time of Novatian, the church needed the episcopal hierarchy in order to prevent her from completely falling into immorality. Novatian was not satisfied with those who lapsed into idolatry and the church's policy of forgiveness. Novatian's soteriology is not based on church membership alone; forgiveness of sins is ultimately an eschatological feat by God. What is pertinent to our discussion is that Novatian's ecclesiology does away with the hierarchy of the church by establishing membership status at the individual level, but only as belonging to the community. Harnack says, "the primary question as regards Church membership is not connection with the clergy (the bishop). It is rather connection with the community, fellowship with which secures the salvation that may indeed be found outside its pale, but not with certainty."[27] So Gunton states that "as Harnack

---

24. Bavinck says that "Montanism wanted to ground the church in the alleged inspiration and prophecy [of their movement] and were averse to all church offices and authority. 'The church is itself properly and principally the Spirit himself'" (Bavinck, *Reformed Dogmatics*, 4:282).

25. "*sed ecclesia spiritus per spiritalem hominem, non ecclesia numerus episcoporum*" (Tertullian, *On Modesty* 21.17 [ANF 4:100]).

26. Ibid.

27. Harnack, *History of Dogma*, 119–20.

represents it, therefore, Novatian's position is a denial of the Constantinian view of the church that we have met in this connection: it is not a mixed community existing in some contingent relationship to the 'real' church."[28] Gunton quotes Harnack, who states, "[a]s the assembly of the baptised, who have received God's forgiveness, the Church must be a real communion of salvation and of saints; hence she cannot endure unholy persons in her midst without losing her essence."[29] Gunton eliminates Novatian's claim that "hence she cannot endure unholy persons in her midst without losing her essence." He is not interested in Novatian's controversial view that the only church is a pure church that consists of a morally pure group of individuals. August Neander states, "Novatian held the following opinion: As the mark of purity and holiness is one of the essential marks of a true Church, every Church which . . . suffers those who have violated their baptismal vow by great sins, to remain in the midst of her . . . ceases thereby to be a true Church."[30] Novatian appears to have created a dualistic vision of the church; a visible church that is mixed with impurity; and an idealistic pure church that is the goal of the visible church. The reason Gunton can overlook this is that Novatian's error is that he formulated two visible communities of believers—one true and one false—so that what constituted the church was very narrow and exclusive. Novatian did not resort to a visible and invisible church, but located the church within the individual believers as they exist as a concrete community. So regardless of Novatian's error of assuming the church must be a collection of morally pure people, what is of import is that Novatian located the real being of the church in the local membership, instead of in a platonic invisible universal church.

Since Tertullian and Novatian developed an ontology of the church which stressed the local community instead of the hierarchy of bishops, Gunton asks, "what is theologically at stake in this contradistinction of 'orthodox' and 'heretics'?"[31] For Gunton the answer is simple: "the heart of the matter is pneumatological."[32] This is a bold statement because neither Tertullian, Novatian, nor Harnack expounded at length on the Holy Spirit in their writings on these controversies. Tertullian does make references to the Spirit, but his primary argument is an eschatological moral argument: willful adultery or fornication is something that should be left in the hands of God at judgment and not the bishops. Per Gunton's judgment, the

28. Gunton, *The Promise of Trinitarian Theology*, 63.
29. Harnack, *History of Dogma*, 119.
30. Neander, *The History of the Christian Religion*, 266.
31. Gunton, *The Promise of Trinitarian Theology*, 63.
32. Ibid.

"orthodox" were driven by a desire for unity, which eventually led them to strengthen the institution. On the other hand, our two "heretics" were driven by a recognition of the community as the place where the church is realized. Tertullian even stated that the community of believers, not the bishops, is the Spirit himself. The "orthodox" view led to a vision of a bifurcated visible and invisible church, which rested in the unity of the bishops. Since the bishops, or the clergy, are the visible representation of God's church, the tendency is to consider the church as imperfect but waiting for a full revelation in the *eschaton*; a visible/invisible dualism is the result. But for the two "heretics," the community is the place where the church is located, meaning that there is a concrete existence in the here-and-now, but with the expectation of a future perfection of *that* community. Gunton says that in the ecclesiology of the "heretics," "there is a considerable emphasis on the eschatological dimensions of the Spirit as the one by whose agency the life of the age to come is made real in the present."[33] The church is not seen as possessing the Holy Spirit but is liberated by the Spirit to be *that* community of Jesus Christ. But as a real community, it is an imperfect community. Just as the Spirit took fallen human nature and perfected it in the person of Jesus Christ, that same divine action is present in the church. The church *is* the body of Christ because it is being perfected in its fallen state towards its future state; a perfection which was achieved by Jesus Christ as a gift to his community. Instead of the church being perceived as an unknown invisible substance underlying the local visible community waiting for God to gather the true church at the end of times, Gunton views the Holy Spirit as creating the church from particular individuals in the here-and-now with an anticipation of perfecting the relationships with God and with the rest of creation. In this way, the teaching of the "heretics" has assisted Gunton to develop his ecclesiology in a relational manner that has an eschatological outlook. The *being* of the church is concrete, it is wherever there are believers meeting in the name of Jesus Christ; and it must be recognized that this gathering of individuals to new networks of relations is an action of the Holy Spirit. Therefore, Gunton's ontology of being-in-relations and his eschatological action of the Holy Spirit has a consistent presence within his ecclesiology.

C. Ecclesiology and Pneumatic Logos Christology

Tertullian and Novatian both stressed the individual in the local church over the universal church; for both theologians, the local community *is*

---

33. Ibid., 64.

the church. For Gunton, it is the agency of the Holy Spirit that constitutes the church as a community of free like-minded individuals. Therefore, the same divine action of the Spirit in the incarnation that liberated Christ to be *that* messiah also energizes the Church to be *that* community of individuals-in-relation. Gunton develops his ecclesiology within the boundary of a pneumatic Logos Christology; for the humanity of Christ is a major determinant for instituting and shaping of the church. It is with Gunton's ecclesiology where much of his earlier criticism and assertions take concrete form, especially the particularity of the humanity of Christ. Instead of the God-man Jesus Christ's role being limited to the forensic, moral, or legal sphere, where his victory is somewhere in the otherworld, Christ's humanity achieved a victory in our world that took shape when he instituted his church. It is a church that is instituted by Jesus Christ but is constituted by the Holy Spirit—God's "two hands" determine ecclesiology. Gunton is concerned that Christology alone has defined the church so that Jesus' history as the one who instituted the church becomes the sole basis of the historical church; a basis which causes it to lose its present reality as the temple of the Spirit. Zizioulas says that "if *becoming* history is the particularity of the Son in the economy, what is the contribution of the Spirit?"[34] Zizioulas answers that the Spirit's contribution "is to liberate the Son and the economy from the bondage of history . . . the Spirit is the *beyond* history, and when he acts in history he does so in order to bring into history the last days, the *eschaton*."[35] There must be an element of the pneumatological in the ontology of the church, meaning that the church is not simply in possession of the Spirit, but is eschatologically constituted by the Spirit. So the same divine action of the Spirit within the immanent Trinity and the incarnation of Christ must be present in the life of the church since the Spirit is the agent of liberation, particularity, and futurity. An overrealized eschatology will associate the deeds of the Church too closely with the Holy Spirit, thereby giving the Church a sense of infallibility in *praxis* and doctrine. In order to avoid this situation, both the fallibility and the visible nature of the church are proper to an ecclesiology which gives place for the particularizing action of the Spirit.

Gunton says that "Christology's tendency is to universalise."[36] For our purposes here, this means that the tendency in dogmatics is to emphasize the divine nature of the Son while expositing an ecclesiology. When the divine nature of the Son is over-stressed in ecclesiology, the church

---

34. Zizioulas, *Being as Communion*, 130.
35. Ibid.
36. Gunton, *The Promise of Trinitarian Theology*, 66.

emphasizes its infallibility, or strives towards a "pure" church now, or associates the works of the church too closely with the works of the Holy Spirit. By considering the humanity of Christ, the church in the here-and-now becomes interesting. For example, Gunton explains Barth's doctrine of election this way: "[t]he moment of truth in the contention is that if election is ordered christologically, and with greater emphasis on the divine Christ than on the human Jesus of Nazareth, the fate of us all appears to have been predetermined in eternity."[37] A direct inference from Gunton's conception of Chalcedon is that the humanity of the Son is a real humanity that is *liberated* by the Holy Spirit to be true humanity. The life that Jesus actually lived in history was not *decided* on the other side of eternity, rather it was *shaped* on the other side of eternity. Jesus' human life was not predetermined in a deterministic sense, but it was shaped by the eternal triune relations; it was shaped by the love of the Father and directed by the perfecting love of the Spirit—Jesus was liberated by the Spirit to be obedient to the loving will of the Father. Gunton perceives that ecclesiology is to be developed with the same systematic trajectory, the same action that the Spirit worked on the human nature of Christ is the same action on the church—a divine action of *liberation to be*. The church's destiny is not conceived in a deterministic or fatalistic fashion, but it is shaped by the will of God, through the work of the Son and perfected by the Holy Spirit. Gunton says, "as the Son institutes the church—gives it immanent historical existence—it is the function of the Spirit to constitute it, to free it from institutional*ism*."[38] As we can see, Gunton's ecclesiology takes shape from his particular Christology: the divine *Logos* assumes human nature, without overwhelming it; the Spirit creates and liberates that human nature to be truly human. So based on Jesus' humanity being a spirit liberated humanity, Gunton argues that in "Chalcedon and the Letter to the Hebrews that Jesus is without sin does not imply that he is omniscient, or even infallible."[39] Since the Son of Man was contingent and fallible, then the church cannot expect to be anything more than our Lord. In other words, how did Jesus overcome sin without a reliance on his divine nature as the eternal *Logos*? Gunton responds by saying, "Not through some inbuilt divine programming, though that is the way it has often been made to appear, but by virtue of his free acceptance of the Spirit's guidance. How far then may the church, consisting as it does of still sinful people, claims more for itself than it claims for him?"[40] The church is

---

37. Ibid.
38. Gunton, *Theology through the Theologians: Selected Essays, 1972–1995*,
39. Gunton, *The Promise of Trinitarian Theology*, 66.
40. Ibid., 66–67.

a human church of Jesus Christ, one that is interesting in the here-and-now with a hope for future fulfillment.

Gunton's ecclesiology is constructed with an eye towards the free acts of Jesus' humanity, and not only by his acts in eternity as the *Logos*; otherwise, the acts of the Father and the Spirit will have a reduced role in ecclesiology. Jesus had a fallen human nature that existed in history, meaning that he had certain human limitations; his perfect communion with the Father and the Holy Spirit maintained his sinless state. So the Church cannot expect to have a perfect nature for it is comprised of people with fallen, but redeemed, natures—the church is fallible and visible. Jesus' resurrection provides hope for humankind, and also the Church: the Church's fallen state is being perfected in its creaturely reality. At this stage, the stress for Gunton is on the humanity of Christ. Gunton's thesis that Christology universalizes and Pneumatology particularizes is given more traction in light of his ecclesiology. Christology brings the universal application of God in Christ as the Savior of the created order, but the Holy Spirit particularizes that divine action so that particulars are liberated in order to reach their intended divine goals. John Yoder's work, *The Politics of Jesus*, can illuminate Gunton's desire for ecclesiology to engage the humanity of Christ positively as part of God's revelation—the humanity of Christ is not merely a place for divine punishment, it reveals something about God.

In his vision of the incarnation, Gunton stresses the importance of Christ's human nature in revealing the ontological relationships of the divine persons, and the epistemological means of understanding the economy of salvation. Gunton says, "and if the Spirit which constitutes the church is the one who was responsible for the shape of Jesus' life, we are still free to teach that he will give the church a christomorphic direction. But it will be a different shape from the authoritarian one of the past, because it will be more oriented to the humanity of the savior."[41] The humanity of Christ is important in Gunton's account of the incarnation, and it is also important for his ecclesiology. In order to understand the place of Christ's humanity in ecclesiology, Gunton says, "it is some such concern which, despite its relative lack of pneumatological content, has informed the ecclesiology of John Howard Yoder."[42] The fact that Gunton is willing to forgive Yoder his apparent lack of pneumatological content informs us that what Yoder has to say concerning the humanity of Christ and the church is important to Gunton's ecclesiology.

41. Ibid., 69.
42. Ibid.

Yoder's argument for political involvement by means of non-violence is not germane to the discussion of Gunton's incarnational approach to ecclesiology; but rather the manner in which Yoder perceives Jesus' humanity as the decisive source for our epistemological understanding of the church's composition and purpose. Yoder begins his work with a brief commentary on the Gospel of Luke; he concludes by saying that,

> Jesus was, in his divinely mandated (i.e., promised, anointed, messianic) prophethood, priesthood, and kingship, the bearer of a new possibility of human, social, and therefore political relationships. His baptism is the inauguration and his cross is the culmination of that new regime in which his disciples are called to share. Hearers or readers may choose to consider that kingdom as not real, or not relevant, or not possible, or not inviting; but no longer can we come to this choice in the name of systematic theology or honest hermeneutics.[43]

The point for Yoder is that we should not look to the immanent life of God to determine Jesus' relevance for our present time, but we should look to the economy; the economy is where we will find the humanity of the Son. Yoder says that the intent of the preamble in John 1:1 "was not to consecrate beside Jesus some other way of perceiving the eternal Word, through reason or history or nature, but rather to affirm the exclusivity of the revelation claim they were making for Jesus."[44] For Yoder, Jesus' human career should not be treated allegorically as pointing to some deeper meaning requiring hermeneutical and spiritual discernment on part of the readers. For this tends to treat the actions of Jesus and the response of others as if they were all mistaken of Jesus' true intents. Recognizing that for some, Jesus' death was predetermined in eternity past as that which either paid the ransom or as substitutionary penalty, Yoder bemoans that, "whatever be the imagery, Jesus knew he had to die, for reasons unrelated to his social humanity. Therefore the social humanity of how that necessity came to be carried out is unimportant."[45] For Yoder, the tradition has stressed the other-worldly Jesus at the expense of his humanity; but this is not the way early Christology developed.

Yoder says, "*First* there was the bare resurrection message; *then* there was the lordship proclamation; *then* it was filled out with the body of memories of the words and works of Jesus of Nazareth. The movement in the formation of the New Testament literature was toward, not away from, filling

---

43. Yoder, *The Politics of Jesus*, 52–53.
44. Ibid., 99.
45. Ibid.

out the picture of Jesus' humanity."[46] For Yoder, Christ's human action indicates that he was socially-politically active as opposed to merely completing requirements in the cosmic law court; Jesus acted within the social-political realm in order to create a new order. It is not Yoder's ethics that concerns us, but that Yoder expects Jesus' humanity to have a bearing on Christology; Christ's actions are to be defined within historical time and space. Yoder says that "Luke's report of the testing begins with the economic option."[47] The temptations of Christ are not written to demonstrate the *homoousia* of the Son with the Father, as if the temptations are a mere enticement to abuse divine omnipotence. Yoder interprets the temptations through a socio-politico lens, meaning that Jesus was establishing his non-violent rule against the violent and power-seeking structures in the world. So for Gunton, the temptations are interpreted through the lens of liberation—the Son's action is free obedience to the Father through the liberating action of the Holy Spirit. Gunton says that "modern theology, for all its stress on the importance of Jesus' humanity, has often failed to come to terms with the dogmatic implications of the theme [i.e., temptations of Christ]."[48] Gunton then says that, "the replies placed on the lips of Jesus express his response in terms of what I have called his vertical relatedness. For him, the relation to God the Father, revealed at baptism, requires a particular response, of free worship and obedience."[49] Both Yoder and Gunton are attempting to account for the humanity of Jesus when developing their respective Christologies; so that instead of over stressing the action of the eternal *Logos*, the actions of Jesus Christ in our creaturely reality has concrete meaning.

So Yoder redefines Christ's ethical teaching away from an overly spiritualized allegorical account to one that is concrete in the daily lives of first century Judaism. Yoder primarily attains this redefinition through the use of the "jubilee." One example will suffice to demonstrate Yoder's approach. In the so-called "Lord's Prayer," Jesus tells his disciples to pray "forgive us our sins."[50] Instead of this being a cry for the release of our moral guilt before God, Yoder says that this "tells us purely and simply to erase the debts of those who owe us money; that is to say, practice the jubilee."[51] The point for Yoder is that we should look to the humanity of Jesus Christ for significance and relevance, especially in regards to the ethics of the church. Instead of the

46. Ibid., 110.
47. Ibid., 25.
48. Gunton, *Christ and Creation*, 54.
49. Ibid., 55.
50. Luke 11:4
51. Yoder, *The Politics of Jesus*, 62.

forgiveness of debt referring to a spiritual relief of guilt, Jesus relieved those overburdened with monetary debt. The essence of Jesus' words and teaching is really an attack on the powers and structures of society. Yoder ultimately defines Jesus' actions from within his creaturely existence, so that Jesus is creating a new social order, one that is antagonistic towards the current political, social, and religious powers and structures. Yoder says, "by watching closely the details and the context of the Gospel narrative, we can see reported the work of an ethical-social Jesus whose words and work, life and death, consistently project and make real a particular pattern of presence in the world."[52] It is no small coincidence that Gunton uses similar language in respect to Christ and the church. In reference to the gift of freedom, Gunton says that "the pattern of Jesus' behavior and obedience, climaxing as it did in the acceptance of death, is for Paul the model for the behavior of the church to which he was writing."[53] Gunton then states that the pattern of Jesus' life "is based on freedom from the slavery of moral self-assertion and religious self-satisfaction. Freedom comes from the denial of self rather than from its expansion."[54] Jesus operated within human structures, so what he accomplished was in relation to those human structures and powers, and not some other-worldly transaction in heaven. The Holy Spirit granted the human nature of Christ the ability to overcome the forces within our human condition that thwart human beings from reaching their intended goal of a real humanity as a diving gift.

What this means for ecclesiology is that Jesus' life, death, and resurrection were a result of the life he lived; Jesus' life was not preordained in a deterministic fashion so that the choices he made were already determined in eternity past. The cross of Christ is a result of his non-conformity to those Powers that have usurped God's authority. Those Powers and Structures are necessary, and are used by God to mediate his will for the human race, but they are now fallen and against God. The church was instituted by Jesus as the nexus of a new social order, to be the reality that is against those Powers and Structures which have wrongly gained authority for themselves. For Yoder, the cross of Christ demonstrated the result of both non-conformity and non-violence: Jesus' death was due to his life, which eventually is what created the church. Yoder says,

> For Paul, as interpreted by Berkhof, the very existence of the church is its primary task. It is in itself a proclamation of the lordship of Christ to the powers from whose dominion the

---

52. Ibid., 93.
53. Gunton, *Enlightenment and Alienation*, 95.
54. Ibid.

church has begun to be liberated. The church does not attack the powers; this Christ has done. The church concentrates upon not being seduced by them. By existing the church demonstrates that their rebellion has been vanquished.[55]

This means that the concrete existence of the church is as a new community that is a new social structure, one that Jesus demonstrated and initiated. For Yoder, it is wrong to think

> that the gospel deals only with personal ethics and not with social structures. Nor . . . the only way to change structures is to change the heart of an individual, preferably the one in power, and then see that he or she exercises control of society with more humility or discernment or according to better standards. What needs to be seen is rather that the primary social structure through which the gospel works to change other structures is that of the Christian community.[56]

For Yoder, Christ in his humanity established a new social order, and as people enter into that new structure, salvation is present—the victory of Christ is revealed in the new structure. The new structure is based on the proposal that Jesus' "victory is both a continuing and an earthly one."[57] For Gunton, Jesus' victory over the temptations is an earthly victory because he triumphed over the "principalities and powers," which are defined as earthly realities. Gunton quotes G. B. Caird, who explains that when Paul "claims that on the cross Christ has disarmed the powers and triumphed over them, he is talking about earthly realities, about the impact of the crucifixion on the corporate life of men and nations."[58] So for Gunton, "the victory is not over forces which inhabit a transcendent world, separate from ours, and intervene from outside."[59] The "principalities and powers," theologically speaking, are those social, political, and moral structures which are not under the immediate control of any particular person(s) or group(s), but nevertheless have undue influence over humanity. This way, Gunton agrees with Yoder that the "principalities and powers" should be defined within our earthly existence, so that Christ's past victory over the demonic social and political structures can remain a victory in our present lives. Christ's victory

---

55. Yoder, *The Politics of Jesus*, 150.
56. Ibid., 154.
57. Gunton, *The Actuality of Atonement*, 57.
58. Caird, *The Language and Imagery of the Bible*, 242.
59. Gunton, *The Actuality of Atonement*, 65.

requires the establishment of a new social and political structure; this new structure finds its concrete reality in the new community—the church.

Gunton says that the mature Yoder turned his attention more explicitly to ecclesiology, and that he argued "for a voluntary community which lives from the historical particularity of its origins. All such enterprises enable us to reappropriate an ecclesiology of the humanity of Christ."[60] Just as the humanity of Christ was assumed from fallen humanity—albeit the person Jesus Christ was sinless—the church is also fallen and not free from error. Just as the Spirit liberated Christ's humanity, the church is liberated within the structures of the world to be what God intended. But the church is perfected by the agency of the Spirit and is being constituted to be *that* people of God in the same way that the humanity of Christ was liberated to be *that* particular person. The church for Gunton is not a group of individuals who have had an inner change of faith, but a new community that was and is ordered by Christ to be a new social order of freedom and liberation. For Gunton, this can only be accomplished if the divine nature of Christ is perceived *as* the Holy Spirit liberating his humanity, so that the same divine action is also liberating the church to be itself in the face of those opposing Powers and Structures. Ecclesiology is then pneumatological because the concrete reality is located in the new social structures that are being reimaged and reappropriated within history as God the Father guides it towards its intended destiny. The Holy Spirit for Gunton creates new and creative networks of relationships in response to the real situation in the world; those new networks are shaped christologically and also eschatologically by the Holy Spirit. The Church is not the Spirit, but it is guided by the Holy Spirit towards its eschatological perfection.

---

60. Gunton, *The Promise of Trinitarian Theology*, 70.

Frank D. Macchia: Pneumatology as Justification

Introduction

PENTECOSTAL THEOLOGY IS CURRENTLY in its infancy due to the circumstances in which Pentecostalism began; but fortunately, there are many Pentecostal scholars who are doing high-level academic work in the area of Pentecostal theology generally and Pneumatology in particular.[1] Dr. Frank Macchia is one of these, a professor of theology at Vanguard University, which proudly proclaims its heritage from within the Pentecostal tradition. Dr. Macchia is also the editor of the international Pentecostal journal *Pneuma*, and has contributed numerous articles as well. Dr. Macchia is also a minister in the Assemblies of God, and as of this writing, serves as an elder at a local church in California. The reason for listing Macchia's achievements is to demonstrate that he is firmly planted within the Pentecostal tradition; he is not an outsider making observations. Contextually speaking, Macchia is an appropriate conversation partner for Gunton due to the influence that Barth and Moltmann had on both scholars. Macchia does not rely heavily on Zizioulas, but there is an element of appreciation for the Eastern Fathers, which parallels Gunton's admiration of the East as witnessed in Macchia's use of *theosis*. Finally, Macchia's primary two works, *Baptized in the Spirit* and *Justified in the Spirit*, are both attempts to recapture the Holy Spirit's role in creation, salvation, and the *eschaton*.[2] Ultimately, this means that the choice of Macchia is somewhat arbitrary, but given his Pentecostal

---

1. For example, Amos Yong, Frank Macchia, James K. A. Smith, Simon Chan, and Allan Anderson, to name a few.
2. Macchia, *Baptized in the Spirit*; Macchia, *Justified in the Spirit*.

commitment[3] and those areas which overlap Gunton's thought, it seems fitting to use Macchia as a positive voice and yet an alternative voice to Gunton's Pneumatology. But before we engage Macchia, a few comments on Pentecostalism are necessary.

A. Pentecostalism Revisited

Gerald T. Sheppard made the following statement:

> An attempt to describe pentecostal movements can be ventured only after admitting that no definition of 'pentecostals' will satisfy all groups claiming that name. For our purposes I prefer an inclusive definition of pentecostal churches, namely those who advocate some form of 'Spirit' baptism replicative of what the disciples received at the first Pentecost described in Acts, chapter two.[4]

Macchia was greatly influenced by Sheppard,[5] and like him understands Pentecostalism as a polyphonic movement in search of a definitive identity. Allan Anderson states that "because of the great diversity within Pentecostal and Charismatic movement, it is very difficult to find some common unifying features or distinctiveness by which they might be defined."[6] Macchia is in general agreement with Anderson's assessment when he says that "the diversity of global pentecostalism makes it impossible to speak of 'a' pentecostal theology, especially since a full-blown theology of the Christian faith from a classical Pentecostal perspective has not yet been written."[7] That said, Pentecostalism is traditionally organized into three groups: (1) classic Pentecostals who can trace their roots to the Azusa Street revival in Los Angeles; (2) Charismatic Renewal, which are basically historical churches that have experienced or practiced some form of the Pentecostal experience; and (3) Charismatic independent churches that represent those self-identified Pentecostal churches that do not trace their existence to the

---

3. Macchia says, "I came to cherish most from my Pentecostal heritage its strong sense of calling from God toward some form of gifted ministry" (*Baptized in the Spirit*, 13–14).

4. Sheppard, "The Nicean Creed," 401.

5. Regarding his time at Basel, Macchia says "later, during my doctoral studies at Basel, I took a hermeneutics colloquium with Heinrich Ott that lasted several semesters. Some of the most significant contributions that I made to those discussions were due to Gerald Sheppard's influence" (Macchia, "Justification by Faith," 223).

6. Anderson, *An Introduction to Pentecostalism*, 10.

7. Macchia, "Pentecostal Theology," 11–20.

Azusa Street Revival. The key concept in all three forms of Pentecostalism is "Spirit Baptism" or the event of being "baptized in the Spirit," so we will examine this in more detail.

Allan Anderson's genealogy of Pentecostalism demonstrates a common experience of the Spirit, "that is a personal encounter with the Spirit of God enabling and empowering people for service."[8] Frederick Bruner states that "theologically, the adherents of the Pentecostal movement unite around an emphasis upon the experience of the Holy Spirit in the life of the individual believer and in the fellowship of the church."[9] Bruner concludes that the primary distinction for Pentecostalism is Spirit baptism, which is "to be understood as experiential Christianity, with its experience culminating in the baptism of the believer in the Holy Spirit evidence, as at Pentecost, by speaking in other tongues."[10] Hollenweger's seminal work titled *The Pentecostals* surveys the historical progress and varieties of Pentecostalism. In it, Hollenweger concludes that the common thread within Pentecostalism worldwide is the bifurcation of Christians into two groups: "Those who have been baptized in the Spirit and those who have not."[11] Macchia states that,

> most Pentecostals have viewed Spirit baptism as analogous to a rite of passage among Christians to an intense awareness of the presence of God and an experience of the kingdom of God in power. Such an experience is regarded among a majority of Pentecostals as an empowerment of Christians for vibrant praise and dynamic witness, both of which are thought to involve signs and wonders of the kingdom that should be experienced to some degree in the everyday lives of ordinary Christians.[12]

---

8. Anderson, *An Introduction to Pentecostalism*, 187. Later, Anderson says, "[A]lthough different Pentecostals and Charismatics do not always agree on the precise formulation of their theology of the Spirit, the emphasis on divine encounter and the resulting transformation of life is always there" (ibid., 188).

9. Bruner, *A Theology of the Holy Spirit*, 20.

10. Ibid., 21.

11. Hollenweger, *The Pentecostals*, 9. Hollenweger presents a thorough survey of Pentecostal movements around the world and demonstrates that for most Pentecostals speaking in tongues is considered a sign of Spirit baptism, but it is not universally agreed that it is a necessary or sufficient sign; neither it is agreed when the *glossolalia* takes place. The one item that is clear as a distinctive for Pentecostals is "Spirit baptism" as a post-conversion experience, regardless of how it is played out by each particular movement.

12. Macchia, *Baptized in the Spirit*, 34–35.

In this way, the issue for Macchia is not the evidence of "tongues," but that "Spirit baptism," however it is used or defined, is a Pentecostal distinctive. "Spirit baptism" is not simply a term used to express *glossolalia* but becomes a metaphor that expresses a more comprehensive and robust theology of the Spirit within a Pentecostal framework. At this point, the problem is that "Spirit baptism" has no specific Pentecostal theological content, it just denotes the presence of the Holy Spirit. One of the primary reasons for the lack of a determinative content behind Pentecostals' use of "Spirit baptism" are the varied beliefs as to when "Spirit baptism" takes place in the life of the believer (whether at initial conversion, or subsequent to the initial conversion). Simon Chan asks "if the term Pentecostal or Charismatic still serves as a useful term of predication. Is it not in danger of death by a thousand qualifications?"[13] The answer for Macchia is that Pentecostalism must retain "Spirit baptism" as its distinctive feature, but in such a way that it encompasses more than merely experiential phenomena. In light of the various strands of Pentecostalism's theology of particular signs and doctrines, Hwa Yung states that "what is central to classical Pentecostalism's self-definition of itself, namely, post-conversion experience of Spirit baptism leading to speaking in tongues, cannot be taken as the defining characteristics of the whole Pentecostal-Charismatic movement today."[14] Pentecostals are in general agreement that "Spirit baptism" is their distinct identity marker, but there is no consensus as to the theological content of the term. So Macchia states that "enough have understood Spirit baptism as a postconversion charismatic experience to make this view of the doctrine distinctly Pentecostal."[15] What this means is that Macchia has framed "Spirit baptism" beyond an initiatory rite, or as part of the sacraments; Spirit baptism *is* a metaphor for some type of experience that happens in the life of the believer after coming to faith. This does not mean that Spirit baptism is not part of the reception of faith, but that from a Pentecostal viewpoint, Spirit baptism *is* part of the life of the believer that is realized experientially by the believer and the community.

Macchia takes the distinctive of Spirit baptism and expands it to a broader theological metaphor, so that the personal Pentecostal experience of empowerment, including the signs and wonders (especially tongues) is still intact; the metaphor actually draws the individual into the redemptive activity of God in Jesus Christ through the Spirit. In this way, there is still the idea of a subsequent Spirit baptism, but as *part of* and *as* the Spirit

---

13. Chan, "Whither Pentecostalism?," 580.
14. Yung, "Pentecostalism and the Asian Church," 41.
15. Macchia, *Baptized in the Spirit*, 20.

baptism metaphor which takes place in the life of the believer. Macchia is free to state that "whatever else it is, Spirit baptism is a powerful experience received with or at a moment distinct from Christian initiation."[16] By framing "Spirit baptism" as a post-conversion experience that is manifested personally and experientially, Macchia accomplishes several things in his theology. First, he establishes "Spirit baptism" as the key Pentecostal identity marker, the one that distinguishes it from other Christian traditions. Second, Macchia redefines and broadens the Pentecostal identity marker of Spirit baptism so that it has more theological weight within systematic theology and the history of the church. Henry H. Knight III says that Macchia "redefines Spirit-baptism in terms of the love of God that renews, sanctifies, and empowers, and uses it to integrate a wide range of theological emphases and movements, as well as to explore the Trinity, ecclesiology, and soteriology."[17] Finally, Macchia develops Spirit baptism into a robust metaphor that can draw Pentecostalism into the eschatological work of the Spirit so that the metaphor can encompass all the categories of theology. In attempting to create a full Pneumatology, Macchia states that "we have been baptized in the Spirit, we are being baptized in the Spirit, and will be baptized in the Spirit."[18] Therefore, as a Pentecostal distinctive, Spirit baptism is a post-conversion experience that is not predicated on *glossolalia*, healings, empowerment for service, or other so-called gifts of the Spirit. As Anderson states, "through their experience of the Spirit, Pentecostals and Charismatics make the immanence of God tangible."[19] As we proceed, we will find that Macchia uses the Pentecostal distinctive, albeit redefined, as the *locus* of his theological project, especially in light of the theological categories of Ecclesiology, Christology, Pneumatology, and the Doctrine of God. Before we proceed to discuss Macchia's theology, we must address the order that the topics are presented in light of the Pentecostal paradigm.

B. Revelation as a Soteriological Project

As we have examined above, Gunton views revelation as a battle between the witness of scripture against human reason. Revelation is a theological

---

16. Ibid., 153.
17. Knight, "Reflections," 5.
18. Macchia, *Baptized in the Spirit*, 154.
19. Anderson, *An Introduction to Pentecostalism*, 187. Anderson later states that, "although different Pentecostals and Charismatics do not always agree on the precise formulation of their theology of the Spirit, the emphasis on divine encounter and the resulting transformation of life is always there" (ibid., 188).

discipline and a science in its own right without having to subordinate itself to other disciplines in academia or society. Gunton has an allergy to any theological endeavor which appears to give preference to human reason over revelation as found in the redemptive act of God as found in the witness of scripture. So it is safe to say that he views revelation as a *noetic* battle, an epistemological contest that is attempting to determine the proper order of knowing the nature of God and his relation to creation. But for Pentecostals, epistemology is not at the fore of theology; the experience of the Spirit is the focus. As we will discover, Macchia also privileges experience, but experience that is framed within soteriological and systematic contexts.

Early in the development of "classical" Pentecostalism there was not a concern with matters of dogma; for some, a systematic account of Christianity was not the primary impetus for a life in the Spirit—the *experience* of the Spirit is *the* experience. Keith Warrington states that "Pentecostals have always emphasized experiential Christianity rather than doctrinal confession. Rather than describe or explain doctrines in the mode of systematic or dogmatic theologians associated with the seminary and scholar, they typically explore them in the biblical narrative and by the testimony of those affected by them."[20] The point Warrington is attempting to articulate is that Pentecostal theology did not develop from creeds but from experience, which in turn led to a distinctive theology. There is a slight privileging of experience over doctrinal developments, but that does not negate the need to develop creeds, theologies or a systematic account of that experience. Douglas Jacobsen says that "[Pentecostal] experience is only half the picture of pentecostal faith. From the very earliest days of the movement experience and theology have been wedded together, and the relationship has always been reciprocal. Pentecostal experience has been circumscribed by theology, and pentecostal theology has been grounded in experience."[21] Since Macchia is a Pentecostal, when he discusses revelation he does so within a Pentecostal paradigm—theology develops from within experience. But for Macchia, the experience is not isolated to a specific point that is subsequent to conversion in the life of the believer, but as an experience

20. Warrington, *Pentecostal Theology*, 15–16. Even though this has been the accepted conclusion, not all agree. Wacker states that "the evidence for pentecostals' determination to exact goose-step conformity in matters of doctrine is so voluminous it is hard to understand how the contrary notion ever arose. We might well begin with William J. Seymour himself, to challenge the myth that the man with the big heart was casual about doctrinal regularity. Though Seymour could speak quite movingly about the importance of charity in the Christian life, his own Azusa Mission issued a formal creedal statement on the inside front page of the first issue of the Mission's paper, *Apostolic Faith*" (Wacker, *Heaven Below*, 77).

21. Jacobsen, *Thinking in the Spirit*, 21.

of the whole of salvation. Spirit baptism is a metaphor that encompasses the new life of the believer—but as an experience of the individual and the community; it is not just the clergy or the most priest who partakes of the divine life, but all believers.

Macchia is in general agreement with Gunton that revelation is to be found within the redemptive acts of God as derived from the economy; but for Macchia it derives from within the experience of the economy in our lives. Macchia says that "God is revealed in the story of Jesus not only as the Son, Jesus Christ, but also as his heavenly Father and as the Holy Spirit who comes from the Father to rest on Jesus."[22] Revelation is not derived from creedal statements or through human reason, but from within the story of Jesus Christ. This would place Macchia on the same field as Gunton, but Macchia moves beyond Gunton's view that revelation is the act of God to a soteriological trajectory. But not a soteriology in the classic sense; rather one that is defined within Macchia's redefinition of Spirit baptism. Pneumatology plays a critical role in soteriology, and by implication, his view of revelation. Wolfgang Vondey says that "what distinguishes Macchia's proposal is that his idea of the divine movement is not based on a distinction of origin but on a mutual participation in the shared, interdependent reality of the Father, Son, and Holy Spirit."[23] D. Lyle Dabney says,

> For the life and death and resurrection of Christ *in toto* and not *in partu* is the mediation of a new gift of the Spirit, a 'baptism' in the Holy Spirit, by which we are made children of God in Christ, by which we are fed in the wilderness and rescued from the storm, by which our sins are forgiven and our bodies healed, and by which we are led into and through suffering and death to new and eternal life.[24]

Dabney continues to say that just as "baptism" in the Holy Spirit involved Christ's entire life, death, and resurrection, that same action of the Holy Spirit that Christ won for us involves our own life, death, and resurrection. This means that Spirit baptism is no longer relegated to a specific moment or activity, but it is that which completes God's promise to redeem his creation. Macchia says that "Lyle Dabney has sought to define Spirit baptism as the eschatological gift of new creation in order to suggest a pneumatologically rich point of departure for soteriology."[25] What we find is that Spirit baptism for Macchia is an experience in the life of the believer that

22. Macchia, *The Trinity*, 2.
23. Vondey, *Beyond Pentecostalism*, 106.
24. Dabney, "Justified by the Spirit," 58.
25. Macchia, *Baptized in the Spirit*, 48.

places him/her in the midst of God's self-giving love; it is an eschatological love in that the life experienced now is a down payment of resurrection to come. For Macchia, "Spirit baptism is a baptism into the love of God that sanctifies, renews, and empowers until Spirit baptism turns all of creation into the final dwelling place of God."[26] More will be said regarding Macchia's vision for "Spirit baptism" in the section on Pneumatology, but for now, the point is to demonstrate that Spirit baptism has a broader meaning than initiation or subsequent empowerment; it is a metaphor which draws Pneumatology into the sphere of creation, redemption, and eschatology. Revelation must be construed in terms of Spirit baptism in such a way that it is experienced soteriologically as an act of the Triune God with an emphasis on the work of the Holy Spirit.

For Macchia, revelation flows from within the Pentecostal experience of Spirit baptism, but only when conceived within God's economic act of redemption: *faith seeking understanding*. Where Gunton relies on an ontology of relation for his theological epistemology, Macchia relies on his Pentecostal roots, which are grounded in personal experience. Vinson Synan states that "John Wesley offered his Methodist followers . . . an instant crisis experience."[27] This crisis experience formed the foundation for Pentecostalism's "baptized in the Spirit" as a personal encounter with the divine: "For Pentecostals, revelation is not just intended to affect the mind but also the emotions; theology is not explored best in a rationalistic context alone but also with a readiness to encounter the divine and be impacted by one's discoveries in a way that will enlighten the mind but also transform the life."[28] Macchia's view of revelation outflows from the encounter with the divine, meaning that the experience of salvation is the *locus* of revelation. For Gunton, revelation begins with the incarnation and moves back into the realization of the Triune God; but for Macchia it is our experience of God as savior that has logical priority. In his popular level book titled *The Trinity, Practically Speaking*, Macchia says, "here's the main point of this book: I believe that a force of logic exists in the Bible concerning God as a trinity. It goes like this: Only God can save. The Father saves; the Son, Jesus Christ, saves; and the Holy Spirit saves. Conclusion: Father, Son, and Holy Spirit are God."[29] Moltmann states that "all the works of God end in the presence

---

26. Ibid., 60.

27. Synan, "Pentecostal Roots," 16

28. Warrington, *Pentecostal Theology*, 21.

29. Macchia, *The Trinity*, 11. A note of caution must be interjected at this point; Spirit baptism is the source of revelation because it is soteriological, but it is also eschatological: creation's redemption is soteriological and eschatological.

of the Spirit,"[30] and Macchia responds by saying that "this statement by Jürgen Moltmann represents the assumption from which this book proceeds. And this insight applies as much to justification as to sanctification and glorification."[31] For Macchia, the presence of the Spirit is the ultimate expression of creation's complete redemption by God.[32] In this way, revelation does not begin with a confrontation between Athens and Jerusalem, but as an encounter with the redemptive activity of God. In his book *The Trinity, Practically Speaking*, Macchia is speaking to a non-academic audience, but there is still much to learn about his theology. In it, he criticizes those past theologies that depended on rationalist interpretations of God's nature:

> The problem is that the entire discussion that has occurred about the Trinity in the history of theology has made the map difficult to read. Theology has historically moved away from the events of the story of Jesus (and our experience of Christ) and increasingly in the direction of the more abstract issues of God's inner life (God's life apart from us or apart from history).[33]

Macchia says that "the doctrine of the Trinity is not only shown in isolated verses of the New Testament; the *entire teaching* of Scripture about salvation demands it."[34] Therefore, revelation is framed within his Pentecostal experience of salvation, which is redefined in terms of Spirit baptism as an experience that involves initiation, sanctification and resurrection to new life. Finally, Macchia says that "to put it more concisely, *only God can save* . . . For one thing, this brief statement has been the chief guiding principle in the steps that the church has taken historically in arriving at its key doctrinal statements about God."[35] The logic is that the experience of God as savior is the starting point for developing theology; the experience is where we meet God.

Since revelation is derived through the lens of salvation as an existential experience, but grounded in the presence of God's Spirit, revelation then must include a Pneumatological element. Macchia says that "through the agency of the Holy Spirit, the risen Christ authenticates Scripture as God's Word by removing the veil of misunderstanding and saving those who turn

30. Moltmann, *God in Creation*, 96.

31. Macchia, *Justified in the Spirit*, 3.

32. Macchia says that "there is potential here for viewing justification within the wide-open spaces of the Trinitarian *koinonia* and self-vindication as the Creator, who makes the creation the divine dwelling place" (ibid., 37).

33. Macchia, *The Trinity*, 13.

34. Ibid.

35. Ibid., 43.

to him in faith when reading the message of the Bible."[36] But he does not want to limit the Spirit's role in revelation to an epistemological awakening, because that would be a return to a Christomonism view of revelation that places all of the stress on Christology. In an article on Bloesch's theology, Macchia explains that "Bloesch's focus on God's self-disclosure in Christ as the foundation of revelation, though praiseworthy, lacks Trinitarian fullness because it lacks an adequate pneumatology."[37] Macchia then rhetorically asks, "Where is the ongoing work of the Spirit in leading the Word today into new and challenging contexts and interpretations?"[38] In other words, revelation is an *act* of God, which is revealed in the economic *act* of the Father, Son, and Spirit. The Spirit's role in revelation is not limited to that of an agent who awakens the believer to the reality of Jesus Christ; the Spirit is also the *act* of revelation. In this way, Spirit baptism is the basis of revelation because the Spirit's *act* is an initiatory and continual presence that leads to the Word through the Pentecostal experience of divine encounter.

Revelation is an experience of the divine, an experience which is shaped by Spirit baptism because as a metaphor it includes God's presence and the experience of that presence. Revelation conceived as God's self-communication returns us to Macchia's complaint that revelation in the past relegated the doctrine of the Trinity to an intellectual enterprise. For Gunton, revelation is grounded in the witness of scripture to the event of the incarnation as an action of the Triune God. But for Macchia, revelation is grounded in the event of salvation as an act of the divine love of God. Macchia says, "through Christ as the Spirit Baptizer, God imparts his divine self as all-embracing love and not just something about God."[39] Emil Brunner makes the point that "God is love" is an essential element of Christian thinking because in it God reveals himself. Brunner says that "love is the movement which goes-out-of-oneself, which stoops down to that which is below: it is the self-giving, the self-communication of God—and it is *this* which is his revelation."[40] This self-giving and self-communication by God does not take place without Spirit baptism; for it is through Spirit baptism that the believer experiences redemption as a continual act of God. This way, revelation is an *event* that culminates in an experience of God's presence due to Spirit baptism. Therefore, it seems appropriate to conclude that

---

36. Ibid., 34.
37. Macchia, "Toward a Theology of the Third Article," 8.
38. Ibid.
39. Macchia, *Baptized in the Spirit*, 261.
40. Brunner, *The Christian Doctrine of God*, 187. Macchia says that "Emil Brunner rightly points to 1 John 4:8 that 'God is love'" (Macchia, *Baptized in the Spirit*, 261).

revelation for Macchia is grounded in the experience of salvation, which overlaps the doctrines of creation, soteriology, and eschatology. Instead of the grounding revelation in the witness of scripture to the incarnation event as Gunton prefers, revelation is an expression of that same Spirit-filled *life* which Jesus lived and imparted to us as the Spirit baptizer. So we find that Macchia's Pentecostal influence slightly alters his perception of revelation so that the experience of the believer and the community is given space in the revelatory event of God.

The previous discussion on revelation explains the chiastic structure of this paper. Macchia's Pentecostal roots almost demands that ecclesiology come first in the order of presentation, because it is in the church where the believer experiences salvation as *koinonia* with the Triune God and other believers. Epistemologically, Macchia recognizes that God's self is the priority in any account of theology; so logically, God as Triune is the place where theology actually begins. But, as a Pentecostal, it is the experience of God as Father, Son, and Spirit that is the proper account of knowing. Macchia begins with the experience of salvation, then builds his theology towards the doctrine of God. Ecclesiology is that place where the Spirit baptizes the believer to be part of the community of Christ. Spirit baptism is only possible because of Christology; that is, Jesus Christ is the Spirit baptizer who pours out the Spirit on his church and all flesh. It logically follows that Jesus, as the Spirit Baptizer, requires that we know something about the Spirit in relation to Jesus—hence, Pneumatology. Finally, since salvation is giving creation back to its creator, then it necessitates an understanding of the Creator. Macchia's doctrine of God is derived from his account of the metaphor of Spirit baptism; all theological categories are framed within the language of Spirit baptism. So, we will now examine Macchia's ecclesiology in light of the metaphor of Spirit baptism.

Chapter 5

Toward a Spirit-Baptized Ecclesiology[1]

Introduction

ECCLESIOLOGY, IN LIGHT OF Pneumatology, for Macchia is a study of communion and is a communal endeavor—"The Spirit is the Spirit of communion."[2] The church is first experienced, and only then can doctrinal development take place. This experience of the church is salvific and relational; the believer is reconciled to the Father through Christ by the Spirit. The experience takes place prior to a robust account of doctrinal commitments or theological organization. For Macchia's approach, the maxim *faith seeking understanding* rings true, and is explanatory to his epistemological presentation of theology. Macchia says, "Given the fact that both the Scriptures and the church assume that salvation is provided by God alone as the Father, the Son, and the Holy Spirit, it is clear that all three must equally be this God; all three together must be a trinity."[3] Later, he stresses the point by saying that, "since only the one God can save, and the Father, the Son, and the Holy Spirit save in loving interaction, the one God must be a loving interaction of Father, Son, and Spirit."[4] The point here is that the experience of salvation drives theology; but salvation does not happen apart from the divine life of the Triune God. Macchia refers to Lesslie Newbigin for a preliminary understanding of ecclesiology, which also concurs with Macchia's Pentecostal heritage.

Newbigin says that "the whole core of biblical history is the story of the calling of a visible community to be God's own people."[5] The church is

---

1. This title is taken directly from chap. 5 of Macchia's *Baptized in the Spirit*.
2. Macchia, *Baptized in the Spirit*, 156.
3. Macchia, *The Trinity*, 107.
4. Ibid.
5. Newbigin, *The Household of God*, 27.

not the invisible community which God alone knows, but is the local visible expression which is located in various and diverse communities around the world. Newbigin says that the "actual community is primary: the understanding of what it is comes second . . . It first of all exists as a visible fact called into being by the Lord Himself, and our understanding of that fact is subsequent and secondary."[6] The Churches of Asia, Ephesus, and Corinth do not make up the entire church, but each instance is *the* church because it is a gathering called by the Lord.[7] This understanding of the local church is consistent with Macchia's Pentecostal tradition because the experience of the local church is where the Gospel is first encountered. Macchia's ecumenical leanings afford him the space to view each church, tradition, and organization as the church of God while encouraging participation between them. At the local level, the church is experienced as a community, one that shares love with the other; at its essence, the church is a community with a mission—a mission towards unity in love: "Spirit baptism implies communion."[8] Considering communion, love, and the local church experience, the church is organized around the dual principles of unity and mission; a mission that is to reach out to the other so that love can be shared. For Macchia, "the church did not just proclaim the gospel, it *participated* in and *embodied* this gospel in its communal life and witness."[9] Macchia references Rodney Starks, who states that "the basis for successful conversionist movements is growth through social networks, through *a structure of direct and intimate interpersonal attachments*."[10] Later, Stark claims that "Christian values of love and charity had, from the beginning, been translated into norms of social service and community solidarity."[11] Stark is more of a sociologist than a theologian, but his point is clear: Christianity's growth was due to its communal nature.

For Macchia, this communal nature of the church is the direct result of Spirit baptism. At this point, it must be interjected that Macchia is also adding a corrective to the traditional model of Pentecostal ecclesiology: "Spirit baptism understood as a communal dynamic can help Pentecostals theologically integrate their concomitant emphasis on Spirit baptism and

---

6. Ibid.

7. In regards to local congregations, Newbigin states that "at the same time it is a real gathering. God is really working. Therefore there is a real congregation. It is these people here whom He has gathered, and this is the Church of God" (ibid., 28).

8. Macchia, *Baptized in the Spirit*, 156.

9. Ibid., 20.

10. Stark, *The Rise of Christianity*, 20.

11. Ibid., 74.

the gifted church."[12] Where Gunton is concerned with particularity being derived from unity-in-relation, Macchia has a constant theme of *participation*. Gunton's ecclesiology is constructed so that the individual derives their personhood through the structures of the community, but Macchia is more concerned that the individual is allowed to be an interactive participant within the community. So for Macchia, "Spirit baptism has a relational structure that has communion at its essence, the communion of self-giving love."[13] Where Gunton stresses the ontology of the person being constituted by the structures of the church, Macchia stresses the experience of the individual who is brought into the communion of the new community.

In order to demonstrate the necessity and influence that Spirit baptism has on Macchia's ecclesiology, we will first examine Spirit baptism and the relation to *koinonia*. *Koinonia* becomes the key rubric for Macchia's understanding of the church as a visible community. So first, we will examine the development of the visible/invisible and local/universal aspects of Macchia's thought. Secondly, we will examine how Macchia infuses the biblical metaphors for the church—People of God, Body of Christ, and Temple of the Spirit—with the Pentecostal concept of Spirit baptism. And finally, we will examine how Macchia derives the classical attributes of the Church from his Pneumatology of Spirit baptism. This way, *koinonia* will be seen as the center of Macchia's ecclesiology because the Holy Spirit is the Spirit of communion.

A. *Koinonia*, Ecumenicalism and Pentecostal Ecclesiology

In commenting on Macchia's theology, especially his ecclesiology, Peter Neumann says that,

> Spirit baptism involves the Trinity opening itself to relationship with humanity and creation—but Macchia believes that this is especially true with regard to the church. The Spirit brings believers into communion with God and one another, allowing the church to participate (and express) the fellowship of the triune Godhead. The concept of '*koinonia*,' then, is a helpful and appropriate way to characterize the nature of the church:[14]

---

12. Macchia, *Baptized in the Spirit*, 159.
13. Ibid., 160.
14. Neumann, *Pentecostal Experience*, 182.

Koinonia provides theological currency for locating Spirit baptism as a mediating concept between Pneumatology and Ecclesiology. *Koinonia* has a dualistic function in Macchia's ecclesiology: it serves as a tool to give Pentecostals space at the table of ecumenical dialogue, and as the *locus* for development of Pentecostal ecclesiology. To this end, Lorelei Fuchs says that "its capacity for such mutual informing has led the biblical concept of koinonia to find its way to the center of the ecumenical language being crafted to express the nature of the church and its unity."[15] Regarding Pentecostal ecclesiology, Robeck Jr. says that as a young movement, Pentecostals "are still finding their place and as a result, they have not yet officially established a clear ecumenical agenda of their own."[16] An issue of the international Pentecostal journal *Pneuma* (where Macchia has served as editor) was devoted to *koinonia,* as reported during an ecumenical meeting between Roman Catholic and Pentecostal Leaders. In one section, an article concludes that

> by listening to the Roman Catholic participants, Pentecostals have been reminded of the importance of the communitarian dimension of the New Testament understanding of *koinonia*. Roman Catholics, on the other hand, have been reminded of the importance of the personal dimension of the same *koinonia* with God which comes from the Holy Spirit who convicts persons of sin and brings them to faith in Jesus Christ.[17]

Therefore, for Macchia, *koinonia is* "at the very substance of Spirit Baptism," and "Spirit baptism offers us the link between the kingdom and the church,"[18] because when both "Spirit baptism" and "*koinonia*" are conceptually conjoined, they determine the framework that allows ecclesiology to reach out to the other—*ad intra* and *ad extra*. The *ad intra* speaks to the *koinonia* within the local churches, especially Pentecostalism; and the *ad extra* speaks to the *koinonia* between different church traditions, denominations, and global communities. The *ad extra* also demonstrates the necessity of including Pentecostal ecclesiology within the current ecumenical conversation, because Spirit baptism reaches beyond Pentecostal charismatic experiences; it is an expansive metaphor that touches on God's redemptive activity as present in the world. God's presence in the world is as the other

---

15. Fuchs, "Communion Terminology in the Lutheran-Roman Catholic," 251.
16. Robeck Jr., "The Achievements of the Pentecostal-Catholic International Dialogue," 167.
17. "Perspectives on Koinonia," 124.
18. Macchia, *Baptized in the Spirit*, 160.

who desires to share *koinonia* with his creation as mediated by the missions of the Son and the Spirit.

Macchia's ecclesiology is Trinitarian in structure and Pneumatological in experience. In other words, God's life as Father, Son, and Spirit bestows their eternal *koinonia* to creation, which is actualized through Christ as the Spirit baptizer. Macchia says that "it is important to note that Pentecostals would not typically formulate their ecclesiology through a concept of Trinitarian *koinonia*."[19] This situation is not due to theological reflection by the Pentecostals, but is an experiential one: the Holy Spirit convicts of sin, and then brings them into fellowship with Christ and other believers. The Spirit is where *individuals* experience God, so a robust ecclesiology is typically an afterthought, or not thought about at all. The Pentecostal scholar Peter Hocken comments that Miroslav Volf's ecclesiology is relevant to Pentecostals because he "comes from a pentecostal background; [his] is the first major work on ecclesiology to take seriously the Holy Spirit's empowerment of every believer; and it does not arise from a charismatic-renewal context."[20] With this in mind, there seems justification for Macchia in citing Volf, who says that "the idea of a correspondence between church and Trinity has remained largely alien to the Free Church tradition. This is to be expected. If one understands the church as a covenant arising insofar as human beings make themselves into a church."[21] This indicates that Macchia justifiably understands the necessity of a relation of the Spirit to Pentecostal ecclesiology; but he also finds it necessary to expand its ecclesiology to take account of God's entire nature as revealed in Christ. In other words, "the Pentecostals do, however, feel challenged by Roman Catholics to develop all the implications for faith and piety which their full trinitarian commitment implies."[22] Philip Ziegler states that "everything decisive in ecclesiology finally depends upon explicating and clarifying the identity and activity of God."[23] So Macchia begins with Spirit baptism as an individualistic experience towards a more robust trinitarian ecclesiology: "Spirit baptism has a Trinitarian structure."[24] Since Pentecostals worship in the Spirit and are given to a theology of the Spirit, a trinitarian structure is not inconsistent with their current practices or theology; they simply need to embrace and reflect on God's triune existence. As people of the Spirit, Pentecostals must embrace and

---

19. Ibid., 162.
20. Hocken, "Theology of the Church," 548.
21. Volf, *After Our Likeness*, 196.
22. Macchia, "Perspectives on Koinonia," 132.
23. Ziegler, "Stumbling upon Peter?," 25.
24. Macchia, *Baptized in the Spirit*, 164.

expand their theology beyond Pneumatology towards the triune God; to be a people of the Spirit begins and ends in the *koinonia* of the Father, Son, and Holy Spirit. Macchia's ecclesiology is trinitarian because the *koinonia* that is expressed in the concreteness of the local community and between various communities is brought about through Spirit baptism. The Spirit *is* the love between the Father and Son, and is that agent who brings about a church that reflects God's eternal and divine *koinonia*. Philip Kariatlis says that "Christian theology would claim that the Father, Son and Holy Spirit exist in interpersonal *koinonia*, dwelling in each other through a movement of reciprocating love, yet without losing their distinctive personal attributes."[25] The idea of *koinonia* as a relational term also explicates that the essence of a proper ecclesiology is shaped by God as Father, Son, and Spirit. Therefore, an ecclesiology which includes Spirit baptism as constituting the church as a *koinonia* has as its foundation the eternal divine life of God as Father, Son, and Spirit. This way, Macchia's use of *koinonia* and Spirit baptism allows him to move into an ecumenical dialogue that is currently reflecting on the relationship between the Trinity and ecclesiology, while simultaneously, he is able to propel Pentecostal theology beyond the Spirit alone to the Spirit in relation to the Father and the Son.

Just as God's nature is relational and moves towards the other, Jesus baptizes the church with the Spirit so that "baptized in the Spirit, the church seeks out the other as well in missionary outreach."[26] In other words, "Spirit baptism means that the *koinonia* of God is not closed but open to the world."[27] The otherness of God is intrinsic to his triune life, and is expressed in Spirit baptism as a "bestowal" of God's self: *koinonia* is that aspect of Spirit baptism in which love moves the individual to the other, as well as the church to the other (i.e., church communities and the world). Macchia says that "Spirit baptism implies a triune life that is motivated by love, not only as an internal dynamic but externally toward the other. Spirit baptism seeks the other for the other's sake, for liberation and communion."[28] For Pentecostals, ecclesiology is Spirit-driven, but that must include a community that is willing to be an open communion towards non-Pentecostals. In other words, *koinonia* imbues ecclesiology with a systematic drive towards ecumenical participation: God has poured out his Spirit on all flesh. Kariatlis explains that, "from the very beginning, the church was understood to be a communal event where God was the One who was responsible for gathering

---

25. Kariatlis, "Affirming Koinonia Ecclesiology," 54.
26. Macchia, *Baptized in the Spirit*, 160.
27. Ibid., 161.
28. Ibid.

his people in order to communicate to them everything that he was and had."²⁹ The Spirit that Christ poured out on believers is an event, a mission to create *koinonia* within creation that reflects God's being. Fuchs says that *koinonia* is a "pivotal concept [that] weaves throughout the states as God's 'gift' and God's 'calling' to both church and world."³⁰ In this way, otherness and mission are two sides of the same coin; Christ has baptized the church with the Spirit so that the church can exist in a community and realize her mission of bringing others into the communion of the triune God. In order for creation to experience God's presence, Spirit baptism becomes the primary metaphor that accomplishes the task of *koinonia* as a vertical and horizontal reality; *koinonia* begins with the triune God and ends with the community constituted by the same triune action.

By grounding his ecclesiology in the relations between the three persons of the trinity, Macchia states that "*koinonia* grants Spirit baptism its relational dynamic and helps us to understand how the outpouring of the Spirit constitutes the church and involves the diversely interactive charismatic structure of the church in the church's living witness to the kingdom."³¹ By associating *koinonia* and Spirit baptism with the church, Macchia is placing himself within current ecumenical dialogue and Pentecostal theology. In commenting on Pentecostal-Catholic ecumenical dialogue, Robeck Jr. says, "the partners in this round of dialogue agreed that *koinonia* is a dynamic term, 'requiring mutuality in its many dimensions' . . . They contended that *koinonia* is rooted in the Trinitarian life of God."³² Again, commenting on models of ecumenism, Fuchs says that "supported by this linguistic exchange, the model of communion of communions expresses relationships of diverse confessional traditions as well as relationships of churches within a single confessional tradition."³³ Donald McLeod explains that Christian unity is achieved relationally as a reflection of God's *enperichoresis* of the triune persons. McLeod says that

> *enperichoresis* within the church is only a pale shadow of that. But it is still a shadow. Believers are defined by each other in a way similar to the way in which the Father is defined by the Son; and they live mutually dependent, mutually beneficent and mutually penetrative lives which reflect the unattainable intimacy

---

29. Kariatlis, "Affirming Koinonia Ecclesiology," 56.
30. Fuchs, "Communion Terminology in the Lutheran-Roman Catholic," 252.
31. Macchia, *Baptized in the Spirit*, 165.
32. Robeck Jr., "The Achievements of the Pentecostal-Catholic International Dialogue," 179.
33. Fuchs, *Koinonia and the Quest for an Ecumenical Ecclesiology*, 66.

which applies within the life of the Trinity. Where we meet one believer we meet the whole church.[34]

In light of their ecumenical trajectory, each of the preceding writers are alerting us to the idea that ecumenical discourse must contain an element of relationality; some type of diversity-in-unity is part and parcel of a healthy ecclesiology. Macchia is impressing upon Pentecostals that Spirit baptism is not simply an individualistic initiation into the church, but is that which brings about *koinonia*—that is, relationality. Macchia states that "the church is not just an association of individual believers but a participation *in the Spirit* in the loving communion enjoyed within God's triune life."[35] Christ brings salvation by pouring out the Spirit of *koinonia* which reconciles believers to God and others, which is manifested in the reciprocal giving and receiving between believers. For Macchia, "Spirit baptism is a profoundly personal but not individualistic experience."[36] The goal is to structure ecclesiology in such a way that it meets the requirements of ecumenism and Pentecostalism.

Pentecostal theology is satisfied because Macchia accents the *individual* experience that is felt as a result of Spirit baptism within the life of the believer. Ecumenical accents are satisfied because the experience is personal, but not isolated; it is a communal and shared experience, both intra- and inter-communally speaking. The relational aspect of ecclesiology maintains the overarching metaphor of Spirit baptism: Baptism in the Spirit "is baptism into an ecclesial dynamic," which results in "communal life and sharing." It requires that "there is no spiritual fullness in alienation from koinonia."[37] Macchia's ecclesiology derives its essence from Spirit baptism because the church is constituted by the Spirit of Christ. The church is constituted so that individuals experience *koinonia* in concrete ways by mutually responding to the needs of others through various and diverse interactions. In this way, the experience of Christ's redemptive work is manifested in the *koinonia* of the Spirit as given in the community, all Christian communities, towards a relational unity that reflects the unity-in-relation of the triune God.

---

34. McLeod, "The Basis of Christian Unity," 110.
35. Macchia, *Baptized in the Spirit*, 164.
36. Ibid., 166.
37. Ibid., 168.

B. The Spirit-Baptized Church:

The church for Macchia exists as a Spirit constituted entity that is manifested in terms of *koinonia* as a reflection of God's triune existence. At this stage, Macchia is still not overly concerned if the universal or local church has privilege over the other. Macchia approaches the ontology and the locality of the church as a dichotomy of "separation or dualism" (meaning the distinction between Christ and his body) and the distinction between "the kingdom" and "the church." Macchia states that "I will show my Barthian colors here and posit between these two extremes a dialectic in the role of the church as *witness or sign*, in which the church holds its treasure as vessels of clay."[38] Theologically speaking, the church is local and universal, but it is primarily an eschatological reality that relies on the work of the Holy Spirit. Simon Chan states that "the understanding of the church as the eschatological community constituted by the Spirit is extremely crucial for Pentecostal spirituality."[39] The constitution of the body of Christ is not a choice between local and universal, or the visible and invisible church, or even the kingdom and the church. The church is simply a possession of the Spirit who is moving it towards eschatological perfection: the church exists as the Spirit-baptized church.

Karl Barth's Christological theology leads him to an analogical existence between Christ and the church. Christ's existence took place in time and space, so the church's existence also takes place in time and space. Barth says that "the Church *is* when it takes place, and it takes place in the form of a sequence and nexus of definite human activities."[40] Later, Barth says that "the work of the Holy Spirit to which it [i.e., the Church] owes its existence is something which is produced concretely and historically in this world."[41] Finally, Barth says that

> for the work of the Holy Spirit as the awakening power of Jesus Christ would not take place at all if the invisible did not become visible, if the Christian community did not take on and have an earthly-historical form. The individual Christian can exist only in time and space as a doer of the Word . . . and therefore in a concrete human form and basically visible to everyone. Similarly the Christian community as such cannot exist as an ideal commune or universum, but—also in time and space—only in the relationship of its individual members as they are fused

38. Ibid., 191.
39. Chan, "Mother Church," 194.
40. Barth, *Church Dogmatics*, IV/1:652.
41. Ibid.

together by the common action of the Word which they have heard into a definite human fellowship; in concrete form, therefore, and visible to everyone.[42]

Kimlyn Bender explains that for Barth, "the true church does not remain invisible in a Platonic or docetic sense, but rather the true church has assumed and assumes a form in history just as God in Christ took on flesh."[43] For Macchia, the local church is the body of Christ only as its existence is as a possession of the Spirit; in the same way, the universal or invisible church exists only as a possession of the Spirit. It is not a matter of a priority of the local against the universal, because their inseparability is based on their creation by the Spirit: "the Spirit and kingdom of God are thus prior to the church and determine its eschatological journey as a pilgrim people."[44] Hans Küng and Volf impacted the shape of Macchia's ecclesiology: both added insight into Macchia's ecclesiology as giving priority to the eschatological action of the Spirit. As a church shaped by the eschatological Spirit, priority is given to the dynamic and free action of God in Christ through the Spirit to shape the particular church towards its perfection as a perfectly united church. This way, the *invisible* church is construed relationally instead of platonically; the perfection is in the unity with God and others.

Macchia expresses an ecclesiology that is constituted by divine freedom that results in a church that is participating in the Spirit's eschatological and global transformation "of all things into the very dwelling place of God."[45] Küng says that "the real Church is first and foremost a happening, a fact, an historical event. *The real essence of the real Church is expressed in historical form.*"[46] The New Testament presents the church in its *reality*, not as a celestial reality or doctrine. There is a conceptual difference between the *essence* and *form* of the church, but in reality the two are inextricably linked. In a sense, the *essence* of the church is its invisibleness or hiddenness; and the *form* is the visible side. This means that the *form* of the church is historical; it is constantly changing, but an eschatological change that is predicated on its true form. Küng says that "only when we distinguish in the changing forms of the Church its permanent but not immutable essence, do we glimpse the real Church."[47] Later Küng states that "the old quarrel be-

42. Ibid., IV/1:653.
43. Bender, *Karl Barth's Christological Ecclesiology*, 72.
44. Macchia, *Baptized in the Spirit*, 192.
45. Ibid.
46. Küng, *The Church*, 23.
47. Ibid., 24.

tween the advocates of an *ecclesia invisibilis* and the advocates of an *ecclesia visibilis* is now long out of date."[48] What has replaced this model is a church that is constituted by the Spirit, one that is *not* the kingdom of God, but one that is praying and anticipating the culmination of God's kingdom. Küng comments that "the Spirit of God comes first; and through the Spirit God in his freedom *creates* the Church, and constantly creates it anew from those who believe ... There is no church which is not created and must constantly be created; and none is created without the operation of the Spirit."[49] For Küng and Macchia, the church is not to be identified with Christ or the Spirit; the church is constituted and perfected by the work of Word and Spirit. The question of the locality of the church is the wrong question: the church is a visible expression of the Spirit's invisible creation, which is being renewed daily. The concrete reality of the Spirit's presence and work in the church is seen in the *koinonia* within particular communities, as well as between those communities. So, based on Küng's ecclesiology, the church is a dynamic reality that is constituted, sustained and renewed as a possession of the Holy Spirit to be a community with an eschatological existence in anticipation of the culmination of God's reign in all creation.

Volf expresses a similar sentiment in that the church is not to be too closely identified with Christ or the Spirit: the church is a product of Christ's work and the Spirit's operation. Macchia states that Volf rejects "transferring the subjectivity of Christ to the church, forming a collective subject, a 'total Christ.'"[50] Volf says that the church "is the *people* who in a specific way assemble at a specific place."[51] It is not the *act* of assembling which creates the church, but that the elect assemble in some type of locality as the church of Christ. Volf, in reference to Otto Weber, says that "the church nowhere exists 'above the locally assembled congregation,' but rather 'in, with, and beneath' it."[52] The *locus* of the church's identity is not found in the local church, but in its constitution by the Holy Spirit. The church is visible, but that is not the entire story; the church is the eschatological church of the Spirit. Volf says, "To preserve the eschatological character of every assembly while simultaneously distinguishing between the church and Christ or between the church and the reign of God, the point of departure must be the priority of the entire eschatological people of God over the local

48. Ibid., 59.
49. Ibid., 232.
50. Macchia, *Baptized in the Spirit*, 193.
51. Volf, *After Our Likeness*, 137.
52. Ibid., 138.

church."⁵³ The question of identifying the church with Christ, or the visible/invisible church dichotomy is not necessary on Volf's account. The local church is part of the larger church, or the universal church, but only if "universal church" is defined as the *eschatological* church. This means that the church, local and universal, is open to its future completion as the church of Christ. Volf says, "this is why the local church is to be defined not from the perspective of its relation to the existing *communion sanctorum*, but from the perspective of its relation to the perfected church in the new creation of God."⁵⁴ The local church *is* the church, and the universal church *is* the church, since both have "*their common relation to the Spirit of Christ, who makes them both into the anticipation of the eschatological gathering of the entire people of God.*"⁵⁵ So for Volf, the church *is* the church only in relation to Christ and the Spirit; the church is not to be identified with either: the church *is* a local gathering, and a universal calling of the elect. What is of import here is that the focus is not on the ontological nature of the church, but on its eschatological existence, an existence that is open to the future. In other words, the church is a dynamic gathering which is constituted by the Spirit of Christ as a communion of people who exist in open relationships *ad intra* and *ad extra* for the sole purpose of fulfilling its divine perfection of *koinonia* with God and others.

Küng and Volf aid in our understanding of Macchia's pneumatological ecclesiology because the local community is an instantiation of the eschatological "universal" church. There is no *real* distinction between the local and universal church; but there is a *real* distinction between the church, Christ, and the Spirit. In order to overcome the problems of the church as the "body of Christ" and the local/universal issue, Macchia turns to his ecclesiology of Spirit baptism. Macchia states that "Spirit baptism is a participatory metaphor that is dynamic, interactive, and eschatological, calling forth understandings of the church that avoid both its separation from, and unqualified identification with, the kingdom of Christ."⁵⁶ The church must be construed in a relationship with the risen Christ as mediated by the action of the Holy Spirit. The church cannot assume an absolute authoritative role that usurps Christ as head and the continual work of the Spirit, as if the church *is* the kingdom of God. There is a priority of the Kingdom of God over the church; the church is the servant of the kingdom. The Kingdom of God is an eschatological cosmic reign of God, that is, God's kingdom rule

53. Ibid.
54. Ibid., 140.
55. Ibid., 141.
56. Macchia, *Baptized in the Spirit*, 193.

is over his entire creation. Therefore, the church must recognize that the world, including society, is part of God's kingdom; and the Spirit of God is using the church to transform the world—the church is not the goal, but the servant of God's kingdom rule. Moltmann finds that God's kingdom is the earth, in the sense that it is not simply those pious few who withdraw from society as a sign of holiness. For Moltmann, "God without the world and the world without God, faith without hope and hope without faith are merely a mutual corroboration of one another."[57] Moltmann is speaking against a "half-hearted" Christianity that withdraws from the world. Moltmann sums up theologians like Bonhoeffer, Kutter and Christoph Blumhardt by saying that they "took the practical step away from religion to the kingdom of God, away from the church to the world, away from concern of the individual self to hope for the whole . . . because they looked for the coming of the kingdom of God in the world among the poor and oppressed."[58] For Macchia, this apparent paradox forms a dialectic of the Spirit in that the Spirit constitutes the church as an eschatological reality, but one that is a historical fallen reality. The church is the Kingdom of God in the sense that it is an eschatological reality, while simultaneously, due to its historical fallen existence, it is not *the* Kingdom of God. The invisible and visible distinction is not crucial for Macchia; it is the eschatological existence of the church that makes that debate unnecessary: the church in its visible reality is the product and possession of the eschatological Spirit, meaning it is an anticipation of its divinely intended goal. In this way, the ecumenical tension between the universal/local or invisible/visible is confronted with the fact that the visible church in each local and global incarnation is only an anticipation of the completed eschatological work of the Spirit; so no church can claim a *realized* eschatological position of being *the* church—the perfected church is simply not yet realized.

On the other side, Pentecostal's emphasis on the invisible church, which stresses a primitive and triumphalist ecclesiology, is also confronted in Macchia's pneumatological presentation. Since the pentecostal church is a work of the eschatological Spirit, Pentecostals must take seriously their place within the historical church that has been a witness to Jesus Christ since Pentecost. Macchia says that, "The visible realization of the unity of the church in history will not be viewed as a gift that merely comes 'suddenly from heaven' but rather through a dialectical historical process involving humble and open ecumenical exchange and genuine repentance and ability

---

57. Moltmann, *The Church in the Power of the Spirit*, 283.
58. Ibid.

to change even the very structures of the church."[59] In other words, in the presence of Christ, ecumenical concerns conflict with Pentecostal concerns. Jesus Christ baptizes the church—Pentecostal and non-Pentecostal—with the Spirit who moves through time. Therefore, the Spirit moves the Church of Christ through the past, affecting the present, towards its intended *telos* of being fully indwelled with the Spirit of God. Macchia's ecclesiology of a Spirit-baptized church then turns to more concrete matters—the three biblical metaphors and the traditional marks of the church.

C. Biblical Metaphors of the Church

Macchia infuses the biblical metaphors of "people of God," "body of Christ," and "temple of Spirit" with his metaphor of Spirit baptism so that the biblical metaphors can be understood as inclusive terms that demonstrate the possibilities for Pentecostal theology. The consequence is that the traditional marks of the church—"one holy catholic and apostolic Church"—are also expressed in terms of Spirit baptism. Spirit baptism becomes the theological glue that allows the models and the terms to have a wider appeal and overlap between traditions. As the *people of God*, the church finds itself in continuation of Israel's existence because Christ is the fulfillment of God's election. Throughout scripture, Israel's prophets had a continual theme of restoration; which is an expectation of a renewal of God's Spirit to indwell Israel. Therefore, "Jesus as identifiable with God was qualified to bestow the Spirit hoped for by Israel."[60] This way, the church is only the *people of God* because of Spirit baptism; the church lives from the fulfilled promise of God to dwell with his people, a promise that Christ fulfilled as the Spirit baptizer.

The same theme is present when the church is referred to as the *body of Christ*. Paul wrote to the church at Corinth that "by one Spirit we were all baptized into one body."[61] Macchia emphasizes that the Spirit not only constitutes the church, but initiates members into the body of Christ. In light of Paul's parallel statements in Galatians 3:28[62] and in the context of 1 Corinthians 12[63] there is an element of diversity in the one church. Since the Spirit is

59. Macchia, *Baptized in the Spirit*, 198.
60. Ibid., 200.
61. 1 Cor 12:13 (NASB).
62. "There is neither Jew nor Greek, there is neither slave nor free man, there is neither male nor female; for you are all one in Christ Jesus" (Gal 3:28; NASB).
63. "For by one Spirit we were all baptized into one body, whether Jews or Greeks, whether slaves or free, and we were all made to drink of one Spirit. For the body is not

the Spirit of communion, and brings diverse people into communion, Spirit baptism is necessary for the diversity-in-unity of the church. Macchia says, "the Spirit-baptized body of Christ lives from diverse *koinonia*."[64] Regarding the Holy Spirit, Küng says, "giving the body unity through himself and through his power and through the internal cohesion of its members, this same Spirit produces and urges love among the believers."[65] For a church to be the *body of Christ*, it must be a Spirit-baptized church which displays true diversity-in-unity, which is brought about by Christ as the Spirit baptizer.

Lastly, the church is the *temple of the Spirit* because of the same divine action of Spirit baptism. Spirit baptism represents the church's dependence on Christ and the Father as the source of its life in the Spirit. The Spirit is the eschatological Spirit, so the church must reflect a sense of *becoming*; that is, moving towards its destiny as the temple of God's dwelling. A Spirit-baptized church is the *temple of the Spirit* when it is open to its future, and does not engage in any (over)*realized* eschatology which opens it to the sin of divisiveness as it claims too much (or even absolute) authority for itself. In summary, all three metaphors require Spirit baptism as the ruling metaphor in order to complete God's will and presence in the church. Spirit baptism also means that the Pentecostal theology of baptism in the Spirit becomes an appropriate metaphor for the ecumenical movement because its ultimate meaning and goal is *koinonia* with God and others. The same action of the Spirit is also seen in the four particular marks of the church: oneness, holiness, catholicity, and apostolicity.

D. The Classic Attributes of the Church

Louis Berkhof distinguished between the *Attributes of the Church* and the *Marks of the Church*. The *Attributes of the Church* are those traits ascribed to the invisible (Protestantism) or the hierarchy (Roman Catholicism); and the *Marks of the Church* as those visible signs "by which the true Church could be distinguished from the false."[66] On the other hand, Heinrich Heppe uses the two tropes as synonyms, and interchanges them quite fluidly throughout his *Reformed Dogmatics*.[67] Pannenberg also does not distinguish between the attributes and marks, but for theological reasons, he is more concerned

---

one member, but many" (1 Cor 12:13–14; NASB).

64. Macchia, *Baptized in the Spirit*, 202.

65. Küng, *The Church*, 299.

66. Berkhof, *Systematic Theology*, 576. Bavinck also separates attributes and marks of the church (Bavinck, *Reformed Dogmatics: Abridged in One Volume*, 601–7).

67. Heppe, *Reformed Dogmatics*, 669–70.

with the simplification of the two *tropes* into symbols of the "one" church. Panneberg states that "these four attributes of the church mutually imply one another, but it is no accident that unity comes first, for it is directly given with the being of the church as the fellowship that is grounded in the participation of believers in the one Lord Jesus Christ."[68] The unity of the church becomes the overarching attribute which directs the development of the remaining attributes or marks, so that clinging to a distinction between attributes or marks is no longer pertinent. In a similar manner, Moltmann lists the four primary attributes from the Nicene Creed, but recognizes that throughout church history other attributes or marks have been accepted by various theologians and churches. The distinction between "attributes" and "marks" are not essential since there is not a unified agreement on their numbers or meaning. Moltmann says that "the church's creeds, however, always stopped short at the four classical attributes. These are undoubtedly the essential ones."[69] But Moltmann does not mean that the church is limited to these four creeds, or limited to their particular contextual meaning; the church has the liberty to address the creeds theologically within its contextual situation. Moltmann says that "we shall permit ourselves to add other characteristics to the theological interpretation of the classical marks of the true church and to show their essential connection with the latter today."[70] So it is not essential to an ecclesiology to develop a robust account that distinguishes between "attributes" and "marks." Therefore, Macchia's ecclesiological goal is to theologically explicate the essential attributes of the church that are commensurate not only with their historical moorings, but also with Pentecostal theology. Macchia does this by construing the attributes within his overarching framework of Spirit baptism. To that end, we will now examine the four attributes of unity, holiness, catholicity, and apostolicity in relation to the metaphor of Spirit baptism.

The unity of the church for Macchia extends beyond the intra-fellowship between members of a local assembly. Macchia comments that "the Spirit-baptized marks are broadly ecumenical in nature."[71] The unity of the Church, which is grounded in the one person of Jesus Christ and is actualized by the Spirit, is to be found within the local and global church. Pentecostals have traditionally tended to emphasize the marks of the church using personal language of empowerment, typically for mission and spiritual gifts. But for Macchia, the Pentecostal accent is located in the Spirit's

68. Pannenberg, *Systematic Theology*, 405–6.
69. Moltmann, *The Church in the Power of the Spirit*, 340.
70. Ibid., 340–41.
71. Macchia, *Baptized in the Spirit*, 206.

indwelling as a continual—as well as momentary—filling(s) that renew apostolic power and faithfulness to Christ to serve a witness to him. Moltmann describes the theological attributes this way: "[t]he church's unity is its *unity in freedom*."[72] In the same way, the church's unity is the *koinonia*, which is an aspect of a Spirit-baptized church. The church is baptized by one Spirit towards a unity that is grounded in the *being* of God. In this way, a Spirit-baptized church is a united church, locally and globally, because the Spirit is the divine agent who perfects communion. Macchia expresses that "divisions between churches that define themselves without reference to the others cannot be justified, no matter how understandable the divisions may have been historically."[73] Regarding divisions, Barth says,

> There is no justification theological, spiritual or biblical for the existence of a plurality of Churches genuinely separated in this way and mutually excluding one another internally and therefore externally. A plurality of Churches in this sense means a plurality of lords, a plurality of spirits, a plurality of gods . . . There may be many things which can be said by way of interpretation and mitigation. But this does not alter the fact that every division as such is a deep riddle, a scandal. And in the face of this scandal the whole of Christendom should be united in being able to think of it only with penitence, not with the penitence which each expects of the other, but with the penitence in which—whatever may be the cost—each is willing to precede the other.[74]

The Spirit brings *koinonia*, and not uniformity. There is a distinction-in-unity that the Spirit-baptized church exhibits; diversity in the church is an expected trait. There is an belief in Pentecostalism that speaking in tongues is an expected trait; but there is not an agreement regarding unity as a church attribute within Pentecostal theology.[75] Macchia utilizes Pentecostals' penchant for "speaking in tongues" (along with other *charismata*) by

---

72. Moltmann, *The Church in the Power of the Spirit*, 341.
73. Macchia, *Baptized in the Spirit*, 211.
74. Barth, *Church Dogmatics*, IV/1:675–76.
75. "While Pentecostals have nearly always affirmed the invisibility of the universal church, they have regularly used the term *assembly* for the visible local congregation. However . . . they do not correlate entire denominations with the theological concept of the church, typically seeing the church in spiritual rather than institutional terms . . . However, for many Pentecostals of earlier generations, only those baptized in the Spirit had the Holy Spirit . . . Thus, for a time some Pentecostals did not readily accept the Christian character of nonpentecostal denominations" (Hocken, "Theology of the Church," 544).

adapting them theologically as signs of Spirit baptism that symbolizes a differentiated unity; that is, tongues are not an identification maker for the true church: tongues indicate the diversity within the body of Christ. On the day of Pentecost, the use of tongues united divergent people groups with distinct languages into a single witness for Christ. In this way, Spirit baptism created an awareness of "otherness" without eliminating the distinction in order to create an absolute homogeneity. Even during the early days of Pentecostalism's foundation, William J. Seymour, who is considered by most to be the key founder of Pentecostalism, did not see tongues as *the* sign of Spirit baptism, but unity was the sign. Anderson explains that "the primary purpose of the coming of the Spirit as it was practised in Azusa Street was to bring a family of God's people together on an equal basis."[76] Therefore, Spirit baptism is not simply a personal experience but that which brings *koinonia*, which should be expressed locally and between churches as a diversity-in-unity as the one church of the one God, one Lord, and one Spirit.

The attribute of holiness is not constructed as an expression of moral discipline, but epistemologically and missionally as a sanctification in truth (John 17:17–19). The truth that is revealed by Christ is the love between the Father and the Son that is expressed as the Father's love for the world. The Son's mission from the Father is to save his world from destruction and redeem it as a gift to the Father. In this way, "the holiness of the church is dependent on Jesus' sanctification and our participation in it through consecration and empowered witness by the baptism in the Spirit."[77] The holiness of the church is as a Spirit-baptized community that is "set apart" and empowered with the holy task of being a witness to the world of the love of God in Christ—holiness is theologically grounded in the work of the self-effacing Spirit which witnesses to Christ. Since God's attribute of holiness is a direct result of the relationship that the Father and the Son have with the Holy Spirit, then being holy must also contain the element of love. The Spirit-baptized church encounters the love of God, which transforms the community into the holy relationship that God enjoys. Being holy does transform the morality of the individual and the community, but holiness is a mark of a Spirit-baptized community that shares in the love of Christ as a witness to the Father's love.

The "catholicity" of the church for Macchia is also an expression of Spirit baptism that overflows from *koinonia*. The term "catholicity" as one of universality has not found a universally accepted meaning in the history of the church. In his work on catholicity, Avery Dulles states that the

---

76. Anderson, *An Introduction to Pentecostalism*, 45.
77. Macchia, *Baptized in the Spirit*, 222.

contemporary understanding of catholicity by the major Christian traditions do not rely on matters of geography or ecclesial historical continuity. Dulles goes on to say that no church, tradition or denomination has now or ever achieved catholicity. Dulles says that ecumenical churches regard

> catholicity as involving an imperative. They view it as linked not to uniformity but to reconciled diversity. They present it as demanding different forms in different times and different cultural settings. Catholicity, as presented in these documents, is distinctive to the Church but positively related to the total human community and the aspirations of that community for peace and harmony. Above all, these documents insist that catholicity, having its source in Christ and in the Holy Spirit, is a gift from above, continually renewed in the celebration of word and sacrament. This gift, they assert, is destined to reach its completion when Christ returns in glory.[78]

For Macchia, this means that he is free to express catholicity within Spirit baptism, as long as he fulfills the requirements of *koinonia* as a gift from God. Spirit baptism, as a means to catholicity, invokes a qualitative and quantitative dimension to Pentecostal ecclesiology. The Holy Spirit brings the qualitative aspect of catholicity epistemologically by illumination to the truth of God's love; soteriologically by the grace received from the Father in Christ; and experientially through spiritual gifts given to the church for *koinonia* and edification. Quantitatively, the Spirit brings about catholicity because the Gospel is spread throughout the world by the gift and task of mission to the church. Pentecostals as a denomination tend not to speak of catholicity; they recognize that the Holy Spirit baptizes individual believers toward an empowerment to service and witness, so that there is an inherent and implicit understanding of missional task. Since catholicity denotes the Spirit's movement in the world, and within the church, Pentecostals must move beyond restorationist and triumphalist views of the church, so that catholicity can be a possession and eschatological work of the Spirit. The Spirit creates catholicity diachronically and synchronically in the diverse, polyphonic, and multivariate expressions of *koinonia*; Pentecostals must reconnect themselves with the diachronic aspect of the Spirit's work in the history of the Spirit-baptized church. The same Spirit that "called out" the

---

78. Dulles, Catholicity of the Church, 29. John D'Arcy May says that "Catholicity, then, is not just geographical spread, a form of Christian globalisation; it is the realisation of the unity and universality of the church, in organisational forms and cultural contexts. On the analogy of 'realised eschatology' as the present form Christian hope, 'realised catholicity' is the form taken by Christian unity in the midst of human diversity" (May, "Visible Unity as Realised Catholicity," 56).

Roman Catholic, Eastern Orthodox, Lutheran, and Reformed Churches also brought about the Pentecostal churches around the globe. In reference to the Roman Catholic Church, Macchia says that *"our reception of this witness draws us to the same source from which she has received it and must continue to receive it."*[79] Pentecostals must recognize the heritage they have received from the historical churches, but those same historical churches cannot claim too much: all churches have their *being* because of the presence of the Holy Spirit. This means that catholicity is a gift *from* and *of* the Spirit's eschatological presence, and for Macchia, this is the essence of Spirit baptism—*koinonia* that leads to catholicity.

Finally, the attribute of *apostolicity* is clothed in the language of Spirit baptism and *koinonia*, instead of being a mere symbol connecting the church to the original apostles through history or doctrine. Apostolicity corresponds to *koinonia*, in that it is derived from the unity of the Spirit and not through the institution or any clerical hierarchy. When developing the concept of *apostolicity*, the community itself must be construed as constituting the attribute of apostolicity; for the Spirit creates and maintains the community and *apostolicity*. Volf explains that neither apostolic succession nor ordained offices are necessary to bring in the presence of Christ, but Christ's presence comes *"through the dynamic life of the entire church."*[80] By making this claim, and associating himself with Volf on this point, Macchia maintains the integrity of Spirit baptism and apostolicity; apostolicity is no longer reliant on some historical connection between individual church officials and the original church, but is predicated on the life of the entire church. The word "apostle" has the basic meaning of "being sent"; the Holy Spirit's mission is as a witness to God's Son. Therefore, "all gifted members within the *laos* or people of God are sent of God with a mission to fulfill in the baptism of the Spirit."[81] In other words, the Spirit baptizes the church to be Christ's witnesses to the world; the apostolic mission is a Spirit filled mission to the community. So, "in this sense apostolic succession not only means following the faith and confession of the apostles, it means, in consequence of that faith, following in the footsteps of the apostolic ministry."[82] The apostles have an honored place in the history of the church, and are in a unique position in relation to their first-hand witness to Jesus Christ. But the Spirit that filled them with the power to witness and serve baptized *all* the believers in Acts 2 with tongues for witness and mighty deeds for service. Macchia says, "the entire church—indeed, all flesh, including those gifted to

---

79. Macchia, *Baptized in the Spirit*, 228.
80. Volf, *After Our Likeness*, 152.
81. Macchia, *Baptized in the Spirit*, 235.
82. Küng, *The Church*, 460.

be apostles—are part of the Spirit-baptized church as a prophetic community... All are ministers of the word in the power of the Spirit."[83] Therefore, apostolic succession takes place within the entire community—*koinonia*, which is brought about by the Spirit, creates a Spirit-filled community that is united as a witness of Jesus Christ to the world: a united community that not only proclaims Christ but serves others in the community and the world. In this way, "apostolicity is thus a mark of the church" because she is a Spirit-baptized community that is participating in the work of the Spirit, and thereby the divine life of the triune God.

Therefore, Macchia's ecclesiology is Spirit-baptized and fulfills his theological requirements of Pentecostalism and ecumenism. Spirit baptism is not simply a momentary event, but a metaphor that places the Holy Spirit at the center; the Holy Spirit is not a possession but is the one who possesses the church by constituting her existence. The experience of Spirit baptism is a real experience for the Pentecostals; but in Macchia's account, the experience leads beyond individual experience to *koinonia*. *Koinonia* is possible because of the Spirit: *koinonia* designates that the Spirit is not limited to one church body, but is the possessor of the local and universal church which makes up the body of Christ. In this way, *koinonia* has an ecumenical element because the Spirit is working to bring a unity within the body of Christ, but a unity-in-diversity that recognizes and respects the individual person, individual congregations, and larger organizations. Ecclesiology represents the culmination of Macchia's overall theological project: Spirit baptism begins with God and ends with God, but demonstrates the overflowing love of the triune God which embraces and takes up creation into that love. The embrace of God created, justified, and perfects humanity by the will of the Father, through the work of Christ, and the perfecting love of the Holy Spirit. That God is love and God is Spirit signifies that the Holy Spirit is essential to conceiving of God as love; as the love between the Father and the Son, the Spirit *is* God's expression of love. When creation, including the church, is baptized with the presence of God's Spirit, Spirit baptism is defined as God's love manifested in the unity of love that Christ won. Macchia's theology is expansive and open to the Spirit's work in the church and the world at large, so that, as a Pentecostal, he can appreciate and participate in the Spirit's work within the historic and contemporary church. So this openness by Macchia should be reciprocated and embraced by non-Pentecostals as a conversation partner who can offer a prominent place for the Spirit without sacrificing the glory of the Father and the Son. A Spirit-baptized existence is an existence in communion with the Father, Son, and Holy Spirit.

---

83. Macchia, *Baptized in the Spirit*, 236.

Chapter 6

Christology: Christ as the Spirit Baptizer

Introduction

MACCHIA'S ECCLESIOLOGY DERIVES FROM within the experience of salvation, which is the expression of the Triune God embracing his creation. The church, the new community, as the location of the salvific experience indicates that *koinonia* reveals God's embrace and God himself. Therefore, *koinonia* is fundamental in determining God's nature and acts, especially in reference to the Incarnation. So Christology for Macchia is developed within the framework of God's economic activity and our experience of it: only God can save, Jesus saves, so Jesus is fully God.

We will examine Macchia's Christological development within a soteriological context that culminates in the kingdom of God. The kingdom of God refers to God's presence with his creation, a presence which is expressed in terms of Spirit baptism. Spirit baptism is the metaphor that integrates the Spirit into all categories of theology; but today, it is the soteriological aspect which has focus because of Christ's redeeming work as the Spirit baptizer. This way, Christology is derived from soteriology. Christ must be the Spirit baptizer because justification culminates in the presence of the Spirit; therefore, the place to begin with Macchia's Christology is in soteriology; that is, in the kingdom of God.

We will see Macchia's argument develop out of Rahner's rule that the economic is the immanent, and the immanent is the economic. Macchia does not take Rahner's rule as absolute; our experience of God's economic activity defines Christ's nature, a nature that is in continual relation with the Father and the Holy Spirit. This ultimately expresses that the Father is the One who bestowed the Holy Spirit on Christ; and Christ won the right to bestow the Spirit on creation in redemption. This way, the Spirit then bestows the kingdom back to the Son, then to the Father. David Coffey's "bestowal" model of Christology will be instrumental in explaining Macchia's particular expression of the Spirit in the Godhead and what it means for Christology. Finally, we will argue that out of this, Macchia's Christology is really a Word-Christology instead of a Spirit-Christology. The differences between the two models are slight and nuanced, but the latter stresses the Spirit's location in the two natures of Christ, and the former stresses the *koinonia* between the three divine persons in the Incarnation. So we will look at how the Kingdom of God motif assists Macchia in developing a Christology from within an experience of the economic acts of God.

A. Christ as God Who Saves

Christ and the Kingdom of God

The Kingdom of God is an important concept for Macchia because of its Christological and Pneumatological implications; it signals both the inauguration of God's presence by Christ and God's eschatological goal for his creation—both acts take place in the Spirit. Christopher Stephenson says that "the kingdom of God is the most consistent theme in Macchia's theology and that it reaches extensive integration with Pneumatology in *Baptized in the Spirit*."[1] Macchia makes use of Walter Kasper to demonstrate that the "kingdom of God" is a theological term that is associated with God's presence. Kasper says that "in the tradition of the Old Testament and of Judaism the coming of the Kingdom of God means the coming of God."[2] For Kasper, this coming of the kingdom will find its ultimate expression when God comes in his fullness to be "all in all." For Moltmann, the kingdom of God is the act of the triune God, which finds its richest expression in the kingdom of the Spirit. So by considering Kasper's and Moltmann's theologies of the kingdom, Macchia can envision the Spirit as the kingdom, and Jesus is the king who will hand it over to the Father in the end. Christ is associated very closely with the Spirit in preparing creation to be the Spirit indwelled kingdom. Kilian McDonnel says that "Gregory of Nyssa identifies the whole kingdom with the Spirit."[3] Macchia says, "there is not critical dialectic between Jesus and the Spirit. He is the king and the Spirit is the kingdom."[4] Jesus is the Spirit baptizer because of his role in redeeming

---

1. Stephenson, *Types of Pentecostal Theology*, 60.
2. Kasper, *Jesus the Christ*, 78.
3. McDonnell, *The Other Hand of God*, 226.
4. Macchia, *Justified in the Spirit*, 277.

creation and preparing it to be the kingdom of God, which is a symbol that connotes creation being indwelled with the presence of God. McDonnell says that Gregory "expresses the Holy Spirit's union with the Son in the anointing—the Son is the king, the Holy Spirit is the kingdom:"[5] John the Baptist recognized the significance of Christ as the messiah because of Jesus' ability to baptize, or anoint, with the Spirit. Macchia says,

> suffice it to say here that the connection that John the Baptist will forge between Jesus as the Spirit baptizer and the inauguration of the kingdom of God to establish God's lordship in history is rooted in the Old Testament assumption that the divine presence will make this lordship a reality as a source of freedom and redemption for humanity.[6]

Jesus saves because of the Spirit, and the Spirit saves because of Christ. Macchia explains that Pentecostals have a tendency to separate Christology and Pneumatology, so that salvation is conceived as the sole work of Christ, with Spirit baptism being an addendum that appropriates or assists in Christ's work. Macchia says, "this christological focal point still did not prevent many Pentecostals from fracturing Christ's saving work from his role as Spirit Baptizer."[7] Christ's role as the Spirit baptizer in the kingdom of God is the defining point for Christology. Where Gunton's Christology is formulated through ontological considerations, Macchia's Christology is formulated along soteriological trajectories: God saves because Christ saves, but Christ saves because the Spirit saves; and the Spirit saves because Christ is the Spirit baptizer. Moltmann is a recurring conversation partner for Macchia, so his insights into the kingdom of God will shed light on Macchia's Christology, which is envisioned as the reign of Christ the Spirit baptizer.

Moltmann creates a scheme that conceptualizes the "kingdom of God" within the doctrine of the trinity so that instead of a simple "kingdom," it is the kingdom of the Father, the kingdom of the Son, and the kingdom of the Spirit. Yet, there are not three kingdoms but one; this is not a chronological conception, but a logical recognition of the labor of each triune person. The kingdom of the Father is seen as the originating force of creation itself, but Moltmann integrates a futurity into that event. This means that even though the Father is perceived as the ruler over creation, there is inherent in that rule a future destiny. This way, "the kingdom of the Son consists of the liberating lordship of the crucified one, and fellowship with the firstborn of many

---

5. McDonnell, *The Other Hand of God*, 226.
6. Macchia, *Baptized in the Spirit*, 94.
7. Macchia, "The Kingdom and the Power," 119.

brothers and sisters."[8] The kingdom of the Son is expressed in soteriological terms, instead of ontologically, as the alleged highest expression of humanity—the Son liberates us from the "servitude to sin" to be like himself, and in fellowship with him. Moltmann then says that "in this he anticipates the kingdom of the Spirit."[9] The Father is the lord over creation because he is the origin of creation, but a creation with a future that is conceived in the kingdom of the Spirit. The kingdom of the Son and the kingdom of the Spirit are intimately connected; one does not exist apart from the other. The Son liberates creation to become the kingdom of the Spirit; as the Spirit baptizer, the Son gives creation its future and destiny. Moltmann says "the kingdom of the Spirit is experience in the gift conferred on the people liberated by the Son—the gift of the Holy Spirit's energies."[10] Through Moltmann, we can see Macchia's stress on the Son as the Spirit baptizer; Spirit baptism is a metaphor that expresses God's triune activity in all phases of redemption as a unit. The kingdom of the Son is intertwined with the kingdom of the Spirit in such a way that the purpose of the Son's kingdom is to inaugurate the kingdom of the Spirit.

Christology is formulated towards creation's future as the place where God's presence dwells—a creation that is fully baptized with the Spirit. Christ inaugurated the kingdom of God during the incarnation by bringing the presence of the Father's kingdom to creation. Christ, the one anointed with the Spirit, became the Spirit baptizer at his resurrection. Macchia says that "Spirit baptism is the will of the Father to indwell the creation through the Spirit in order, by the Spirit, to involve creation in the relationship between the Father and the Son (John 17:20–23)."[11] The kingdom of God is that which Christ inaugurates as the *eschatological* kingdom in the present with a goal towards the final consummation of God's presence. Christologically speaking, this has a soteriological orientation which expresses Christ's work in terms of salvation, but that also expresses the intimacy between the Father, Son, and Holy Spirit. Christ is the second person in the experience of redemption, a redemption which is part of the divine *taxis*: the Father's kingdom has a logical priority; the Son's kingdom is second in the order of redemption; and the Spirit's kingdom is third as the culmination of creation's future. Therefore, the kingdom of God is the kingdom of the Trinity which culminates in Christ baptizing creation with the Holy Spirit.

8. Moltmann, *The Trinity and the Kingdom*, 210.

9. Ibid.

10. Ibid., 211. Moltmann goes on to say "that is the reason why the kingdom of the Spirit is as closely linked with the kingdom of the Son, as the kingdom of the Son is with the kingdom of the Father" (211).

11. Macchia, *Baptized in the Spirit*, 107.

Christ and Koinonia

Macchia's Christology develops from within *koinonia* in a way that parallels his doctrine of God, that is Pneumatically. Macchia says, "the Spirit is the Spirit of communion. Spirit baptism implies communion."[12] It is no coincidence that Macchia prefers the term *"koinonia"* over community; by giving preference to this term, he is able to avoid some of the pitfalls of other social trinitarian models. Macchia states that he is "open to the social analogy of the Trinity, which means [I am] critical of Augustine's psychological model of the Trinity."[13] We can interpret this to mean that for Macchia, it is the distinctions between the divine persons that defines who God is; as an expression of the unity of the divine substance. Macchia is "open" to the social trinity, but by privileging the use of *"koinonia"* over "community," he is avoiding the pitfalls of tritheism. Robert Letham says that "with the recent reawakening of interest in Eastern theology in the West, a social model of the Trinity has arisen in the West that focuses on the distinctiveness of the three persons, often tending toward a loose tritheism."[14] On the other hand, Sarah Coakley, who is quite critical of social trinitarian models, explains that those who adopt social trinitarian models are not necessarily justified in turning to the Cappadocians for undisputable support. Coakley claims that Gregory of Nyssa adhered to a *koinonia* and not to a community of three persons. In reference to Gregory of Nyssa's theology, Coakley says that *"the talk is of 'communion'* (koinōnia) *between the 'persons,' not of 'community.'"*[15] Later she states that *"Gregory's favored analogies for the Trinity stress the indivisibility of the 'persons' and even a certain fluidity in their boundaries."*[16] So for our purposes, Macchia's use of *koinonia* is not by chance, but is grounded in the idea that God saves as Father, Son, and Spirit; not as a committee but as a communion of persons. Therefore, Christology signifies that Christ is the God who saves because God is a *koinonia* of Father, Son, and Spirit. *Koinonia* retains the *perichoretic* interpenetration of the divine persons, where "communion" may be construed as retaining vestiges of a social model; a social model which has bearing on Christ's divine nature.

Christ's divine nature is revealed from his relation in the economy as an expression of *koinonia*, so that the relation with the Holy Spirit is critical to Christ's divinity. Jesus's divine nature is not based on presuppositions

---

12. Ibid., 156.
13. Macchia, "Pinnock's Pneumatology," 172.
14. Letham, *The Holy Trinity*, 3.
15. Coakley, "'Persons' in the 'Social' Doctrine of the Trinity," 134.
16. Ibid.

regarding the two natures, or a binitarian view that is only concerned with the relationship between the Father and the Son. Christ's eternal nature is an expression of his economic work in our time and space as our savior in light of his action with the Holy Spirit—Jesus' role as Spirit baptizer defines his deity. Macchia says, "The basic assumption throughout the New Testament that Jesus was raised from the dead as one who imparts or baptizes in the Spirit points more than anything else to Jesus' identification with God."[17] Jesus is identified with God due to his soteriological activity, as opposed to metaphysical speculations regarding *ousia*, *homoousia*, etc.; only God can pour out Godself. The connection between Christ's divine status and the Spirit is expressed by Macchia through the words of Augustine. Augustine asks, "how then can he who gives the Holy Spirit not be God? Indeed, how much must he who gives God be God!"[18] Veli-Matti Kärkkäinen comments on Augustine—this passage in particular—saying,

> the Spirit proceeds 'originally' from the Father and also in common from both the Father and Son, as something given by the Father. In other words, Augustine is careful in safeguarding the Father as the primary source of the Spirit. And even when the Son is included in the act of procession of the Spirit, it is not from two sources but rather from a single source in order to protect divine unity.[19]

The Son is conceived by Macchia in terms of act and *koinonia*: the Son *acts* as the second person in the divine *koinonia* who receives the Spirit from the Father, thereby sharing in the love, glory, and communion of the Godhead. This is not surmised from speculation but from the economic activity of the Son as the Spirit baptizer. The Father originates, and the Spirit perfects but it is the Son who actualizes the Father's will and the Spirit's perfections. Jesus, identified as the giver of the Spirit, indicates that Jesus' self-identification was more than imparting a "God consciousness"; he was imparting the Spirit of God—thereby, making himself divine. Without Pentecost, and the outpouring of the Spirit, there is no reason for the church to associate Jesus with God; the church began as the risen Christ poured out the Spirit on his followers to establish the Kingdom. Pentecost is the place where Christ, as the firstborn among his brothers, filled the believers with the justifying Spirit. The Spirit justified Christ as the Son of the Father, and through Christ baptized believers, so that justification is truly a divine act of the triune God.

---

17. Macchia, *Baptized in the Spirit*, 181.
18. Augustine, *The Trinity (De Trinitate)* 15.6.46 (trans. Hill, 431).
19. Kärkkäinen, *The Trinity*, 48.

B. Spirit Christology: The Anointed One Who Anoints

Christ's Divinity Pneumatically Shaped

Macchia is faithful to the Chalcedon tradition, while shaping his Christology using soteriological language that expresses the experiential nature of Pentecostal theology. Macchia's theology is experiential; he stresses an "objective pneumatology" in order to avoid the pitfalls of liberal theology, which gives priority to the subjective intuition of the individual. Macchia says that "an objective pneumatology is inspired by Karl Barth, who accused Schleiermacher of making the tragic error of concentrating his pneumatology on religious consciousness rather than on the outpouring of the Spirit at Pentecost."[20] Barth criticizes Schleiermacher because his Christ is nothing more than an incomparably quantitatively better Christian than us; our inherent subjective awareness of God is a lower degree than Christ. So Barth says, "*The word is not so assured here in its independence in respect to faith as should be the case if this theology of faith were a true theology of the Holy Spirit.*"[21] For Macchia, the Spirit anoints Christ to be the incarnate Son, and continues to anoint him during his earthly mission. In a sense, the Son is sent from the Father and the Spirit: "if the Spirit already rested on the Son in the bond of love enjoyed eternally with the Father, then the incarnation allowed the Spirit, too, to rest on the body of Jesus within the circle of love and justice enjoyed within the triune life."[22] Macchia's Pentecostalism pushes him towards an inclusion of an experiential element in his theology, but not as an inherent property of human consciousness—the experience is shaped within the triune economy. Bengt Hägglund comments on Scheleirmacher's theology as follows:

> The claims of faith do not represent objective knowledge; they are, rather, expressions of devout self-consciousness. They do not describe the object of faith; they describe the personal function of faith. The Christian articles of faith are legitimized by the fact that they correspond to the devout Christ consciousness of faith, or to the Christian's inner experience.[23]

On the other hand, Macchia's experiential theology is pneumatically based in that it is shaped by Christology because justification is *in* and *through* the Spirit but as a divine act that takes place in Christ, who is

---

20. Macchia, *Justified in the Spirit*, 132.
21. Barth, *Protestant Theology in the Nineteenth Century*, 457.
22. Macchia, *Justified in the Spirit*, 132.
23. Hägglund, *History of Theology*, 355.

justified as the Son of the Father and the man of the Spirit. Macchia says that "Spirit baptism is the place where the 'objective' and 'subjective' (or interpersonal) meet. In the context of Spirit baptism, justification is based on the former but involves the latter."[24] The point is that Macchia's Christology develops epistemologically from within soteriology, but theologically within the objective work of the acts of the Triune God. In this way, Macchia's Christology is intimately relational; that is, the Son is the Son because he proceeds from the Father and the Spirit; the Father is the origin of the Son but the Spirit also participates in the Son's origin; the Son also participates in the Spirit's procession, for the Father sends both the Son and the Spirit but not without the full participation of each person, respectively. The result is that Macchia's Christology is fully dynamic, *perichoretic*, and relational, for Christ as the Spirit baptizer conveys that Christ proceeds from the Father, and as the God-man, proceeds from the Spirit into the world (Luke 1:35). It is the eternal dynamic relationship where the Father sends the Son by the Spirit, and the Father pours out the Spirit through the Son that defines the eternal relationship of the Son. The Kingdom of God relies on the reciprocal activity of the triune persons; the Father anoints the Son with the Spirit; the Son in turn anoints creation with the Spirit; the Spirit indwells creation with the presence of God, thereby allowing creation to reach its divine *telos* as God's dwelling place—in this, the kingdom of God is actualized. There is not the problem of eternal subordination because the Father receives his kingdom from the Son and the Spirit, thereby guaranteeing their equality in the kingdom.

At this point, Macchia's Christology can be further illuminated with the assistance of the Catholic theologian David Coffey. Macchia briefly refers to Coffey's "incarnational" Pneumatology in the context of his own concept of "objective" Pneumatology. There are three reasons for interjecting Coffey at this juncture; first, Coffey's incarnation theology expresses Macchia's Christology quite favorably due to his focus on the Holy Spirit; second, Coffey is a Catholic theologian, and this comports well with Macchia's ecumenical inclinations; and third, Coffey represents a connection between Macchia and Gunton due to his method that accounts for the role of the Holy Spirit in the "incarnation" of Christ. We will use Coffey's article titled "The 'Incarnation' of The Holy Spirit in Christ," because he states that, even though another of his books covers this theory, in this article he "will take advantage of the opportunity to update a number of things said in the book."[25] So Coffey's incarnation theology is called an "incarna-

---

24. Macchia, *Justified in the Spirit*, 133.
25. Coffey, "The 'Incarnation' of the Holy Spirit in Christ," 466.

tion" of the Holy Spirit not because of the ontological location of the Holy Spirit within the *hypostatic* union, but due to the role the Spirit exhibited in the incarnation. Coffey relies on Rahner's transcendent anthropology, because ultimately it signifies that "the divinity of Christ is not something different from his humanity; it *is* the humanity."[26] For Coffey, Christology is developed from within salvation history instead of metaphysical speculations regarding the two natures of Christ. Christ's humanity is the maximal expression of the eternal *Logos* that human nature is capable of expressing. Coffey says, "the divine person is not given *absolutely* perfect expression in the human nature of Christ, but only the perfect expression *relative* to the capacity of human nature."[27] The economy is where Christian epistemology takes place, and only then should the theologian construct Christology. This way, the scriptures portray Jesus as being anointed by the Father with the Holy Spirit, revealing that the Spirit must be conceived as an essential relation in the incarnation. As we will see, this will have a bearing on Coffey's Christology, and in turn, explain Macchia's Christology.

Coffey makes the following claim: "the anointing of Jesus by the Father with the Holy Spirit. The acquisition of this insight had been impeded throughout the history of theology by the domination of the belief that the divinity of Christ was ontologically different from his humanity."[28] It is Macchia's contention that Veli-Matti Kärkkäinen "wrote correctly that the Pentecostal movement has placed the doctrine of Spirit baptism at the forefront of the theological agenda in modern theology."[29] Christ's deity associated with his humanity and the ascendency of Spirit baptism gives Coffey theological purchase to solidify the role of the Holy Spirit in *the* incarnation and view "the Incarnation [as] the work of the Holy Spirit, Spirit of Sonship."[30] Coffey develops his Christology in a slightly different trajectory than the tradition. Instead of the eternal *Logos* assuming humanity by the will of the Father, and receiving grace by the Holy Spirit to be obedient to the Father's will, Coffey describes the Incarnation itself as a triune act, with an emphasis on the increased role of the Holy Spirit. The humanity of Christ was created by the act of the Triune God, but the Holy Spirit radically sanctified the human nature so that it could receive the person of the Son—the Father's will was completed and the eternal Son became the Son of God in humanity. Macchia explains that "the Spirit gives the Word an anointed and indwelt

26. Ibid.
27. Ibid., 468.
28. Ibid., 469.
29. Macchia, *Baptized in the Spirit*, 19.
30. Coffey, "The "Incarnation" of the Holy Spirit in Christ," 469.

body as a gift in order that Christ could give all bodies the gift of the same anointing."[31] Therefore, for Coffey and Macchia, the Spirit initiated, preserved, and maintained an intimate relationship with the human nature of the Son of God; the Holy Spirit was not an addendum after the Son assumed his human nature. In a way, the Holy Spirit deifies the human nature, which moves humanity towards God as an act of reconciliation. This corresponds precisely to Macchia's soteriologically oriented theology because justification is an act of the Triune God instead of merely a forensic declaration. This way, Spirit baptism demonstrates that the Father anoints Jesus' human nature with the Spirit and eventually anoints his creation with the same Spirit.

At this point, there is a correspondence between the theological methods of both Macchia and Coffey. Coffey explains that the doctrine of the immanent Trinity "developed over a period of about 300 years as a framework to give needed support to the basic data of Christian experience once these were translated from functional into ontological categories."[32] Coffey is specifically referring to the *filioque* of the West as that point where the Holy Spirit's role in the incarnation was diminished due to the supposition that the Spirit proceeds from the Father and the Son; thereby leaving little conceptual space for the Spirit in sending the Son. But Macchia frames the issue thusly, "I note favorably Pannenberg's rejection of the *Filioque* . . . Indeed, the clause is also to be rejected because it implies that the Spirit is ontologically inferior to the Son and it threatens to present Christ's Lordship in a way that is not adequately differentiated from that of the Father."[33] So, Macchia and Coffey find that the *filioque* indicates an ontological subordination of the Holy Spirit, which then influences how the role of the Holy Spirit in the economy is perceived; the result is that the Holy Spirit has a subordinated role in the incarnation. Coffey's theology overcomes this issue by stressing the lesser utilized trinitarian model, which is framed around the internal *manner* of the "processions" instead of the outward movement based on the processions themselves.

Coffey's theology begins with the inner movement of love between the Trinitarian persons, that is, God's *aseity* is perfected by the agency of the

---

31. Macchia, *Justified in the Spirit*, 180.

32. Coffey, "The "Incarnation" of the Holy Spirit in Christ," 470. Kelly says that the early fathers' "most fruitful efforts . . . were expended in considering the Triad as manifested in creation and redemption, and in attempting to show how the Son and the Spirit, revealed in the 'economy' as other than Father, were at the same time inseparably one with Him in His eternal being. Economic Trinitarianism of this type continued to find exponents in the late second and early third centuries" (Kelly, *Early Christian Doctrines*, 109).

33. Macchia, "Baptized in the Spirit," 19.

Holy Spirit. Instead of emphasizing Aquinas' discussions on the "relations of origin," which are derived from Christ's status of "being sent," Coffey chooses to focus instead on Aquinas' position of God's self-sufficiency in which the Holy Spirit closes the circle of the Godhead. So instead of relying on God's "processions," which involves the missions of the Son and the Spirit to go out and save humanity, God's redemption is viewed as a free movement that reaches out to humanity in order to deify his creation by bringing humanity into God's circle of love. Gilles Emery says that "Thomas' Commentary on the *Sentences* is guided by this central thesis: The procession of the divine persons in their unity of essence is the cause and the reason for the procession of creatures."[34] But elsewhere, Emery says,

> St Thomas shows that since God's actions in the world ("procession toward external nature") add nothing to the processions which constitute a perfect "circle," they are not to be numbered amongst the intra-Trinitarian processions. God's actions in the world are of a different order, even though they are attached to the intra-Trinitarian processions.[35]

What Emery explains is that Aquinas' trinitarian theology is complicated and multifaceted. So Coffey is not wrong in explaining Aquinas' twofold trinitarian theology *per se*; Coffey's goal is simply to stress Aquinas' use of immanent procession of the persons towards each other, instead of the linear movement of the processional missions of the Son and Spirit. The movement that is central for Coffey is the movement of love between the Father and the Son, which in turn gives place for the Holy Spirit as well as defining the nature of the Son and the Spirit in the incarnation.

For Coffey, by aligning his theological method with New Testament accounts of the love between the Father and the Son, his Incarnation theology is based on the position that "the Holy Spirit is the mutual love of the Father and the Son."[36] Coffey is attempting to move beyond Augustine's usage by denoting his model as a "bestowal" model, as opposed to a "procession" model. To quote Coffey again, "I call it the bestowal model because according to it the Holy Spirit, as mutual love of the Father and the Son, is the love which the Father bestows on the Son and the answering love which the Son bestows of the Father."[37] Coffey is taking into account the relationship between the Father and the Son, which is realized in salvation history at Jesus' conception and baptism; a relationship that takes place through the ac-

---

34. Emery, *The Trinitarian Theology of Saint Thomas Aquinas*, 36.
35. Ibid., 73–74.
36. Coffey, "The "Incarnation" of the Holy Spirit in Christ," 471.
37. Ibid.

tivity of the Holy Spirit. This movement by Coffey is analogous to Macchia's Spirit baptism, for the Spirit anointed Jesus to be the Spirit baptizer sent by the Father; as Spirit baptizer, Jesus answers the Father's love by redeeming creation and returning it to him. Taking Macchia and Coffey as a unit, their Christology is formed economically in such a manner that love becomes the operative arena—which is associated with the person of the Holy Spirit. The humanity of Christ is formed in love, that is, the Holy Spirit; and the love between the Father and Son *is* the person of the Holy Spirit. Therefore, the *taxis* of the trinity is maintained because the Father is the first in love, and the Son answers in love, and the Holy Spirit is third by being the love that is *bestowed* between the Father and Son. At this point, Coffey's methodology is to develop a Christology that is based on the historical activities of Christ as that between the Father and the Son as mediated by the Spirit.

The foundation for Coffey's Christology is in the relationship between the persons of the Father and the Son, rather than between the two natures of the *hypostatic* union. Pannenberg states that "Jesus' self-consciousness has shown him to be related to God, to be sure, not directly to 'the Logos' as the second Person of the Trinity, but to the heavenly Father."[38] And later, that

> one cannot properly understand Jesus' Sonship without taking his relation to God the Father as the point of departure. The question of the unity of the man Jesus with the eternal Son of God cannot be put and answered directly. That is the common mistake of all theories that attempt to conceive the unity of God and man in Jesus on the basis of the concept of the incarnation of the Logos.[39]

So instead of beginning with two natures, Coffey constructs his Christology from the unity between the Father and the Son, which determines the direction for his Christological developments. Epistemologically speaking, Jesus' relation with the Father determines his unity with God through the Spirit; but logically, the Christological ontology is deduced from "a direct communication of being, of subsistence, from the Father to the humanity of Christ constituting him Son of God in humanity."[40] The unity between the Father and the Son is located in the person of the Holy Spirit, as an equivocal love that is unique between the Father and the Son; but is also asymmetrically analogical because the Spirit is poured out by Christ as the love of the Father. Coffey says that "we have received, ultimately from the

---

38. Pannenberg, *Jesus- God and Man*, 334.
39. Ibid.
40. Coffey, "The 'Incarnation' of the Holy Spirit in Christ," 474.

Father, a bestowal of the Holy Spirit which makes us sons and daughters of the Father and draws from us a response of love for the Father."[41] The love that the Father "bestowed" on the Son is the person of the Holy Spirit; the Holy Spirit is the unity of the Father and the Son as an outcome of Coffey's "bestowal" model.

So taking Macchia's overarching metaphor of Spirit baptism along with Coffey's Incarnational theology, it is apparent that Christology is a triune endeavor which is shaped by the love between the Father and the Son in the person of the Holy Spirit. Barth's well-known trinitarian axiom of "Revealer, Revelation, and Revealdness" can be restated using Coffey's terms as "Bestower, Bestowed, and Bestowedness." In Macchia's case, the Father bestowed Christ with the Spirit, so that Christ is the gift to creation as the Spirit baptizer who redeems and returns creation as a gift to the Father. The key is that all three sets of terms are connected by love that is expressed in the humanity of Christ from conception to death and resurrection. The love between the Father and the Son, expressed in the person of the Holy Spirit, signifies both the economy of experience and the logic of theological reflection. In the economy, the Father's love is expressed in the sending of his Holy Spirit to anoint the humanity of the Son to be the Immanuel, the savior of the world. The Son of God then redeems humanity, thereby giving a Spirit-anointed creation back to the Father. The analogy in the immanent trinity is that the Father's love for the Son, and the Son's love for the Father is seen in the eternal person of the Holy Spirit as the love shared in the Godhead. Coffey states that "the sending of the Holy Spirit upon the Church by Christ, begun at Pentecost and continued over the centuries through the Church's ministry of word and sacrament, is nothing other than Jesus' love for his brethren, an essential dimension of his love of the Father."[42] Based on Coffey's "bestowal" Christological model, it is safe to assert that Macchia's Christological model of Christ as Spirit baptizer shares a methodology that stresses the divine action of the Holy Spirit within the incarnation event.

For Macchia, the *hypostatic* union is important, but it must not overshadow the relationship between the Father, Son, and Holy Spirit. Christ's personhood is defined by his relationship with the Father and as the Spirit baptizer. As we will see, this in turn defines his divinity through soteriological terminology because it is as the one who saves that we can recognize his divine status. Considering that Coffey's Christological presentation of "bestowal" theology represents Macchia's method and material content, then we can understand that Christ's divine and human natures are also

---

41. Ibid., 475.
42. Ibid., 478.

apprehended from the experience of salvation. Concerning the incarnated Son, Augustine says that "where it is written of him that he received the promised Holy Spirit from the Father and poured it out, both his natures are indicated, that is to say the human and the divine. He received it as man, he poured it out as God."[43] Macchia appropriates this aspect of Augustine's theology to shape and determine the ontological basis for the two natures in Christ. Christ's divine nature is predicated on his relation to the Father as the one who pours out the Father's Holy Spirit. Macchia says that "Pannenberg has convincingly noted that later Christological statements about the Son's preexistence with the Father evolved from the early proclamation of Jesus as raised from the dead. I wish to stress that this emphasis on the resurrection of Jesus involves Jesus as the one raised from the dead *to bestow the Spirit*."[44] Notice that Macchia uses the same language of "bestowal" as Coffey; and that he engages Pannenberg's doctrine of God, which overcomes ontological subordination by stressing an onto-relational conception of the persons.

Pannenberg's logic is rather nuanced, but serves the purpose of grounding Christ's divinity in the person of the Father, and not metaphysical speculations about natures. Pannenberg argues that notions of the Son's preexistence did not necessarily lead to the conclusion of the deity of the Son; for preexistence could refer to a non-divine preexistent state. Pannenberg concludes that what lead to the deity of the Son "was the use of the Kyrios title for the exalted Jesus. Decisive here was the relating of Ps. 110:1ff. to the exaltation of the Risen Jesus."[45] So for Pannenberg, because of Jesus' exaltation to the right hand of the Father, as the risen Christ the *kyrios* of the Old Testament—as a reference to God—is now applied to Christ. So Macchia has appropriated Pannenberg's resurrection theology to determine the deity of Christ; he also mapped Pannenberg's theology onto his own Pneumatological concerns in such a way that Jesus' status as deity is derived pneumatically as the Spirit baptizer. Jesus' divine nature is developed from theological reflection on his ability to save; an ability that is reliant on his very *being* and not an epistemological awakening to a God-consciousness. In other words, since only God can give God, and Jesus' ability to save is predicated on his role as Spirit baptizer—that is, one who pours out God's self—then it follows that Jesus must be divine. Macchia is aware of the Chalcedon creed, but his understanding of the deity of Christ is soteriological and ecumenical. Jesus is divine because of our experience of salvation, which Jesus Christ won for us by his life, death, and resurrection to become the Spirit baptizer. So

---

43. Augustine, *The Trinity (De Trinitate)* 15.46 (trans. Hill, 432).
44. Macchia, *Baptized in the Spirit*, 109–10.
45. Pannenberg, *Systematic Theology*, 1:265.

Macchia defines Christ's divinity in relation to the Holy Spirit in a reciprocal manner, the Spirit baptizes Jesus to be the Messiah, and Jesus pours out the Spirit as the Spirit baptizer. Christ's divinity is revealed because only God can give God, and Jesus gives God in the person of the Holy Spirit. So in the same manner, Macchia explicates Christ's human nature in relation to the activity of the Holy Spirit.

Christ's Humanity Pneumatically Shaped

As discussed above, the humanity of Christ becomes an ontological concern within Gunton's scheme because of his stress on freedom as an essential component of personhood. The situation is different for Macchia. The humanity of Christ is discussed within a soteriological framework; reconfiguring or correcting the Chalcedon creed is not on his agenda. For Macchia, the concern is pneumatological: his focus is understanding the role of the Holy Spirit within the incarnation; a role which allows for a proper realization of Christ's humanity. Macchia's project is soteriological, but the pneumatological aspect corresponds to a greater emphasis on the Spirit's work as bearing on creation; including the humanity of Christ. Macchia says that,

> Part of the reason for the neglect of such a broad pneumatology at the base of justification has been the gradual neglect in the west of the essential role of the Spirit in creation and the kingdom in Jesus' work as Redeemer. Historically, the gradual victory of logos christology over the typically Jewish spirit christology involved the danger of eclipsing Jesus' humanity, including his need of the Spirit and his history of openness to the Spirit. From the foundation of a logos christology, the possibility existed of neglecting the Spirit's essential role in the church's understanding of Christ's redemptive work.[46]

So even though Macchia's Christology begins soteriologically from the axiom "only God can save," the humanity of Christ is an essential element for our salvation. The concern is that a Logos Christology determines in advance what is primary in developing a picture of Jesus; it develops from philosophical speculations regarding the divine nature of the Logos in relation to the human nature of the Son of God. This is what Macchia wishes to avoid by giving stronger emphasis on the humanity of Christ in Christology. Pannenberg, Kasper, and Haight have all done work on Logos-Christology; and all three have had an impact on Macchia's theology. So we will review

---

46. Macchia, "Justification through New Creation," 209.

their comments in order to further clarify Macchia's approach to the humanity of Christ.

We find that Pannenberg and Kasper represent scholars who Macchia has already referenced throughout his work; but Roger Haight represents a recent theologian, one who represents the more Liberal and Catholic approach to Christology. Pannenberg explains that the Logos Christology of the second century developed as a means of avoiding the early Christological errors, especially modalism, Arianism, and the various forms of monophysitism. Regarding the early church's development of Logos Christology, Pannenberg says, "as one who has gone forth from God, the Logos remains a being of subordinate rank in comparison to the Father who has no beginning."[47] Later, Pannenberg says that "a second weakness of the Logos Christology is the precarious loosening of the connection of the Son's divinity with Jesus of Nazareth, God's historical revelation."[48] After presenting a complementary survey of the development of early Logos Christology, Walter Kasper asks, "[d]oes the classical Logos-christology adequately express the intentions of the biblical theology of the Word, as these are shown to us in the Prologue of John?"[49] Haight describes the problem with classical Logos-Christology by saying that "the pre-existent Logos of God, its character, how it becomes present and operative within Jesus, make up the issues that in fact take over the conversation so that Jesus of Nazareth recedes to the background."[50] The three theologians all agree that in a classic Logos-Christology, the humanity of Christ becomes secondary in Christology to the divine preexisting Logos. This leaves us with the impression that within the thought of the three theologians, and by implication Macchia, there is an implicit agreement and continuity with the Chalcedon creed, that the person of Jesus Christ has two natures—divine and human. The issue is that the humanity of Christ in the economy has little bearing on the construal of the two natures; the eternal *Logos* is where Christology really takes shape. This is what Macchia desires to overcome.

In order to present the humanity of Christ in a positive aspect, one that is systematically coherent with his soteriological axiom that "only God can save," Macchia invokes Pneumatology in the form of his overarching metaphor of "Spirit baptism." Macchia says that "Spirit baptism is the most unique Christological claim made of Jesus in the New Testament."[51] In other words, the Jewish expectations were for one anointed by God who

---

47. Pannenberg, *Jesus- God and Man*, 164.
48. Ibid., 165.
49. Kasper, *The God of Jesus Christ*, 188.
50. Haight, "Logos Christology Today," 93.
51. Macchia, "Baptized in the Spirit," 18

would be their redeemer, as one who would inaugurate a new era of the Spirit. Macchia refers to this as a "Jewish Spirit Christology"; but this view of Christ was ultimately relinquished in the history of theology in favor of a high Christology from above, which did not have much room for the presence of the Spirit along with the humanity of Christ. Macchia's implicit Christology develops soteriologically in that Jesus' human nature is perceived as one who is anointed *with* the Spirit to be *that* messiah. There is no need to discuss the communication of attributes, or the will of the eternal *Logos* against the will of the human nature and so on; reconciliation can only take place when that Spirit-anointed human achieves the right to pour out the Spirit on creation. Macchia says that "Jesus was the justified and the sanctified man as the man of the Spirit and as the one who inaugurated the new creation through the resurrection power of the Spirit."[52] In order to maintain a Trinitarian systematic account of creation, redemption, and the consummation, it is necessary for Christ to redeem creation as part of the created order; the way for that to happen is in a Trinitarian manner. That is, Christ as part of creation is led by the will of the Father and empowered through the anointing of the Spirit. Macchia says that "ultimately, Jesus imparts God's Holy Spirit to us so that we can share in Jesus' sonship and commune with his heavenly Father (Romans 8:15–16)."[53] In this way, Jesus takes on our flesh, so that he can impart to us God's presence in the gift of the Holy Spirit. Therefore, it is safe to assume that Macchia's Christology is based on the tradition's use of the Chalcedon creed, without any major modifications, with the exception of the stress on the Holy Spirit.

For Macchia, Christ's humanity is based on an eternal and infinite quality in the relationship between Jesus and the Spirit. In some mysterious manner, the man Jesus Christ was anointed by the Spirit from conception, and his death and resurrection allowed him the honor of pouring out God's self upon creation—in the person of the Holy Spirit—as a down payment towards the final culmination. Instead of the communication of attributes between the two natures in Christ, Macchia stresses the saving power of Christ as the anointed man who in turn becomes the Spirit baptizer. So Christ's humanity demonstrates what it means to be real humanity, and that is to be in a complete relationship with God, which is defined by Macchia as being fully Spirit-baptized. Therefore, Macchia's Christology is soteriologically driven, but it is shaped pneumatologically because the axiom "only God can save" leads to two natures in Christ: the divine eternal Logos who is the God that saves, and the Spirit-anointed human who redeems by becoming the Spirit baptizer.

---

52. Macchia, "Toward a Theology of the Third Article," 9.
53. Macchia, *The Trinity*, 75.

Chapter 7

Pneumatology as Baptism in the Spirit

Introduction

THE QUESTION THAT PROPELS Macchia's Pneumatology is simply this: how are we saved by the Spirit?[1] Macchia is not attempting to subvert Christology in favor of Pneumatology, which would be to misunderstand Pentecostals as people of the Spirit. His goal is to locate the work of the Holy Spirit throughout all categories of theology, instead of viewing the Holy Spirit as an epistemological addendum that is limited to awakening the believer to the work of Christ and the Father.[2] As a Pentecostal scholar, he begins with the experience of salvation then moves towards more speculative matters of theology. It is not simply a matter of beginning with the economic activity of God from a doctrinal viewpoint. Macchia begins with the experience of salvation, and only then does he develop a soteriology that gives a strong emphasis to the role of the Holy Spirit. As we work through Macchia's presentation of Spirit baptism, our goal is to see that Spirit baptism develops from a specific Pentecostal framework to a more expansive term which explains the Holy Spirit's role in all economic activities of God, as well as solidifying the acts of creation, redemption, and the final consummation as a complete act of the Triune God.

So far, it is safe to state that the Kingdom of God—which finds its fullest expression in the presence of God, that is, the Holy Spirit—is what

---

1. I am grateful to Dr. Macchia for several conversations regarding Spirit baptism, and especially when he delivered this bit of insight regarding his view of Pneumatology.

2. Macchia says, "My goal will be to show that the Spirit brings about justification not only through participation in Christ by the divine embrace but also through Christ in the mutual love and *koinonia* of Father, Son and Spirit" (Macchia, *Justified in the Spirit*, 293).

binds Macchia's Ecclesiology, Christology, and now his Pneumatology. The presence of the Spirit is identified with Spirit baptism; it gives theological purchase for the development of a Pneumatology that is faithful to the Pentecostal tradition. The experience of God's redemptive activity heavily influences the direction of his theological construction for Pneumatology as well as Christology and Ecclesiology. Therefore, we will first show that Spirit baptism is a metaphor which gives room to the Spirit's role in justification; a term which is expanded by Macchia to be more inclusive. It will then be necessary to explore the meaning and impetus of Spirit baptism being declared a "root metaphor" by Macchia. He makes the case that as a "root metaphor" Spirit baptism encompasses all theological categories, thereby allowing the incorporation of the Pentecostal distinctive into modern systematic expressions. Once the "root metaphor" has been explored, we will undertake the task of understanding the role of the Holy Spirit in creation of *koinonia* as otherness-in-relation: the *perichoretic* action of the Triune God is reflected in creation due to the work of the Holy Spirit. The Holy Spirit who *is* the "bond of love" that perfects communion. The same action of the Spirit that creates community is responsible for creation—the Spirit is the creator Spirit. Spirit baptism signifies that the work of creation should be construed as an event that relies on the work of the Holy Spirit—the Spirit creates *ex nihilo* and perfects creation at the *eschaton*. As we will discover, the common thread for Macchia is that he develops his Pneumatology from within the Pentecostal experience of Spirit baptism. So, we will look at the relation between Pneumatology and justification.

A. The Holy Spirit as Beginning and End of the Economy

Macchia develops his Pneumatology from within a soteriological context, one that stresses justification as the redemptive act of God towards humanity and creation. There is an appreciation for the *ordo salutis*; but the problem in modern theology is that justification is typically defined in the context of impartation (Protestantism) and imputation (Catholicism). It appears that Christology serves as the locus for soteriology; the work of Christ provided all that is needed for salvation. Macchia says, "without the Spirit, the Protestant and the Catholic emphases fly apart or, at best, are awkwardly knitted together."[3] The Catholic stress on the imputation of grace through Christ's ubiquitous nature and the Protestant stress on the union with Christ indicate Western theology's tendency to equate atonement as a work of the

3. Ibid., 294.

Son of God; a work which is expressed as a revelation from the Spirit, or that which is appropriated to the believer by the Spirit. Whether revelation or appropriation, justification is conceived as either a declarative act of God or as an ontological change in the virtues of the individual, with all of the stress placed on Christology.[4] In other words, it is Christ's work alone that decides the status of the believer either by *fiat* or by divine imputation. Even though this is a simplistic view of historical theology, it shows that Macchia desires to locate Pneumatology and soteriology within a Pentecostal framework; the experience of God by the Spirit is the place to begin an investigation into the role of the Holy Spirit.

By beginning with the location of the Spirit within justification, Macchia is remaining true to his Pentecostal heritage, while engaging recent advances in trinitarian theologies. Macchia says that "only by placing the Spirit at the very substance of justification is it possible to arrive at a Trinitarian integration of imputed and imparted righteousness."[5] The aim here is to integrate imputed and imparted righteousness, the doctrine of God, and soteriology through Pneumatology as an indispensable component of justification. Elsewhere Macchia says, "I believe that more work needs to be done along the lines of a pneumatological understanding of justification from the beginning to the end of the doctrine."[6] Then later he says that

> I will seek to replace this Roman understanding of distributive justice with the biblical model of redemptive justice or saving righteousness which can be viewed as pneumatological from beginning to end. I come at this issue from a Pentecostal theological reflection that seeks to remain true to our emphasis on the healing and new-creation thrust of the "full Gospel."[7]

The place to initiate a discussion of the Holy Spirit is within a Pentecostal framework that focuses on the experience of salvation, while simultaneously developing a theology of justification that begins with a proper recognition of the action of the Holy Spirit from beginning to end.

By emphasizing the Holy Spirit within the economic activity of God, the Holy Spirit is conceived as an active participant in all aspects of creation, redemption, and the *eschaton*. Macchia says of Spirit baptism that "the term

---

4. Macchia says, "More recent ecumenical efforts have focused on bridging the typically Protestant forensic understanding of justification as a declaration of our righteous standing and the Catholic understanding of justification as a transformation or a being made just" (Macchia, "Justification and the Spirit," 5).

5. Macchia, *Justified in the Spirit*, 294.

6. Macchia, "Justification and the Spirit," 6–7.

7. Ibid., 7.

'participation' (*koinonia*) helps to bring together an emergent eschatology (from below) with a futuristic eschatology (from beyond)."[8] So Pneumatology is the experiential locus, but one that is shaped within a Pentecostal construct that places personal experience of God's economic activity alongside the creeds, doctrinal discourse, and the sacraments. In repetition of Macchia, but more complete, he says that

> without the Spirit, the Protestant and the Catholic emphases fly apart or, at best, are awkwardly knitted together. They lose their grounding and link because they lack adequate substance in the indwelling Spirit. This substance is not only declarative or ethical but is more interactive and truly relational, involving indwelling and communion.[9]

So in order to maintain a Pentecostal identity, it is necessary to begin with the Holy Spirit as a present reality within creation who is working to redeem it, as the perfecting agent in the Trinity. But, the Holy Spirit is also experienced in the life of the believer throughout the entire *ordo salutis*. Therefore, in order to move Pneumatology from an addendum to Christ's atoning work, a more robust metaphor is needed, and to this end Macchia develops the metaphor of Spirit baptism.

B. Spirit Baptism as a Pentecostal Root Metaphor

Spirit baptism, as a root metaphor, impacts the conception of the relationship between soteriology and Pneumatology as extending beyond conceptual delimiters to an integrated systematic doctrine. Macchia puts it this way,

> justification as a Trinitarian act must be accessed by the Spirit and in relationship to the Son. It is thus possible to bring a Trinitarian framework to justification by restoring the baptism in the Spirit to its roles as the root metaphor of salvation . . . it also makes the Spirit essential to Christ's identity and mission, including Christ's work of atonement.[10]

Spirit baptism is the "root metaphor" in that it forces the theologian to consider the location of the Spirit within all the acts of God in creation, redemption, and eschatology; the Spirit is not relegated to awakening the

---

8. Macchia, "The Kingdom and the Power," 125.
9. Macchia, *Justified in the Spirit*, 294.
10. Ibid.

believer to what Christ accomplished, the Spirit himself accomplishes atonement with the Father and the Son. Macchia interprets "justification" along the lines of "rightwising" in order to move justification within the arena of relationship instead of relegating it to the legal sphere: justification, or "rightwising," is a reference to God's saving activity. Brevard Childs states that "Yahweh's righteousness consists, above all, in acts of the saving deeds of redemption . . . by which he maintains and protects his promise to fulfill his covenantal obligations with Israel."[11] Instead of justification being understood as a declarative act or an act of infusing grace, justification is an act of God's love, which restores something lost—the relationship between God and his creation. Macchia says that

> I am convinced after reading Alister McGrath's two-volume history of the doctrine of justification that the problem with forensic justification as it was described by Melanchthon and others was in its dependence on a secular, Roman understanding of distributive justice, which sees justice as primarily punitive, and is thus connected easily to a notion of righteousness as merited favor.[12]

Since justification is defined as God's acting to save, Macchia links this saving action with God's indwelling. Where Gunton defines redemption in relational terminology, Macchia understands salvation as creation becoming the dwelling place of God—Spirit baptism is the means and the *telos* for creation to become *that* dwelling place. By envisioning Spirit baptism as both the means and *telos*, "finally makes the gift of the Spirit essential to justification, as well as all other soteriological categories."[13] Macchia configures justification this way so that the metaphor of Spirit baptism becomes the final place in the economic *taxis*, the Holy Spirit becomes essential in accomplishing and defining Christ's work of atonement. First, Christ's work of atonement was not completed by Christ at his resurrection "but in his pouring out the Spirit as the Spirit baptizer."[14] Second, the atonement is really an at-one-ment, Christ brought about God's justification by pouring out the Holy Spirit: "the atonement is not fulfilled without the gift of the

---

11. Childs, *Biblical Theology of the Old and New Testaments*, 488. In reference to Childs, Macchia says, "By the time we near the New Testament period, justification is ultimately defined as the justice or righteousness that God's final act of redemption will create in the resurrection of the faithful and the transformation of creation" (Macchia, "Justification and the Spirit," 8).

12. Macchia, "Justification and the Spirit," 7.

13. Macchia, *Justified in the Spirit*, 294.

14. Ibid.

Spirit."[15] The gift of the Spirit is not the initiation or conversion gift, which awakens believers to Christ; the gift of the Spirit is God's dwelling with all of his people. Spirit baptism is the goal for creation because it represents God's final dwelling with his creation in a restored relationship won by Christ. In this way, the Holy Spirit "is essential from the first to last in all of the categories of salvation,"[16] because the Spirit baptizes creation with life, and then baptizes Christ to become the messiah, who eventually becomes the Spirit baptizer. As Spirit baptizer, Jesus baptizes creation in an anticipation of the final and ultimate baptism of the Spirit as God's final indwelling of creation.

Spirit baptism is the root metaphor—but it is not a replacement for other soteriological categories; as if one could simply speak of election, atonement, sanctification, or glorification as being synonymous with Spirit baptism. Spirit baptism is a root metaphor for Pentecostals because it gives room for the Holy Spirit in each of the theological categories. Spirit baptism is beyond issues of impartation or imputation because the concern is not the final status or nature of the individual, but the way the Holy Spirit embraces creation as a perfecting action of the Triune God. This way, the twin issues of impartation and imputation find their respective theological content in that it is the Spirit who perfects; that is, actualizes their theological content. Macchia says, "The righteousness of Christ is alien to us because of our sin and weakness in the flesh (the Protestant emphasis), but it is experienced among us by faith within the realm of the Spirit of life (the Catholic accent)."[17] The Protestant emphasis on imputation of God's declared status of righteous is real because Christ pours out the Spirit upon his community and by extension his followers. Barth states that,

> There is no room for any fears that in the justification of man we are dealing only with a verbal action, with a kind of bracketed "as if," as though what is pronounced were not the whole truth about man. Certainly we have to do with a declaring righteous, but it is a declaration about man which is fulfilled and therefore effective in this event, which corresponds to actuality because it creates and therefore reveals the actuality. It is a declaring righteous which without any reserve can be called a making righteous.[18]

For Macchia, this "actuality" becomes a reality because Spirit baptism is where God's love embraces humanity as a completion of the Triune act.

15. Ibid.
16. Ibid., 295.
17. Macchia, *Baptized in the Spirit*, 139.
18. Barth, *Church Dogmatics*, IV/1:95.

God's declaration of righteousness is effective because "the Word of justification in Christ glides on the winds of the Spirit and only performs in the Spirit's embrace. This is true in part because the Father who justifies imparts the Spirit, and the Son who justifies is the Spirit baptizer."[19] Spirit baptism, as a root metaphor, allows for a more *robust* Trinitarian view of soteriology because the Holy Spirit is an actor in all phases of soteriology, the incarnation, and the final vindication of God in Christ when God indwells his people and the Spirit is fully poured out by Christ. On the Catholic side, Spirit baptism also expands the impartation view because the Spirit infuses the community with virtues that individuals are free to emulate and are drawn in to participate and experience by the embrace of the Spirit. Macchia says, "justification is the Spirit's embrace of the creature and the creature's *liberating participation* by the indwelling Spirit in Christ as crucified and risen and in the *koinonia* that will pervade the new creation and the final communion of saints."[20] Spirit baptism as a Pentecostal distinctive is related to an experience by the individual, but it is an experience that is grounded in the event of justification; an event that began in creation, achieved in the life of Christ, and made a reality in creation by the God's embrace. Spirit baptism implies that in creation the Holy Spirit indwelled creation to give it life; in redemption, the Spirit prepared a body for Christ from the Spirit indwelled creation, so that Christ would be the Spirit baptizer; and in justification, the Spirit *is* God's justification so that in the *eschaton*, the fullness of Spirit baptism will be achieved. God will be all in all, as Father, Son, and Holy Spirit.

Salvation is a triune event, for due to Spirit baptism being conceived as a root metaphor, justification is conceived as a Christological *and* Pneumatological event. Kilian McDonnell surveys the early fathers, especially Athanasius and Gregory of Nyssa, and states that "we have that essential reality: as the Spirit is the sole mediation of the sole Mediator, so the Spirit is the sole kingdom of the sole King."[21] Later, McDonnell says that, "If the Spirit is the touch by which one has communion in the mystery of Christ, and if the Spirit is the only access to God, then the goal of the Christian life is the "acquisition" of the Spirit. The Spirit as goal is the kingdom Christ hands over to the Father."[22] For Macchia, "Spirit baptism" then means that Christ is the king and the Holy Spirit is the kingdom. Spirit baptism is that which affords both Christology and Pneumatology equal weight as the Father's "two-hands," as that which brings about the justification of his creation; especially in light

---

19. Macchia, *Justified in the Spirit*, 295.
20. Ibid., 296.
21. McDonnell, *The Other Hand of God*, 226.
22. Ibid., 227.

of the Protestant and Catholic views. Macchia's use of the metaphor "two-hands" means that Christ is anointed by the Spirit so that God's declaration of justification can become a reality: "justification thus means that Christ himself is our righteousness."[23] As the Spirit baptizer, Jesus Christ anoints creation with the Spirit so that the Spirit brings creation into participation with God: "Spirit baptism brings the reign of the Father, the reign of the crucified and risen Christ, and the reign of divine life to all of creation through the indwelling of the Spirit."[24] In other words, imputed righteousness is satisfied because Christ himself was baptized with the Spirit to be our righteousness; and imparted righteousness is satisfied because Christ became the Spirit baptizer through his life, death, and resurrection.

By formulating justification through the lens of Spirit baptism, Macchia is giving room for his Pentecostal roots. Even though he does not explicitly express that the Pentecostal foundational tenet is a personal experience of the Spirit, it seems evident that this is what he has in mind when using Spirit baptism as a root metaphor. J. Rodman Williams explains that "it is a pentecostal distinctive . . . to affirm that salvation precedes baptism in the Spirit."[25] Later, Williams says that "whether evidence or sign, the point made is that the distinctive event of Spirit baptism is primarily exhibited through speaking in tongues."[26] There is a stress in Pentecostalism on the experiential nature of the Spirit in the individual believer; a tangible expression of the Spirit's presence. Macchia's theology develops out of this theological milieu, so that when he expands Spirit baptism as a metaphor, the individual Pentecostal experience still underlies his work.

As we have seen, both Christology and Pneumatology are essential elements towards developing a theology of the experience of baptism in the Spirit, or an indwelling of the Spirit: "we share in Christ through the Holy Spirit."[27] The key phrase here is "share" for this indicates some type of experience in Christ; Christ's life was a reality in time, so our sharing is a reality in time. But this reality is a mediated reality that is shaped and actualized by the Holy Spirit; the Holy Spirit is not simply an instrument to awaken the believer to that which was accomplished in Christ. The Holy Spirit *is* that which was accomplished by Christ when he won the right to pour out his Spirit so that we can "share" or experience Christ. Spirit baptism includes the notion of God's presence; the believers are participating and sharing in

---

23. Macchia, *Justified in the Spirit*, 297.
24. Macchia, *Baptized in the Spirit*, 89.
25. Williams, "Baptism in the Holy Spirit," 357.
26. Ibid., 358.
27. Macchia, *Justified in the Spirit*, 297.

God's actual presence: "Baptism in the Spirit implies a baptism into Christ and into God, a participation in the divine life by which we place on God our death, sin, suffering and isolation in order to partake of his life everlasting, righteousness, healing and fellowship."[28] This way, "sharing" or "participation" are ciphers which point to a Pentecostal understanding of soteriology as a "crisis event" which is experienced by the believer. Macchia appropriates Robert Jenson's theology in order to rebuild the chasm between Protestant and Catholic views of justification so that the participatory aspect may find purchase.[29] For our purposes, Jenson says that "we are made righteous in the church; as we have seen, baptism 'justifies' because it initiates into the community whose *telos* is righteousness and whose reality is anticipation of her *telos*."[30] Later Jenson adds, "I become ontically righteous as I hear the gospel—which is in itself true for me independently of my righteousness—and in hearing am formed by the righteousness that its narrative displays, that is, God's own righteousness of love."[31] This means that Spirit baptism is a real experience in the life of the believer as the believer is drawn into the community that is a bearer of God's Triune life. The communal aspect of ecclesiology is not based on abstract social Trinitarian analogies, but as a participation in the *koinonia* between the Father, Son, and Spirit; that is, as a participation in the communion of God's triune life. This is more than just a communion with believers, but a partaking of God's own life as a *being* in communion. The church's participation in Spirit baptism is "through repentance, faith, water baptism, the Eucharist, *koinonia*, and, especially, empowerment for witness."[32] Spirit baptism expands justification to include the full Triune life of God as God's economic activity becomes an experienced reality in the life of the believer—the Holy Spirit brings us into God's circle of love: the Father, Son, and Holy Spirit are all active and present in the event of justification.

So it seems that Spirit baptism is not simply a replacement for soteriological categories, or a nuanced way for Pentecostals to include their theology within the Western tradition. Spirit baptism is more. Macchia says,

> Justification transforms believers by conforming them to the image of Christ and to the impress of the Spirit in the justice

---

28. Macchia, *Baptized in the Spirit*, 48.

29. Macchia says, "Jenson's proposal is helpful as a point of departure for a deeper discussion of the challenges we face in developing a Trinitarian theology of justification" (*Justified in the Spirit*, 298).

30. Jenson, *Systematic Theology*, 291.

31. Ibid., 295.

32. Macchia, *Baptized in the Spirit*,

of divine *koinonia*. The just relationship with God is a mutual indwelling and participation in life. Faith is not simply a believing of a message or a moral response to the enabling of grace. Faith is an embrace and participation in the life that has possessed us deep within. It must be a faith working in love and nourished by hope.[33]

God's economic triune life, as an act of salvation, should fully account for the acts of the Father, Son, and Holy Spirit. So in this regard, Macchia is in agreement with Gunton that a modalistic view of God is not appropriate, for God's fullness must be located in all his acts. Spirit baptism represents Macchia's attempt to account for the work of the Spirit from creation, to the incarnation and resurrection, to justification and our final redemption. Spirit baptism also represents our real experience of God's work in all theological categories—our experience of creation, in that we are created; our experience in soteriology as experienced in the community; and also as a personal experience of our conversion and continuing experience of our new life. It also represents our life eschatologically because the new community and our justification are a down payment for what is yet to come. It was necessary to rehearse Macchia's use of Spirit baptism as a root metaphor—one that derives from our experience of God's redemptive work—so that it will be easier to understand later Pneumatological developments in respect to the immanent life of God. Since Macchia's work is not a full-blown systematic account of the doctrine of God, we will have to search for clues in order to complete his Pneumatology.

C. *Perichoresis*, The Holy Spirit and the Immanent Trinity

Up to this point, Macchia's Pneumatology is framed within a Pentecostal experience in such a way that the experience of salvation becomes the starting point for his doctrine of God. Again, this is a consistent view within the tradition because it is the Pentecostal equivalent to *fides quaerens intellectum*. So instead of viewing Spirit baptism as an illumination or limited to sanctification, Spirit baptism is an act that encompasses the entire scope of soteriology—Jesus Christ and the Holy Spirit are the Father's justification. So in each of the major theological categories, the Father, Son, and Spirit act together: "all three are present and accounted for, cooperating

---

33. Macchia, *Justified in the Spirit*, 309.

and interacting, in every event of Jesus' life."[34] As noted earlier, the Spirit anointed Christ to indwell creation, so that Christ will be the Spirit baptizer, then the Spirit will indwell creation, albeit in a different manner than the Son. This mutual giving and receiving of the Spirit and the Son is where Macchia develops his doctrine of God; and not merely in the relationship between the Father and the Son. The Spirit is where Pentecostal soteriology is experienced, so it is expected that any doctrine of God will develop from the standpoint of the Spirit. The reciprocal giving and receiving of the Son and the Spirit is the vehicle for Macchia to integrate the doctrine of *perichoresis* that will serve as the foundation for his doctrine of God, especially in respect to Pneumatology. Perichoresis serves to create an analogous relation between God and his creation; God's divine essence is based on otherness-in-unity of the triune persons, and so the Spirit creates by perfecting creation's existence as otherness-in-unity.

Gunton begins his doctrine of God with the personhood of the Father in relation to the Son and the Holy Spirit. Macchia assumes the personhood but is more interested in the mutual indwelling of the persons. Notice the order in which Macchia presents the immanent life of God:

> The accomplishment of justice through incarnation and indwelling is rooted theologically in the nature of God as the Spirit baptizer or as the God who indwells the other and takes the other into God's very self. Such is true of God's life of communion as Father, Son and Spirit. Trinitarian *perichoresis* involves the three persons of the Godhead emptying themselves into each other and receiving from each other's fullness.[35]

God's nature is equated to that of the Spirit baptizer because God's internal movement is outward towards the other, the Father loves that which is other, the Son; the Son and Spirit both have the same reciprocal outward movement of love. The Holy Spirit is the love between the Father and Son, and therefore he baptizes both in a reciprocal and perfected love. In a way, Macchia's presentation is similar to Gunton's in that he is beginning with the persons and then moves to the unity of God. Perichoresis is not so much about maintaining the divine unity, but rather about explaining the nature of existence of the Trinitarian persons. An existence explained not in simple terms of relation, but as an interpenetration of giving and receiving. Spirit baptism then takes on a different meaning because it cannot be limited to special empowerment or graces given to the individual, but represents a giving of God's self to that which is not God. Geoffrey Wainwright explains

---

34. Macchia, *The Trinity*, 5.
35. Macchia, *Justified in the Spirit*, 301.

that being in the "image of God" is a reference to our ability to communicate with him; our God-given potential for a relationship. We glorify God by living our lives in a way that is shaped by God's nature as Father, Son, and Spirit: the Spirit of Christ shapes our lives towards communion. So Geoffrey Wainwright develops a liturgical basis for giving and receiving; that is, what "God graciously sets up with mankind comes to expression in the language of worship where God and human beings each give and receive in an exchange which is their mutual communion."[36] It was through the communion and communication of Jesus with his Father that we learned *who* God is—the Father of Jesus Christ. In Jesus Christ we witness the perfect sacrifice; the perfect communion between God and humanity. Jesus' communication, or self-giving, and communion with the Father "may even correspond, within the sphere of time, to that eternal *perichoresis* by which, according to highly developed trinitarian theology, the divine Persons empty themselves into each other and received each other's fullness."[37] For Wainwright, it is in the liturgy where God, as Father, Son, and Spirit, is experienced; then theology reflects upon the experience to give doctrinal expression to God's nature. So it is with Macchia: the Pentecostal experience has logical priority to the objective reality of God as expressed in doctrinal reflection. Following Wainwright's direction, our communion with God is based on God's eternal triune communion, so that *perichoresis* is essential to God's nature—a communion of mutually shared love that is communicated to his creation. The eternal communion of God's self is then shared with creation by the agency of the Holy Spirit.

With the agency of the Holy Spirit who creates *koinonia* in mind, Macchia states that, "the Spirit contributes to the essence of the love involved in this mutual indwelling, actively participating in it to inspire and bear witness, creating a circle of divine *perichoresis* that is dynamic and celebrative, a holy dance of love."[38] The Holy Spirit is essential because the communication between God and his creation involves an outward movement that is provided by the person of the Holy Spirit. The Holy Spirit is not *the* love between the Father and the Son, but is intertwined in an eternal relation of reciprocal give and take with the Father and the Son. The Holy Spirit is not *that something* which completes the divine communion; the Holy Spirit's existence is an existence predicated on being in communion with the Father and Son, in the same way the Father and Son's existence are predicated on existence in the divine communion. The Holy Spirit is eternally in the divine

---

36. Wainwright, *Doxology*, 19–20.
37. Ibid., 23.
38. Macchia, *Justified in the Spirit*, 301.

communion, there is no need to think otherwise. So the Holy Spirit ushers in God's presence by reaching out to the other to the embrace of the divine communion of love.

For Macchia, God's essence is his *perichoretic* life—the mutual indwelling of the Other within the divine triune nature. Even when God reaches out to his creatures, Macchia finds that "God's embrace of the other through self-giving and indwelling thus has its roots within the triune life."[39] But for Macchia, God's otherness is also appropriated to the agency of the Holy Spirit; the otherness of God is intrinsically associated with the Holy Spirit as the agent of communion. In a rebuttal to Moltmann, Macchia states "that there is something about Barth's notion of God's 'otherness' . . . that Pentecostals do appreciate in the context of their experience of the eschatological Spirit in worship, despite the theological problems involved in these concepts."[40] The crux of the matter is the connection of God's otherness with the felt presence of God in the person of the Holy Spirit. God's otherness is important for understanding the nature of the divine essence, because within the Trinity, "otherness is constitutive of unity."[41] There is not an underlying substance that we need to determine how the three persons fit into the unity of the substance, for the divine substance is the unity of the three. Zizioulas locates the unity of God within the three persons, so that otherness and communion are conceived of as ontological categories.[42] Regarding the Holy Spirit, Zizioulas says that "when the Holy Spirit blows, He does not create good individual Christians, individual 'saints,' but an event of communion, which transforms everything the Spirit touches in to a *relational being*."[43] Again, the presence of God is experienced in the life of the Pentecostal, but it is an experience that is a gift by the Father of the Holy Spirit (through Christ), so that the believer(s) can enjoy the life of communion with the Triune God and others. Therefore, Macchia can move backwards from a life of worship and experience to appropriate the Holy Spirit as the spirit of *koinonia* who establishes otherness-in-communion. Since the Spirit is the agent who provides communion and otherness as an eternal participant in the divine *perichoretic* life of God, the question is: what role does the Spirit have in the immanent life of God in relation to divine *koinonia*?

39. Ibid.
40. Macchia, "The Spirit and Life," 123.
41. Macchia, *Justified in the Spirit*, 301.
42. Zizioulas, "Communion and Otherness," 352.
43. Ibid., 354.

For Macchia, the answer is to be found within a nuanced version of Augustine's analogy of "bond of love." It is in the "bond of love" where Macchia's ontological understanding of Pneumatology gains traction. Where Gunton is quite critical, Macchia takes a more cautious approach when engaging Augustine's analogy.[44] Macchia recognizes that there is an inherent problem when viewing the Spirit as the "bond of love," in that the Spirit can be de-personalized in such a way that he is conceptualized as a relation. Macchia says that we must be careful when conceiving the Spirit in relational terms as the "bond of love," otherwise we could be in danger of "eliminating the Spirit's participation as person in the *koinonia* of Father and Son, relating to them in ways appropriate to the Spirit."[45] Eugene Rogers becomes Macchia's interlocutor at this stage because of his work on the Spirit. Macchia says that "Rogers argues that the Spirit is not the bond of love or deity between the Father and the Son in some *unqualified* sense."[46] Macchia is stressing Rogers' position that the Spirit adds an "excess" and "superfluity" to the love and deity of the Father and the Son. What is interesting is that Rogers does not engage much with Augustine's "bond of love"; so that is not Macchia's concern. His focus is that Rogers is stressing the action of the Spirit within the life of Christ as the source for determining the person of the Spirit, instead of speculations on the immanent life of God. So Rogers says that "the only interaction of the Spirit with plot and circumstance that could *distinguish* the Spirit from the Son, will be the Spirit's interactions *with* the Son."[47] Macchia is correct, for Rogers the Spirit is not the "bond of love" in an *unqualified* sense, as if the Spirit is conceived as an accidental property in the Godhead. For Rogers and Macchia, the Spirit as the "bond of love" indicates the Spirit's personhood: for "if the Spirit 'adds' superfluity to the Father and the Son, one might say that the Spirit adds infinity, and therefore divinity, even to God."[48] Rogers concludes that the Holy Spirit conceived through "her" relations with the Son leads to the concept of the deification of human beings, albeit with a caveat of qualifications. In other words, the human nature of Christ did not become divine, it remained human, but it was deified in the sense that it was brought into an intimate relation with the Holy Spirit during Christ's earthly life. Rogers says "what

---

44. Macchia states, "I am open to the social analogy of the Trinity, which means I am critical of Augustine's psychological model of the Trinity. Yet I also cherish Augustine's notion of the Spirit as the bond of love between the Father and the Son" (Macchia, "Pinnock's Pneumatology," 172).

45. Macchia, *Justified in the Spirit*, 302.

46. Ibid.

47. Rogers, *After the Spirit*, 7.

48. Ibid., 47.

the Spirit does is join human beings to the *koinonia* of the trinitarian life."[49] So for our purposes, Augustine's "bond of love" is not to be rejected, but qualified and expanded through the relation that the Son has with the Spirit. The Holy Spirit related to Christ by preparing a body, prepared him for ministry in the desert, vindicated him as the Son of God in power at his baptism, empowered him to be obedient to the Father, and raised him from the dead. The Spirit in Christ's life moved him towards the redemption of the lost and the restoration of *koinonia* between God and his fallen creation. It is the "bond of love" which determines that the Spirit has an outward movement towards others; the Spirit's movement is one of communion; and the otherness and communion activities of the Spirit is what allowed for the incarnation of Christ to come about—which is our salvation.

So the "bond of love" determines the Spirit's divine activity as "the one who opens God's communion and mutual indwelling beyond the 'I-Thou' relationship between the Father and the Son in order to include the many."[50] Macchia's theology of Spirit baptism directs him to conceive of God's economic activity in terms of reaching towards the *other*, which must include God's actual divine life. The monarchy of God is not based on the Father as the source of the divinity, but the Father as Lord of that which is given back to him by the Son and the Spirit. The "bond of love" is that which allows the monarchy of God to take place only in and as a communion of love between the three divine persons. In this way, the "bond of love" includes the concept of communion, or *koinonia*. Macchia says that "through the Spirit, God becomes an abundant gift poured out from the rich relationship and communion enjoyed between Father, Son, and Spirit."[51] Macchia interprets John 17:21[52] as an explicit witness to the *koinonia* that is intrinsic to God's very essence. Therefore, the Holy Spirit as the "bond of love" which moves outward to the other, and God's essence being structure as *koinonia*, means that Pneumatology is *koinonia* and is the essence of the divine communion. In this way, *koinonia* is a useful concept for Pentecostals because it involves the very life of God as God. This is Macchia's specific contribution to Pentecostalism: since *koinonia* relies on Pneumatology, Pentecostals as people of the Spirit must engage themselves with *koinonia*; this will enable them to develop their theology along Trinitarian grounds.[53] Macchia emphasizes

49. Ibid.
50. Macchia, *Justified in the Spirit*, 302.
51. Ibid., 303.
52. "That they may all be one; even as You, Father, are in Me and I in You, that they also may be in Us, so that the world may believe that You sent Me."
53. In an article, Hocken states that "the concept of the church has not generally been central to Pentecostal faith, though it has been more prominent among

that Pentecostals have not adequately focused on the *koinonia* that Christ as the Spirit baptizer gives to creation; especially as people of the Spirit. So the "bond of love" is better defined as a willful participation by the *person* of the Spirit in sharing the love between the Father and the Son, thereby making this love a love of communion. The Spirit then opens up the love between the few (i.e., the Father and the Son) to the many: "Spirit baptism incorporates the many into this communion, being rooted in this eternal openness of God as love."[54] In this way, "creation comes into direct and full communion with God and in God when it becomes the dwelling place of God's Spirit in the very image of Christ, which I define in the light of 1 Cor. 15.20–28 as the fulfillment of God's kingdom."[55] So Spirit baptism is intimately connected with the "bond of love analogy" and serves as a means to protect against the tendencies of Pentecostalism towards a Christomonistic theology. For if the Spirit *is* the "bond of love," then Christ would be simply pouring out divine love as an accidental universal property that is not located within our human condition. But, if the Spirit as the "bond of love" is the person who shares in the love between the Father and Son, thereby creating communion, then when Christ as the Spirit baptizer pours out the Spirit, then the personal agency of the Spirit liberates humanity so that it too can share in the love that leads to *koinonia*. Love then becomes a real love because it is generated within our creaturely condition, just as the human Christ displayed love to the Father and his community. The Spirit is necessary for a proper *koinonia*, and since Christ initiated and inaugurated the community in the incarnation, the Spirit as the "bond of love" is essential to the incarnation.

In a similar register as Gunton, Macchia does not define salvation as the forgiveness of sins quantitatively speaking. Salvation for Gunton is a restoration of the broken relationship between Creator and his creatures, as well as between creatures. For Macchia, the concept is similar except that the focus is more on renewal towards fellowship that begins with the embrace from and within the triune God. It is apparent that this embrace and renewal of fellowship takes place in Spirit baptism. Since Jesus Christ descended to our time and space in order to redeem the lost, and since

---

those churches formed and living in situation of hardship and oppression" (Hocken, "Theology of the Church," 544). Hocken also purports that even when Pentecostals are concerned with ecclesiology, it is more for doctrinal or denominational unity, and not as a community grounded in the Trinitarian life of God. Commenting on several Pentecostal authors, Hocken states, "while none of these authors systematically studied the relationship between fellowship in the Spirit and understanding of the church, their concern for unity necessarily had an ecclesiological component" (ibid., 546).

54. Macchia, "Baptized in the Spirit," 20.
55. Ibid.

Spirit baptism is where the embrace of the Triune God finds its *locus*, then it is easy to conceive that the Holy Spirit is necessary for salvation as the "bond of love." For Macchia, salvation rests in the inner life of the Triune God as a love story between the persons of the Trinity; in this way, the "love story [is] about the bond of love in the Holy Spirit between the Father and the Son."[56] The "bond of love" is necessary because the Spirit moves towards creation by anointing a body for the Word, who in turn baptizes creation with the Spirit; the Spirit who brings creation back to the Father through divine love—a type of *theosis* in that humanity is drawn into the "bond of love" by the Holy Spirit. The incarnation is an act of love, which is only accomplished with the agency of the Holy Spirit because all the external works of God are indivisible. Therefore, the "bond of love" defines the Spirit as a person who acts in a dynamic movement of love towards the other, establishing *koinonia* within the immanent life of God, which eventually is experienced in the economic activity as Christ becomes the Spirit baptizer at his resurrection and ascension. The Spirit as the "bond of love" is also involved in creation, which affords Macchia the space to further his Pneumatology in the doctrine of creation.

D. The Holy Spirit Creates

For Gunton, the idea that the Holy Spirit creates draws from his doctrine of mediation, which states that the Word and the Spirit are the two divine persons who are the Father's "two-hands" who complete his will to create. The Holy Spirit is the agent who moves the love of God outward and perfects it. This way, the Spirit is the agent of perfection, or to be more precise, of eschatological perfection. Therefore, for Gunton, the Holy Spirit as creator is associated with the doctrine of God. As we will see, Macchia's view of the Spirit as the Creator emerges from within a soteriological framework; the Spirit creates because the Spirit is active as the perfector of the final consummation of creation. We will begin with a lengthy quote from Macchia, so that we can begin to unpack his understanding of how the Spirit is the Creator:

> The Father is the Creator who makes the creation as the household of the firstborn Son and the place of the divine indwelling. The Son is the one who takes on flesh in order to be the preeminent Son of the household, but he does this by pouring forth the Spirit. The Spirit fashions the creation from the void in order to anoint this creation as a gift to the Son and the Father. The

---

56. Macchia, *The Trinity*, 139.

Spirit gives anointed flesh to the Son in order that all flesh could under this anointing receive the Son and the Father, indeed, the divine *koinonia* as well. The Son receives the anointed body so that he might, as divine, pour forth the Spirit on all flesh. The Spirit offers the incarnate Son to the Father in the Son's death and resurrection in order that the Son may offer the Spirit to the Father along with the redeemed creation in the *eschaton*.[57]

The Father, Son, and Spirit are the Creator in Macchia's theology; the triune persons are involved in a creative dance that exhibits the mutual indwelling of the three persons. The passage indicates that the triune God creates, which for our purposes means that the Spirit creates; but we still need to unpack the soteriological basis for Macchia's claim.

The Father and the Son are the Creator because their divine work ends with the indwelling of the Spirit; either by election of the Son, or by the Son pouring out the Spirit. For Macchia, the *telos* of creation is to be the dwelling place of God, and salvation is a restoration of this promise. The presence of God is mediated and realized in the presence of the Spirit because this indwelling by the Spirit opens creation to God's self and his redemptive activity. Revisiting the theme of McDonnell,[58] Macchia says that "the Son is the King and the Spirit is the kingdom in the fulfilment of the Father's will."[59] In other words, when the Spirit indwells creation—as the will of the Father through the Son—the Father is creating by redeeming creation from sin and death, moving creation towards its eschatological goal of becoming God's dwelling place. The Son creates because he is the incarnate Son of the Father who is Lord over creation as the Spirit baptizer. Creation realizes its goal because the risen Christ pours out God's presence in the person of the Holy Spirit. The Son is Lord over creation because God's Lordship has always found its content within redemptive divine acts in history: God declares his lordship over Israel due to his acts of deliverance. In the same way, God's Lordship is found in the historical act of the life, death, and resurrection of Jesus Christ; a life that was victorious over sin and won Jesus the right to be the Spirit baptizer. Macchia says "suffice it to say here that the connection that John the Baptist will forge between Jesus as the Spirit baptizer and the inauguration of the kingdom of God to establish God's lordship in history is rooted in the Old Testament assumption that the divine presence

57. Macchia, *Justified in the Spirit*, 304.

58. "If the Spirit is the touch by which one has communion in the mystery of Christ, and if the Spirit is the only access to God, then the goal of the Christian life is the 'acquisition' of the Spirit. The Spirit as goal is the kingdom Christ hands over to the Father" (McDonnell, *The Other Hand of God*, 227).

59. Macchia, *Baptized in the Spirit*, 91.

will make this lordship a reality as a source of freedom and redemption for humanity."[60] What this means is that God the Father and God the Son are always present in the act of creation; the goal for creation is to be indwelt with God's presence. Creation is an event, the event of God coming to his creation, which takes place as a divine action in the will of the Father, and by the incarnation of the Son who baptizes with the Spirit.

Therefore, the idea that the Spirit creates has a soteriological and eschatological thrust. Macchia does not go into any detail about the metaphysics regarding the void in the Genesis account—the event of creating is more important. The Spirit creates out of the void to "anoint," which is another term for "baptize"; the Spirit creates so that the presence of God will indwell creation and return it as a gift to the Father and the Son. Creation *ex nihilo* is not the focus, the focus is that God creates in the Spirit, that is, as an ongoing presence of the Holy Spirit actively redeeming creation. Spirit baptism is not merely an individual human feeling, but is a soteriological metaphor which intimately connects creation to redemption and eschatology. For Macchia, to speak of the creation activity of the Spirit is to think of all three categories: the three categories are logically distinct but in actuality the reference is to one event, the event of Spirit baptism. In a review of Clark Pinnock's Pneumatology, Macchia offers his own theological insights regarding the Spirit and creation; he states that "redemption is not an abandonment of creation."[61] Generally speaking, Pentecostal's eschatology is an "other-worldly" enterprise that is seeking a release from this fallen material existence in anticipation of a new and different kind of existence. There is a discontinuity with this creation and the new creation, ontologically speaking; the only continuity is with the immortal soul. One author states that "Pentecostals should concentrate not just on being removed from the sin and depravity of this world but also how best to introduce the Kingdom of God and righteousness into society prior to any return of Jesus."[62] D. J. Wilson expresses the same conclusion that Pentecostals, generally, do not see God working for the redemption of *this* world, but are anticipating Christ's bodily return, which will destroy this material world and create a new one, along with a new kind of physical body for his believers.[63] On the other hand, Macchia says, "it has been clear to me ever since then that the

---

60. Ibid., 94.

61. Macchia, "Tradition and the *Novum*," 37.

62. Warrington, *Pentecostal Theology*, 323.

63. Wilson states that for Pentecostals, "since the end is near, they are indifferent to social change and have rejected the reformist methods of the optimistic postmillennialists and have concentrated on 'snatching brands from the fire' and letting social reforms result from humankind being born again" (Wilson, "Pentecostal Perspectives on Eschatology," 605).

gospel of the resurrection redeems and transforms creation and is not the escape of the immaterial soul to another world."[64] Creation is an event that involves this world—creation, redemption and eschatology are connected because Jesus Christ has baptized "all flesh" with the Spirit. The dispensationalist model of older Pentecostal theologians creates a disconnect between the doctrines of creation, redemption, and eschatology, because the work of the Spirit is only conceived in the moral sphere. But Spirit baptism for Macchia means that the Spirit creates as an event that includes redemption that restores creation back toward its final destiny of being indwelled with the presence of God.

So the doctrine of creation in respect to the Spirit is soteriological, in that creation and redemption are interconnected and incomprehensible without each other. Returning to his review of Pinnock, Macchia says that, "Pinnock adds that the Spirit as the Spirit of creation is the connecting link between creation and redemption, for it is the same Spirit involved in both acts of God. The Spirit of creation is also the Spirit of redemption who transforms the powers of the old creation into the powers of the new."[65] This review of Pinnock by Macchia is a parenthetical remark expressing Macchia's views regarding the Spirit and creation; this indicates that Pinnock serves as a voice of support for Macchia's own views regarding the Spirit and creation. Pinnock says that the "Spirit is involved in implementing both creation and new creation. There could not be redemptive actions unless first there had been creative actions. The creative acts underlie the salvific acts. The Spirit who brings salvation first brooded over the deep to bring order out of chaos."[66] For Pinnock, the Spirit is the creator because the Spirit redeems creation. The Spirit is not limited to subjective moral experiences, or pietism as expressed in the church; the Spirit is located in the history of creation creating avenues for creation to reach its destiny. Again, Pinnock expresses that,

> Only the Spirit who brought life to the world in the first place can bring new life to it. Redemption does not leave the world behind but lifts creation to a higher level. The Spirit has been implementing God's purposes for creation from day one and is committed to seeing to it that they issue in restoration. Creator

---

64. Macchia, "Tradition and the *Novum*," 37. Macchia is referring to the reading of Oscar Cullmann's *Immortality of the Soul or Resurrection of the Dead?*

65. Ibid.

66. Pinnock, *Flame of Love*, 50.

Spirit inspires hope for a world beyond the reach of humanity, in which God's power raises the dead and makes everything new.[67]

For Pinnock, creation, redemption, and perfection correspond to the creation activity of the Holy Spirit *in toto*; the Spirit acts *within* creation to bring about its perfection in Christ. That creation is an *event* of the Holy Spirit and not simply a punctiliar act of creation *ex nihilio* is seen when Pinnock says that "in one sense creation is complete, in that God has called it forth and it exists. But its goal has not been reached, and it is in that sense incomplete and unfinished. Only at the end of history will it be clear what the creation was meant to be, because it will have reached the goal."[68] For Pinnock, this completes the account of the work of the Spirit in creation; the Spirit is the Creator because his action is to perfect creation by giving life and perfecting it at the end.[69] The Spirit perfects *this* creation; eschatology is not an escape from *this* creation, but the anticipation of the perfection of it through and in Christ. For Pinnock, the Spirit creates the conditions for creation, and therefore humanity, to reach its intended goal of a complete relationship with God as Father, Son, and Holy Spirit. For Macchia, in light of Pinnock, the Holy Spirit is the creator because of his redemptive activities, which correspond to the doctrines of creation, salvation, and eschatology. Creation is not simply the initial act of creating—it does include *ex nihilo*—but a continual act that encompasses all of creation, and not just an illumination of believers to the work of Christ. Creation is baptized by the Spirit at the initial creation event; creation is again baptized in the redeeming activity of the Father's Son; and finally, creation will be baptized by the Spirit fully when it is perfected with God's presence. Finally, Pinnock says that "the Spirit is not restricted to religious spaces; he is the giver of life itself and present in all aspects of it."[70] This way, Macchia finds content for the metaphor of Spirit baptism in the work of the Holy Spirit in all aspects of creative activity. Creative activities that take place in creation which are moving it towards its *telos*. A *telos* that is shaped by the love between the Father and the Son; that is, a Christologically shaped *telos* that is driven by the Holy Spirit in Spirit baptism. The Spirit is moving creation towards its divine goal in the face of those forces that are attempting to thwart God's

---

67. Ibid., 54.

68. Ibid., 58.

69. Pinnock states, "Spirit is perfecter, then, of the creation of which Jesus is the highest expression. Spirit is at work in history, first bringing humankind into existence and then moving it toward the goal of union" (ibid., 61).

70. Pinnock, *Flame of Love*,

plan. The Spirit is the presence of God in the world, liberating creation so that it can reach its divine destiny of being indwelled by its Creator.

Macchia's Pneumatology is grounded in the saving activity of the Spirit, which is steeped in the Reformed tradition of grace as God's free activity. The Holy Spirit is free to create, redeem, and perfect; the freedom in the economy is a reflection of the freedom in the immanent trinity. The Spirit is the liberating agent of creation and within God's self. The mutual indwelling of the three persons culminates in the outward movement of the Spirit that liberates the trinitarian persons to reach out to the other. Macchia says that, "It is not that God enjoys communion within Godself by necessity but gives to creation freely. Through the Spirit, it is all abundantly and excessively free, both in the context of God's self-determination within the immanent Trinity and God's self-disclosure and vindication in the economic Trinity."[71] For Gunton, the Spirit is presented as that which liberates the other; the Spirit brings freedom to be. The Spirit liberates the Father and the Son to be *that* divine person; and the same divine action liberates creation to be the other-in-relation—liberation means the freedom to be *that* other. For Macchia, the *perichoretic* action of the immanent trinity means that the Spirit liberates the Father and the Son to be self-determined. There is a soteriological accent because liberation focuses on the outward movement of God that embraces creation within the triune life. In a sense, the Spirit liberates God to be Other over against creation, thereby strengthening God's divine personhood and otherness. Oscar Cullmann argues that the Holy Spirit's role in salvation is the resurrection of the body, and is not limited to the preservation of an immortal soul.[72] Liberation is characterized soteriologically through Jesus Christ's *victory* over death, and not simply the freedom to be real humanity. Cullmann explains that for Paul the term "flesh" is something which acts outside of humanity, albeit because of humanity's sin that eventually culminates in death. Even though "flesh" does have the idea of the physical body, because that is where this outside force has the most impact, "flesh" is really a term for life apart from the Spirit, which leads to death. So,

> deliverance will come when the power of the Holy Spirit transforms all matter, when God in a new act of creation will not destroy matter, but set it free from the flesh, from corruptibility. Not eternal Ideas, but concrete objects will then rise anew, in the

---

71. Macchia, *Justified in the Spirit*, 305.

72. Macchia says that "when I read Oscar Cullmann's classic little book, *Immortality of the Soul or Resurrection of the Dead?* It has been clear to me ever since then that the gospel of the resurrection redeems and transforms creation and is not the escape of the immaterial soul to another world" ("Tradition and the *Novum*," 37).

new, incorruptible life-substance of the Holy Spirit; and among these objects belongs our body as well.[73]

Liberation is an act of the Holy Spirit to create, redeem, and perfect; liberation is an act of God that finds its origin in the *perichoretic* dance between the Father, Son, and Spirit. In this way, even the concept of liberation for Macchia finds its original meaning in salvation; instead of beginning with the relation between the persons, it is in the redemptive work of the economy that defines liberation. God's lordship is rooted in the Old Testament idea that God's presence will bring historical deliverance for Israel. God's presence is a "source of freedom and redemption for humanity."[74] Liberation is intimately connected with God's presence, a presence that brings redemption—liberation's concreteness is located in freedom from sin and death. Macchia says that,

> God's presence is promised in the *Shekinah*, which that guaranteed Israel's liberation from her oppressors and from the hopeless of sin and death. In a word, the law cries out for the Spirit. It is ultimately through the promise of the Spirit that the law becomes a living reality that witnesses to the enhancement of righteousness and life.[75]

The Spirit's action of liberation is not simply an ontological predication as in Gunton's relational model; liberation is from the effects of sin which leads to death. There is also a relational element to the Spirit's liberation; the Spirit liberates so that relationship can be restored and koinonia can be experienced: "Spirit baptism thus frees us to give ourselves wisely and redemptively in love to others."[76] The Spirit perfects the Father's will in creation by liberating creation towards a Christ-like existence; an existence which is defined within the new community—an otherness-in-relation existence. Macchia concludes that "justification is the Spirit's embrace of the creature and the creature's liberating participation by the indwelling Spirit in Christ as crucified and risen and in the koinonia that will pervade the new creation and the final communion of saints."[77] Therefore, Macchia's Pneumatology begins logically and epistemologically from within the economy, and proceeds into the imminent life of God, so that the divine

---

73. Cullman, "Immortality of the Soul or Resurrection of the Dead?," 28–29.
74. Macchia, *Baptized in the Spirit*, 94.
75. Macchia, *Justified in the Spirit*, 117.
76. Macchia, *Baptized in the Spirit*, 172.
77. Macchia, *Justified in the Spirit*, 295–96.

perichoresis is witnessed in the economic activity of God and culminates in the work of the Spirit.

The Spirit who liberates and brings relationships does so because of the divine life of God as *perichoretic* action of the persons; the persons who freely give and receive from each other. As seen from the above survey, Macchia's Pneumatology is Pentecostal because he begins with the economic activity of God as experienced by the individual and the community. The constant thread throughout the discussion of Macchia's Pneumatology has been *koinonia* and perfection: the Spirit is the perfector of community. In Macchia's pneumatology, the Spirit is conceived within the same framework as Gunton, but with different accents. Macchia finds that the Spirit is the one who completes God's love because that love is essentially defined as pouring out to the other. For Gunton, the other is the Holy Spirit, who completes the divine communion of love. Gunton is attempting to maintain God's integrity and freedom by locating the essence of love within God's self. For Macchia, the other is creation, because that is where we experience God's presence in the Spirit. Macchia maintains God's freedom because God is not under any compulsion to pour out that love; it is the Spirit that opens God to his creatures, thereby perfecting his outward love. This love is not yet perfectly experienced by creation; the Spirit is perfecting the experience of God's love by creating a new community—a new networks of relations because of the victory of Christ as the Spirit baptizer. So yes, Macchia's and Gunton's pneumatologies overlap, but Macchia would add that it is necessary to realize the ongoing relationship that Spirit baptism brings to creation. Spirit baptism means that God's full presence within his creation is creation's divinely ordered goal; a goal which is being eschatologically realized by the Spirit. At the end, the Spirit will hand the perfected creation to the Son who will deliver the kingdom to the Father, and then creation's *telos* will be complete as an experience of the baptism in the Spirit.

Chapter 8

Doctrine of God—The Spirit-Baptized Divine Life

Introduction

So far, Macchia's theological program is propelled by his root metaphor of Spirit baptism—it is the center by and from which Ecclesiology, Christology, and Pneumatology all find their moorings. The experience of God begins theological reflection and development; it is the church where the Word and Spirit are *experienced* by the believer. Christ is *experienced* as the one who is anointed with the Spirit as the Spirit baptizer baptizing creation. The Spirit fulfills God's plan to dwell with creation through the eschatological *experience* of his Spirit. This way, Macchia's Doctrine of God develops from within the Pentecostal experience of the Spirit: the Spirit mediates the presence of the Father and the Son so that the Triune God indwells creation.

Although Macchia's doctrine of God is presented last, this does not mean that it is of least importance to Macchia, or that Spirit baptism as a metaphor has priority over the *being* of God. At this stage, Macchia is more concerned with developing Pentecostal theology in a systematic fashion in such a way that the experience of salvation has epistemological priority. So out of our experience of salvation, we can develop a doctrine of God: we have received God's grace in the church—a grace based on the work of Jesus Christ through the mediating work of the Spirit—and based on that experience we can assemble a theological account of the God who saves. It is the God who saves, not the God who is omnipotent, omnipresent, and omniscient, that drives Macchia's quest for a doctrine of God. The classical attributes of God are part of our theological reflection after we have come to faith. So instead of beginning with questions of substance and attributes, Macchia begins with the economic activity as revealed in Scripture to develop an account of God's *being*. Instead of formulating God's essence based on speculative relations of origins, it is the language of the Incarnation—"incarnation" and "indwelling"—that frames our talk about God. The Father's "two-hands"—the Son and the Holy Spirit—mediate salvation by securing God's Lordship, and also by constituting it. We will see that for Macchia, the Lordship of God is based on the conception that the Father's monarchy is grounded *in* the three persons, instead of merely viewing the Father as the source of the monarchy. Instead of grounding personhood in the constituting activity of the Spirit, Macchia grounds personhood in the *koinonia* of the Trinity; the Holy Spirit completes the love between the Father and the Son in a way that is reminiscent of Spirit baptism, which completes the divine communion. So Macchia's doctrine of God culminates in Pentecost, for Pentecost is where we meet the Triune God. It is extremely difficult to give an account of Macchia's doctrine of God when he has yet to produce a systematic account of God. The reader is left to interpret those areas in Macchia's writings that approximate a doctrine of God, which leaves the exegete open to inserting his/her own biases into Macchia's thought. Also, the impetus for Macchia's work is to produce a systematic and robust presentation of the Pentecostal distinctive of Spirit baptism and not a full systematic work. So we will look at Macchia's doctrine of God with the understanding that there are overlaps with the earlier sections, which means we will only discuss areas which express those unique and important conceptions in Macchia's doctrine of God.

A. Doctrine of God as Pentecostal Experience of the Spirit

For Gunton, God's personhood is absolute and is constituted from within his eternal communion as Father, Son, and Spirit; but the creature's personhood is constituted first from God and secondarily by relations with others. As we will see, Macchia is in general agreement with Gunton's project, but his development is slightly nuanced towards a Pentecostal stress on the work and experience of the Holy Spirit. Macchia says that he "will use the mutual indwelling of Trinitarian *koinonia* as a context for understanding the overlapping and integrated nature of justification and sanctification and, more broadly, the theological categories of creation, redemption, and the giving of life."[1] In this way, for Macchia, it is the "mutual indwelling," or the perichoretic activity of the three persons, that gives him purpose to understand God and redemption, but as we will

1. Ibid., 293.

see, there is also a stress on the Spirit that fully integrates his Pentecostal identity into the doctrine of God.

In two of Macchia's primary works—*Justified in the Spirit* and *Baptized in the Spirit*—he reflects on aspects of soteriology instead of speculating on the inner nature of God. In *Baptized in the Spirit*, it is the experience of "Spirit baptism" as a "strong sense of calling from God toward some form of gifted ministry"[2] that frames the remainder of his theological formulations. As we saw in the section on Pneumatology, Macchia uses the Pentecostal distinctive of Spirit baptism as a mediating doctrine between Catholic and Protestant views on justification; but he does so without neglecting the significance of the two traditions, or by creating an admixture of the two doctrines. Both Catholic and Protestant views of justification begin with metaphysical ideas about God's essence and attributes, then they attempt to explain how this kind of God relates or redeems fallen creation. Macchia does not decry this method, but as a Pentecostal it is the experience of the Holy Spirit that is central to a pentecostal account of theology which does not begin with speculative ideas about God's *being*. Macchia says that "nothing short of a full-blown Trinitarian integration will be sufficient, and the place to start is with the most neglected participant, namely, the Holy Spirit."[3] The place to begin any discussion of the doctrine of God for Macchia will be from the standpoint of experience, which is not merely a subjective experience, but the experience of God's economic activity as an experience of the Spirit. It is not in the subjective experience of the individual alone, but as God's economic activity is experienced within the subjective individual and the community in the presence of the Holy Spirit. This is not a post-Kantian subjectivism that locates our religious beliefs within the mind or consciousness of the individual. Macchia states that "Spirit baptism is a profoundly personal but not individualistic experience."[4] The Holy Spirit is the link between Christ's work and our justification with the Father; our experience derives from the revelation of God's divine life. Baptism in the Spirit is justification—the Father willed our justification, the Son won our justification, and the Spirit completed our justification because justification is ultimately defined as God indwelling creation. The event of revelation as an economic activity is where the nature of God is revealed; it is not in speculative reason, but in the experience of salvation—which for a Pentecostal requires that adequate space be given to the work of the Spirit. Macchia states that "the Trinitarian God emerges in the story of Jesus as the Christ,

---

2. Macchia, *Baptized in the Spirit*, 13–14.
3. Macchia, *Justified in the Spirit*, 294.
4. Macchia, *Baptized in the Spirit*, 166.

the man of the Spirit, who is constantly accountable to the Father as the source of all life."[5] It is the revelation of Jesus Christ in history which is the foundation for Macchia's understanding of God, but it is the involvement of the Holy Spirit in our justification that distinguishes his particular doctrine of God. Wolfhart Pannenberg concludes that "to find a basis for the doctrine of the Trinity we must begin with the way in which Father, Son, and Spirit come on the scene and relate to one another in the event of revelation. Here lies the material justification for the demand that the doctrine of the Trinity must be based on the biblical witness to revelation or on the economy of salvation."[6] So for Macchia, this statement by Pannenberg develops the necessary stress on the Holy Spirit, for "Pannenberg shows that the involvement of the Spirit in the relationship between the Father and the Son in the story of Jesus prevented the early church from becoming binitarian."[7] So it is the economic activity in the revelation event of Jesus Christ that Macchia develops his doctrine of God, but it is interrelated to the work of the Holy Spirit because that is where the Christian experience of salvation is mediated. Since "the Spirit is at the very substance of justification and all soteriological categories (1 Cor. 6:11),"[8] and Spirit baptism—the presence of God—expresses the Pentecostal soteriological distinctive, then it follows that soteriology as an expression of God's economic activity is Macchia's starting point for developing his doctrine of God.

Macchia is not that interested in making his starting point from any philosophical notions of the one God, or ideas derived from apologetic arguments such as causation, ontological arguments, teleology, etc. Macchia's doctrine of God develops from the three persons of the Godhead with a stress on the Holy Spirit as a corrective to the Western approach that has a tendency to reduce the role of the Spirit by stressing the covenantal relationship between the Father and the Son.[9] So instead of beginning with

5. Ibid., 118.

6. Pannenberg, *Systematic Theology*, 1:299.

7. Macchia, *Baptized in the Spirit*, 118. Macchia is referring to Pannenberg when Pannenberg states, "The source of the specific mode of the Spirit's presence in the church is to be sought, however, in his function of mediating the fellowship of the Son with the Father. If the Spirit were not constitutive for the fellowship of the Son with the Father, the Christian doctrine of the deity of the Spirit would be a purely external addition to the confession of the relation of the Son to the deity of the Father" (Pannenberg, *Systematic Theology*, 268).

8. Macchia, *Justified in the Spirit*, 295.

9. Moltmann explains that the reason for the stress on the Father and the Son was due to the issues over Arianism and Sabellianism. The basic questions for the early church were "what is the relationship between Christ and God, and how is the divine revelation of Christ to God the Father related to the unity of God himself? And how is

the relations of origin—"begotten" and "procession"—as the central idea in determining God's nature, Macchia prefers economic language of "incarnation" and "indwelling." Terms like "begotten" and "procession" have an implicit focus on the other side of eternity, they are couched within the immanent life of God. But "incarnation" and "indwelling" both give preference to God's existence in our history as the Father's "two-hands": God the Son and God the Holy Spirit are present and active in our reality. Macchia says that "the accomplishment of justice through incarnation and indwelling is rooted theologically in the nature of God as the Spirit baptizer or as the God who indwells the other and takes the other into God's very self. Such is true of God's life of communion as Father, Son, and Spirit."[10] The nature of God is the Spirit baptizer; he is the one who reaches out to the other as a reflection of our experience of God. Creation did not experience God from within the inner trinitarian relations, or as the "sending" of the Son, but as the Spirit indwelled it and perfected it so that the creative work of the Son could be experienced. God is experienced in creation by his "two hands," the Son who is the Lord of the Kingdom and the Holy Spirit who is the Kingdom. The Son and the Spirit work to establish God's Kingdom, and then hand it back to the Father so that God is Lord over all. Our experience of God is as the incarnate Son and the indwelling of the Spirit, an experience which is a fulfillment of the Father's will. We experience God because he has baptized his creation with the Spirit—Spirit baptism reveals God. Therefore, God is the Father who baptizes; God is the Son who baptizes; and God is the Holy Spirit who baptizes. Spirit baptism expresses who God is, he is the God who thrice reveals himself as indwelling his creation; but God thrice reveals because he is three. But we experience only one baptism (water baptism is intimately related to Spirit baptism), so God must be one. Spirit baptism defines God from our experience of God's presence instead of relying on rational speculations about God. Our experience of God reveals his Lordship over our lives and creation itself. So we will look at the connection between Spirit baptism and God as Lord.

B. The Lord is the Spirit

The Lordship of God is based on God as the Spirit baptizer, rather than as the One who has supreme authority as the sole and powerful Creator. Macchia says, "if, as I maintain, however, the establishment of divine lordship

---

the adoration of Christ as God reconcilable with God's unity?" (Moltmann, *The Trinity and the Kingdom*, 130).

10. Macchia, *Justified in the Spirit*, 301.

in history (the establishment of the kingdom of God) is defined biblically as a baptism in the Spirit, this lordship cannot be defined abstractly and certainly not by a solitary ego that acts unilaterally on the world."[11] When the Lordship of God is defined in reference to the Holy Spirit as an expression of baptism by the Holy Spirit, then God's eternal nature as Father, Son, and Spirit can come into focus. This way, the lordship of God develops in light of Spirit baptism; the Spirit is not an addendum, but is vital in determining God's lordship. This way, the Father is still the source of the Godhead—not because of relations of origin, but because he willed creation to be indwelt by the Holy Spirit. Macchia says that "in creating all things by the divine Word and Breath (Gen. 1:1–2; John 1–3), the Father earmarks the creation as that which will be involved in the bond of love through the Spirit that exists between the Father and the Son . . . The creation is thus made through the Spirit by and for the favored Son (John 1:14; Col. 1:15–16)."[12] In a sense, the Holy Spirit is not a result of the monarchy of the Father, but is that agent, along with the Son, who constitutes the divine monarchy: meaning that the Father is dependent on the Spirit (and the Son for that matter) for his monarchy. Macchia turns to Pannenberg who states that,

> By their work the Son and the Spirit serve the monarchy of the Father. Yet the Father does not have his kingdom or monarchy without the Son and the Spirit, but only through them. This is true not merely of the event of revelation. On the basis of the historical relation of Jesus to the Father we may say this of the inner life of the triune God as well . . . The Son is not subordinate to the Father in the sense of ontological inferiority, but he subjects himself to the Father. In this regard he is himself in eternity the locus of the monarchy of the Father. Herein he is one with the Father by the Holy Spirit. The monarchy of the Father is not the presupposition but the result of the common operation of the three persons. It is thus the seal of their unity.[13]

For Pannenberg, the monarchy is constituted by the Father, but only through the Son and Spirit. In this way, the monarchy, and by implication the Lordship of the Father, is dependent on the role of the Spirit: the Father is Lord because he wills the baptism of the Spirit by the Son. Macchia says that "the Son is thus not Lord without the Spirit, just as the Son is not Lord without the Father."[14] Again, Macchia says, "in other words, Jesus is Lord as the Spirit

---

11. Macchia, *Baptized in the Spirit*, 125.
12. Macchia, *Justified in the Spirit*, 119.
13. Pannenberg, *Systematic Theology*, 1:324–25.
14. Macchia, *Baptized in the Spirit*.

Baptizer and delivers the kingdom back to the Father as the Spirit-anointed man and, at the culmination of the kingdom of God, through the Spirit's indwelling and renewing creation after the Son's image."[15] The Son is Lord because he completes the Father's will to baptize with the Spirit. There is priority given to the divine *communion*; Jesus as the Spirit baptizer and the Holy Spirit as the baptism returns creation back to the Father an action that completes the work of God as Father, Son, and Spirit. Macchia says, "the divine monarchy has communion at its core,"[16] because the Spirit contributes to the love that is God's essence; a love that is a result of the mutual indwelling that is the divine *perichoresis* of the three triune persons. The communion of God is completed and perfected by the Holy Spirit because that is the way we experience God through the indwelling Holy Spirit who opens us to the Word of the Father.

Macchia explains the communion of God as an "embrace of the other through self-giving and indwelling thus has its roots within the triune life."[17] Spirit baptism brings us into relation with the communion of God as Father, Son, and Spirit; in this way, Macchia's conception of God is formulated in relational and communal terms. Personhood is conceptualized in terms of relation and communion: Macchia says, "as a result of this insight, we should define personhood as 'otherness in communion and communion in otherness."[18] John Zizioulas' article on "Communion and Otherness" sheds light on Macchia's understanding of the economy in developing his doctrine of God towards a model of personhood. In the article, Zizioulas develops otherness and connects it to soteriology by saying that the fear of the other can be conceived as our current state of sin. So in order for the church to realize her fallen state and generate a desire for repentance, a higher model of otherness and communion is needed; and this model is to be found in the Trinity. Zizioulas says that "there is no other model for the proper relation between communion and otherness either for the Church or for the human being than the Trinitarian God. If the Church wants to be faithful to her true self, she must try to mirror the communion and otherness that exists in the Triune God."[19] The relational communion of the Triune God is the model

---

15. Ibid., 123.
16. Ibid., 124.
17. Macchia, *Justified in the Spirit*, 301.

18. Ibid. Macchia is referring to the insights of Moltmann on the "pathos" of God, which is a criticism against the Western concepts of God as either an absolute substance or absolute subject. In order to escape those non-relational ideas, Moltmann purports that God must be discussed in terms of Father, Son, and Spirit then search for the unity (Moltmann, *The Trinity and the Kingdom*, 10–15).

19. Zizioulas, "Communion and Otherness," 352.

for ecclesiology and anthropology, so that otherness and relationality constitutes the *being* of creation, as a reflection of God's *koinonia*. Zizioulas says that the monarchy of the Father is not defined from the divine substance but from the communion that the Father has with the Son and the Spirit. Zizioulas understands that there is an inherent otherness in God that is the ground for the development of relationality and communion as ontological categories. In this way, "otherness is inconceivable apart from relationship. Father, Son, and Spirit are all names indicating relationship. No Person can be different unless He is related. Communion does not threaten otherness; it generates it."[20] Because of Zizioulas' ontology of otherness-in-communion, Macchia concludes that "God thus exists as a communion of persons that embraces otherness and does not dissolve it."[21] The unity of God is maintained in the otherness-in-communion; the persons constitute the unity of the divine substance.

For Moltmann, God's unity is not located in the substance or the sole divine subject, but in three persons. Theologically speaking, the biblical history of the three divine persons created the problem of determining the unity in God. For Moltmann, the divine persons are united by their intimate communication; but that communication is open and inviting to others, it is a unity that is "*capable of integration.*" Moltmann says that 'the *homogeneity* of the divine substance is hardly conceivable as communicable and open for anything else, because then it would no longer be homogeneous."[22] Within God there must be an inherent means for self-differentiation, that which is capable of communicating love to the other. Within Moltmann's scheme, there is the idea that the communication of love requires a self-giving, a pouring out of oneself to the other; in the case of God, this involves the reciprocal and mutual self-giving of the three persons to each other. Moltmann concludes that only persons are capable of being at one with one another; modes of being or modes of subjectivity cannot be at one with each other. So the unity of God is based on the "unitedness" or the "at-oneness" of the three divine persons; there is no need to postulate the unity of the divine substance. The persons are united in their fellowship as Father, Son, and Holy Spirit; personhood involves the unity with one another and in one other. Moltmann says, "the concept of person must therefore in itself contain the concept of unitedness of at-oneness, just as, conversely, the concept of God's at-oneness must in itself contain the concept of all three Persons."[23]

20. Ibid., 353.
21. Macchia, *Justified in the Spirit*, 353.
22. Moltmann, *The Trinity and the Kingdom*, 149–50.
23. Ibid., 150.

Finally returning back to our original subject of personhood, Macchia remarks concerning Moltmann that "personhood is to be defined as the self-giving to the other and the reception of the other in the freedom and justice of divine love, a mutual sharing of life."[24] For Gunton, personhood is grounded in relations; but for Macchia, personhood is grounded in the self-differentiation, the giving and receiving, the distinct otherness within the Trinity that is brought into unity by divine love. The difference between the two theologians is quite negligible; it is the experience of the other—that is, the triune God—which shaped Macchia's conception of personhood.

Divine love for Macchia is a communal event that must include the Holy Spirit as the *person* involved in the love, instead of merely the outcome or relationship of love itself. In other words, God is love not because of the reciprocal love between the Father and the Son, but because of the union of the three persons in love. Macchia stresses the role of the Holy Spirit in the phrase "God is love" without diminishing the love that the Father has for the Son. Macchia explains,

> central to the Trinitarian structure of the story of Jesus is the Father's loving bestowal of the Spirit lavishly ('without limit,' John 3:34) on Jesus at his baptism as the sign of divine love and favor and to declare Christ's sonship (Matt. 3:17), an anointing that begins at Christ's conception (Luke 1:35), is found at his crucifixion (Heb. 9:14), and culminates in his resurrection (Rom. 1:4).[25]

It is not just the love between the Father and Son as an abstract psychological activity between them that describes God's being, but love in its concrete form that pours out the Holy Spirit upon the Son. The Father "baptizes" the Son with the Holy Spirit; the Son returns the love of the Father by "baptizing" the Father with the Holy Spirit. "Baptizing" is a metaphor for the action of love between the Father and Son in the person of the Holy Spirit. This divine action of love, which culminates in the Son being baptized with the Spirit and becoming the one who gives the Spirit, is the same action which God displays as love for his creation. The Spirit is the bond of love because the Father pours out the Spirit on his Son, and through his Son, on creation. In agreement with Gunton, Macchia says that "we need to exercise caution here so that we do not de-personalize the Spirit by eliminating the Spirit's participation as person in the *koinonia* of Father and Son, relating to them in ways appropriate to the Spirit."[26] Elsewhere, Macchia adds "as we will

24. Macchia, *Justified in the Spirit*, 301.
25. Macchia, *Baptized in the Spirit*, 118.
26. Macchia, *Justified in the Spirit*, 302.

note, however, this notion of Spirit as bond of love must be defined so as to enhance the sense of mutual dependence and reciprocity between the Spirit and both the Son and the Father so that the Spirit is not stripped of personhood."[27] The Spirit is not the "love" itself between the Father and the Son, but "the Spirit adds excess and superfluity to the love and deity of the Father and the Son in their bond of love, thus opening this love to the radically other . . . as well as to the eschatological . . . expanse of love's reach."[28] In this way, the Spirit is the third person of the Godhead who opens God's communion and mutual indwelling beyond God's self to the other; the Father-Son relationship moves to the other, the Holy Spirit, who in turn opens communion to the many of creation. So that "through the Spirit, God becomes the Spirit baptizer, the one who opens the mutual love and indwelling of Godhead to all flesh."[29] The experience of God's love is located in the presence of the Holy Spirit when creation, especially the Church of Christ, is baptized with the Holy Spirit.

So the Pentecostal experience of Spirit baptism is central to Macchia's vision of revelation, that is where we meet God: "within a proper Trinitarian soteriology, there is no election, incarnation, atonement, or resurrection without Pentecost."[30] For "all flesh is to be justified by the Spirit and in the Son through Spirit baptism and participation in the just *koinonia* of God."[31] In order to recover Augustine's analogy of the Holy Spirit as the "bond of love," thereby maintaining that the Holy Spirit is essential for God to be love, Macchia appropriates Athanasius as a corrective to Augustine's psychological analogy. In his *Defense of the Nicene Definition*, Athanasius argues that the Arians, by denying the eternal nature of the Son, eliminated the possibility of the Father's eternal existence as the Fountain of the Son. Athanasius bases his argument on the Arians' premise that there was a time when the Son was not. So in Athanasius' estimation, the Arians are claiming the Son was *created*—that is, had a beginning—from nothing. Therefore, the Father as the Fountain is not the eternal source of the Son. In response, Athanasius says that the Arians have reduced the Fountain to a pool because it is not really the eternal source of anything—there is nothing eternally existing except the pool: a fountain is not a fountain if it is not producing anything.[32]

27. Macchia, *Baptized in the Spirit*, 118.
28. Macchia, *Justified in the Spirit*, 302.
29. Ibid.
30. Ibid.
31. Ibid.
32. Athanasius concludes his rhetorical tirade against the Arians by asking, "till they have the daring to say, 'The Son came of nothing;' whence it will follow that there is no longer a Fountain, but a sort of pool, as if receiving water from without, and

Macchia appropriates Athanasius at this point, but stretches his metaphor to include the Holy Spirit. Athanasius' argument is that the Father is not the eternal source if there is not an eternal Son for him to be the source of. Macchia's doctrine of God leads him to attribute the same logic to the Holy Spirit—the Father is not the source if the Holy Spirit is not an ontological part of the Godhead. Macchia says,

> in fact, we can qualify Athanasius's statement to say that, without the Spirit, the Father would still not be a fountain but a kind of pool, a deep and circulating pool of love enjoyed with the Son, to be sure, but a pool nonetheless. But the Spirit makes the Father a fountain and the Son a river, both leading to the eternal ocean of the many in God. Incarnation is possible and is not static.[33]

Athanasius defined the Fountain as the Father eternally begetting the Son, so that without eternally begetting the Son, the Father is a mere pool. By changing the scope of Athanasius' analogy to include the Holy Spirit, the Father is the Fountain because he is eternally the source of the Son and the Spirit. Macchia's construal of the analogy is still more nuanced, for the Spirit creates the *koinonia* that the Father and the Son generate. Without the Spirit as the "bond of love" creating the triune *koinonia*, the Father and the Son are only participating in a "deep circulating pool" of reciprocal love. The Spirit provides the outward movement towards the other that establishes the divine *koinonia* of love, which established God as a Fountain of dynamic love—God's *being* is an outward expression of love. This outward expression of God's love is manifested in our experience of God's grace. For Macchia this is so because we have experienced the Father's election through Spirit baptism; the Father elects the Son to become the Spirit baptizer, and the Spirit completes the Father's will as the source of our election. Macchia is not overly concerned with relations of origins,[34] for "the issue is the interdependence of the persons of the Trinity in the fulfillment of divine love and of redemptive history."[35] Again, Macchia's focus is on revelation as an event in the economic activity of God, as experienced through Spirit baptism. In other words, the place to begin a proper doctrine of God is with the presence of the Spirit, who was poured out by Christ by the will

---

usurping the name of Fountain" (Athanasius of Alexandria, *De Decretis or Defence of the Nicene Definition* 15 [NPNF² 4:160]).

33. Macchia, *Justified in the Spirit*, 303.

34. Macchia states that if pressed, he would hold to the view that the Spirit proceeds from the Father *through* the Son (ibid., 305).

35. Ibid., 303.

of the Father. In this way, the immanent is the economic but only because of Spirit baptism—that divine action by which God reaches out to the other. Macchia says that "the immanent Trinity is the economic Trinity (to use Rahner's axiom) but mainly because of the metaphor of Spirit baptism as descriptive of both the interdependent dynamism of divine love within God and from God in redemptive history."[36] God's purpose for Creation is for it to be God's dwelling place; that is, for God to indwell Creation through the presence of his Holy Spirit.

Therefore, Macchia's doctrine of God is driven by his Pentecostal expression of Spirit baptism as a root metaphor; it is the presence of the Spirit where God in Christ is mediated and presented to the believer. Spirit baptism encompasses all categories of theology so that even in the event of revelation, it has to be given due weight. The doctrine of God is construed not as an intellectual exercise, or as a means to overcome philosophical disciplines that have dominated since the Enlightenment—God is understood and defined within the experience of his economy of salvation. The question of "what does it look like if the Holy Spirit saves us" is partially answered in the formulation of the doctrine of God that begins with Spirit baptism, and also understands Jesus as the Spirit baptizer who is the gift of the Father to his creation. From Spirit baptism God is comprehended as the Father who is the source of the Son; as the Son who is anointed by the Spirit to become the Spirit baptizer. This way, in the *eschaton*, creation will become the dwelling place of Father, Son, and Spirit. God as the triune God of salvation who redeems in the economic action within our history. God is the Father who saves; the Son who saves; and the Holy Spirit who saves—salvation culminates in the presence of the Spirit in creation, when it is baptized with the full presence of God. Until the end, Spirit baptism is a downpayment of God's presence in the here and now as a concrete experience of God's love—for the individual and the community—that is awaiting completion in the end.

---

36. Ibid., 305.

Conclusion

Now that we have come to the end of this thesis, we have discovered two different approaches to Pneumatology in the persons of Colin Gunton and Frank Macchia. We did not attempt to create an amalgam of the two approaches, neither did we attempt to prioritize one over the other. Rather, we explored two approaches to Pneumatology, in a critical and sympathetic manner, while offering a systematic appraisal of their respective strengths and weaknesses. As outlined at the outset, we discussed their projects using a chiastic structure in order to emphasize that the church is where their respective projects—of construing the Holy Spirit as One who brings about communion—reaches its apex. Even though both theologians draw their insights from the Protestant tradition, they both developed their pneumatologies on the basis of divergent epistemological beginnings. For Gunton, it is the personal mediated revelation from God that is the logical starting point of our theological knowing; including our understanding of the Holy Spirit. For Macchia, it is the *experience* of God, as revealed in scripture, that is the starting point developing theological content. In other words, Gunton begins with theological revelation and Macchia begins with the experience of salvation. Hence, for Gunton, the term "communion" expresses his commitment to an onto-relational theology because God has revealed himself in a triune manner. Whereas for Macchia, the term *"koinonia"* expresses a Pentecostal commitment that stresses the experience of salvation in the *koinonia* of the church—a salvation which is experienced in the Son, by the Spirit, to the glory of the Father. In both accounts, we explored how the Holy Spirit is essential in developing an accurate understanding of all theological categories, with an emphasis on God, Pneumatology, Christology, and Ecclesiology.

The Doctrine of God: The Triune Community

Our examination of Gunton and Macchia led to the conclusion that the doctrine of the Trinity is not an afterthought to theology, it is that which begins and ends theology. The doctrine of God must have priority in a theological project because God has revealed himself epistemologically and soteriologically. As Christian theologians, both authors have stressed that God cannot be thought of axiomatically and then scripture adapted to align with prior metaphysical conceptions of the divine. As Christians, we come to know God in our lives and in the scriptures as a triune being. William Placher states that "we do not know an abstract God first and then have to attach this Trinitarian talk, but, from the start, we encounter God in Jesus Christ, in the one he called Father, in the Holy Spirit."[1] This sentiment aligns well with the theological underpinnings of the doctrine of God for our theologians. Even though they have distinct accents—revelation and experiential—they are in agreement that our discussion of God and his relation to creation must begin with a recognition of his self-revelation as Triune. The implications of beginning with the Triune God has significant implications. First, God is allowed to reveal himself as an independent agent and not as an object of our creaturely inquiry. Second, the Scriptures—including propositions and narratives—become the chief source and basis of which we define the attributes of God and not *a priori* philosophical commitments and assumptions. This way, the doctrine of God determines and shapes our investigative methods, our definitions and limits concerning our understanding of who God is.

One of the pressing issues in these two theologies is the relation of theological form and material content. After examining their respective doctrines of God, it seems safe to conclude that they have expressed a formal doctrine of God without giving much weight to the material content. The doctrine of God serves as the formal principle for the other theological *loci*; as a result, the doctrine of God also shapes the form of Pneumatology, Christology, Ecclesiology, Soteriology, etc. Revelation is the formal principle which determines *how* we think about God, but not necessarily *what* we think about God. Revelation determines that our discussions must begin with God's self-disclosure as a Triune being, a being-in-communion. All other theological *loci* develop around the formal principle that God has revealed himself in a tri-personal manner, so that relationality becomes a central organizing tenet in theology. We do not find much attention given to defining attributes such as simplicity, impassibility, or omnipotence in light

---

1. Placher, "The Triune God," 104.

of revelation within and from God's acts. This only becomes problematic if one holds to an Aristotelian substance metaphysics position. It must be admitted that even though our theologians are not committed to traditional metaphysics, at times they still use terms like substance, attributes, subject and predicate to define God, without fully clarifying how this comports with their strongly relational view of reality. That said, by framing their doctrine of God as a formal principle, our theologians have established the authoritative source for knowing God: God is the one speaking for himself in his self-revelation. The question of what is revelation is addressed by Gunton, and only hinted at by Macchia, but what is important is that it is God's revealing—a personal revealing from a subject to another. Regarding God's revelation as triune, Gunton says that,

> This does not mean that we have a private view into the being of God, but that the general characteristics of God's eternal being, as persons in relation, communion, may be known from what he has done and does in the actions that we call the economy of creation and salvation.[2]

Revelation serves as the theological means to develop a doctrine of God as that which is determined by the object under investigation. This way, the doctrine of God is the theological rubric—the formal principle—for developing the material content of all remaining Christian theological categories.

Revelation drives both Gunton and Macchia, albeit differently, in that it determines the shape of theology both epistemically and experientially. Placher says, that "if the triune way in which we know God does not disclose the triune way in which God really is, then God has not revealed God's own self, and a hidden God remains unknown behind the revealed God."[3] As theologians influenced by Barth, it is not surprising that revelation is pitted against *a priori* conceptions of God which are derived from either speculation or natural theology. This means that many of the attributes of God must be reconsidered in light of revelation and the experience of God's economic work of redemption. Even though our theologians do not provide exhaustive accounts of the attributes in relation to revelation, they do offer a few examples that allow us to extrapolate the material content of their method. In commenting on the attributes of God as formulated since the Scholastics (i.e., omnipotence, simplicity, etc.), Brunner says that "all these 'ways' are possibilities of knowing 'God' in a human manner; they are natural, rational theology."[4] Brunner continues by stressing that,

---

2. Gunton, *The One, the Three, and the Many*, 230.
3. Placher, "The Triune God," 90–91
4. Brunner, *The Christian Doctrine of God*, 246.

all this has nothing to do with the Christian Idea of God, and with the way in faith, on the basis of the divine self-revelation concerning God, knows of His Nature and His Attributes. All this is rational metaphysics, it is not Christian theology; it is *theologia naturalis*, not *theologia revelata*.[5]

Emil Brunner expresses our theologians' view of God's self-revelation. The doctrine of God establishes that God's revelation as Triune has priority in theology, which includes the order of knowing and presentation. We only know God because God has revealed himself as three concrete divine persons, albeit in a perfect unity as one divine being. The point being that abstract ideas of threeness, oneness, perfect being, and other concepts of being should not initiate and/or determine our understanding of God. Metaphysical concepts can assist us in understanding God, but only after we have reviewed the revelation of God in Jesus Christ. As Pannenberg says,

> to find a basis for the doctrine of the Trinity we must begin with the way in which Father, Son, and Spirit come on the scene and relate to one another in the event of revelation. Here lies the material justification for the demand that the doctrine of the Trinity must be based on the biblical witness to revelation or on the economy of salvation. On this approach there is no material reason to append the doctrine of the Trinity to that of God's essence and attributes.[6]

Pannenberg asserts that in order to know God as triune, we must either turn to the biblical witness or the economy of salvation. Our two theologians have met Pannenberg's requirements, for Gunton stresses personal mediated revelation, and Macchia stresses the soteriological accent of theology. Revelation and salvation are both actions by God which are grounded in his eternal divine free will; which theologically speaking is grace. Beginning with speculative ideas about the divine or ultimate source of being is to work outside of the concreteness of grace. Our theologians are attempting to integrate the doctrines of election, grace, and God's divine decrees by beginning with God's self-revelation and economic acts of redemption. God freely elects to reveal himself as an act that is fully located in God's divine will; an action that is completely contained and originates within the divine essence.

For our theologians, since God's self-revelation is a triune revelation which begins with the three persons, it is no longer viable to assume that

5. Ibid.
6. Pannenberg, *Systematic Theology*, 1:299.

the Old Testament reveals the singleness of God, and the New Testament reveals the threeness of God. The Christian theologian must begin with what Jesus Christ has revealed, that he is the Son of the Father, and that both are in an inseparable relationship with the Holy Spirit. This way, the Old Testament reveals the supremacy, sovereignty, uniqueness and *the only* God; whereas the New Testament reveals the threeness nature of this God. A social view of the Trinity is necessary, albeit, one that does not venture too closely to a tritheistic view of God. The problem is that there is no consensus to what constitutes a social model of the Trinity. Gunton does not like the term because of the problem with three centers of consciousness which leads to a tritheistic view; and Macchia's theology does not allow for any type of tritheistic or modalist view. It is interesting that our theologians do not identify themselves as social Trinitarians, but their approaches clearly follow some aspects of a social model. Macchia does say that "I am open to the social analogy of the Trinity, which means I am critical of Augustine's psychological model of the Trinity. Yet I also cherish Augustine's notion of the Spirit as the bond of love between the Father and the Son."[7] McCall and Rea explain that "neither the defenders of nor the detractors from Social Trinitarianism (ST) have been especially clear about the core tenets of their view."[8] According to McCall and Rea, the core tenets of a social model of the Trinity includes the idea of one essence or nature, but not the same substance; each divine person is in full possession of the divine nature, while in a particular relation R to one another. At this point, they offer four types of relation R, but for our purposes, this definition is most appropriate: "being necessarily mutually interdependent, so that no divine person can possibly exist apart from the other divine persons."[9] Based on this definition, our theologians are basically Social Trinitarians. The question is: do they avoid the problems associated with a social model which "Latin Trinitarians" find difficult to accept?

For Gunton, the doctrines of *perichoresis* and the monarchy of the Father prevent his model of the Trinity from moving into a social model of those like Moltmann or Swinburne. Gunton says that his transcendentals of *perichoresis* and substantiality suggests a sociality in the doctrine of the Trinity. But, he further states "that is not the same as what has come to be called a social theory of the Trinity, with its suggestions of three almost independent deities."[10] For Gunton, there is one divine source of the

---

7. Macchia, "Pinnock's Pneumatology," 172.
8. McCall and Rea, *Philosophical and Theological Essays*, 2.
9. Ibid., 3.
10. Gunton, *The One, the Three, and the Many*, 214.

divine substance, and that is in the *person* of God the Father. Gunton is more concerned that God's nature is grounded in the *persons* of the Father, Son, and Spirit, instead of perceiving the divine substance as the basis of the Godhead. Since substance is to be found in particularity—meaning those sets of relations which constitutes personhood—then personhood becomes necessary for establishing substance. As we saw earlier, this is a logical concept—substance and personhood are reciprocal concurrent realities. Gunton can thus begin with the three while maintaining that there is only one divine nature or essence because it is grounded in the person of the Father. *Perichoresis* means that the three persons are distinct, yet they exist in an interdependent relation with each other. Each person receives their personhood and personal subsistence in full relation with the other two. This way, the divine persons constitute the Godhead, maintaining the unity, while each subsists in the one divine essence. On the other hand, Macchia also holds to a monarchy of the Father, but it is derived from the action of the Son and the Holy Spirit. Spirit baptism is an action that is a gift from the Father through the Son, one that culminates in the Spirit establishing a "bond of love" between them. What this means is that the Father's monarchy is established when the divine action of Spirit baptism is completed by the Holy Spirit. In other words, the Father's monarchy is real, but is only a monarchy because of the presence and work of the Son and the Spirit. This affords Macchia room to begin with the three without requiring three centers of consciousness or being. Our theologians are social Trinitarians, whether they admit it or not, but they have established limits that avoid the pitfalls of tritheism. It seems permissible to conclude that Gunton and Macchia have opened the way for a social model that allows for an engagement with classical Trinitarian views, wherein God's unity is derived from the three persons without lapsing into analogies drawn from our creaturely existence. In other words, for our theologians, there is simply one divine nature, grounded in the person of the Father as the source, and three divine persons who *are* the one divine essence. To state things negatively, without the three persons, there is no divine substance and without the divine substance, there are not three persons.[11] Therefore, the doctrine of God is the

11. McCall and Rea explain, "Perhaps the core tenets of ST might be helpfully summarized as follows: (ST1) The Father, the Son, and the Holy Spirit are 'of one essence,' but are not numerically the same substance. Rather, the divine persons are consubstantial only in the sense that they share the divine nature in common. Furthermore, this sharing of a common nature can be understood in a fairly straightforward sense via the 'social analogy' in which Peter, James, and John share human nature. (ST2) Properly understood, the central claim of monotheism that there is but one God is to be understood as the claim that there is one divine nature—not as the claim that there is exactly one divine substance. (ST3) The divine persons must each be in full possession

formal principle that directs the material content for Pneumatology, Christology, and Ecclesiology.

Pneumatology: Eschatological Perfector of Communion

For our theologians, Pneumatology provides additional material content to their theological projects, while also solidifying the form of their respective approaches. The doctrine of the Holy Spirit receives its formal content from the idea of necessity. That is, the Holy Spirit must be conceived as a necessary divine person in order for God to be the God of revelation. The tradition established the personhood of the Holy Spirit, but it did so as a result of the *homoousia* between the Father and the Son. Our theologians have established that a stronger account of the personhood of the Holy Spirit is necessary in order to fully grasp God's nature and work in the redemption of his creation. Pannenberg says that "theology has often neglected the relation between the soteriological operations of the Spirit in believers and his activity both as the Creator of all life and also in its eschatological new creation and consummation."[12] Formally speaking, our theologians have devised schemes which rely on the eternal *taxis* of the divine nature in such a way that all three persons have a logical priority in order for God to be God. As we will see, our theologians created a Pneumatology that is based in the revelation of God as Triune.

To begin with, neither theologian is concerned to explain or defend the personhood of the Holy Spirit by using scriptural proof texts to demonstrate that certain pronouns or personal acts of will distinguish the Spirit from the Father and the Son. The personhood of the Holy Spirit is predicated on the idea that God is Triune: the Holy Spirit is conceived as the third person who constitutes the divine communion. No longer should theology be preoccupied with explaining the eternal generation of the Son and how that differs from the eternal procession of the Holy Spirit. Since the Trinity is an eternal divine communion that has been revealed to have a

---

of the divine nature and in some particular relation R to one another for Trinitarianism to count as monotheism" (McCall and Rea, *Philosophical and Theological Essays*, 3). It seems to me that if by "substance" they are referring to "hypostasis," then even classical proponents would agree with this statement. But if by "substance" they are referring to the Aristotelian understanding, then Gunton and Macchia would not hold to this model, because this would be equivalent to three divine independent persons. So again, a rethinking of what it means to be a social Trinitarian must be considered for future discussions of a social model.

12. Pannenberg, *Systematic Theology*, 3:2.

divine order, that order should be expressed relationally instead of substantively. This way, the Holy Spirit is the divine person who is necessary for the perfection of the divine nature, the personhood of the Father and the Son, and the completion of the divine communion. What is revealed is that the eternal generation and procession is based on divine love, and not an impersonal divine nature. Moltmann says that "the Holy Spirit has a wholly unique personhood, not only in the form which it is experienced, but also in its relationships to the Father and the Son."[13] Gunton exemplifies this in his assertion that the Holy Spirit is the person who perfects the love between the Father and the Son. Macchia on the other hand, expresses this sentiment when he uses the metaphor "Spirit baptism" to differentiate the Spirit's role as the gift that the Father gives to the Son, and as the gift that the Son returns to the Father as a response. Both theologians are attempting to expand Augustine's analogy of "bond of love" so that the unique personhood of the Holy Spirit is expressed in fuller terms.

The result is that the Holy Spirit cannot be conceived in a way that endorses a double procession. The Holy Spirit as the one who seals the bond between the Father and the Son proceeds from the Father as the source of the Godhead, and is also "sent" from the Son as a response to the Father's original sending. For our theologians, the point is that instead of relying on language of causality, which results in a subordination of the Son and the Holy Spirit, the three persons must be thought of as eternally existing in some type of eternal relationship. This way, the *filioque* debate is considered a mistake; our theologians are in agreement with the East on this point. The one problem with this approach is that the scriptures indicate some type of functional subordination in the acts of the three divine persons. The Father sends the Son and he sends the Holy Spirit in the name of the Son. Elsewhere, Jesus himself claims that he will send the Holy Spirit. Jesus also claims that the Holy Spirit will only speak on behalf of the Son (cf. John 15:26; 16:13), and testify concerning him. Both theologians acknowledge the self-effacing Spirit, but their schemes do not stress enough the functional subordination of the Son and the Spirit. It is my contention that the subordination in scripture is an expression of the divine *taxis* within the Godhead; it is an order of the divine operation, not of the divine ontology. With that said, the point is that there is a relational equality between the divine persons that requires the equal personhood and relational status of the Holy Spirit. This gives both theologians a concrete footing to conceive of the Holy Spirit as a necessary agent who completes the Trinitarian relationships of the Father and the Son, and who also receives his own person through

13. Moltmann, *The Spirit of Life*, 12.

the relationships from the Father and the Son—a mutual interpenetration of relationships that orders and establishes the divine communion of God.

Our theologians are in agreement that the Holy Spirit should not be relegated to the areas of human subjectivity, such as, illumination and sanctification. For Gunton, the Spirit is the agent of eschatological perfecting of communion, a communion which begins by reconciliation with God and then with other human beings. This way, sanctification is a work of God, which culminates in the divine order with the work of the Holy Spirit. Macchia defines sanctification through the lens of Spirit baptism by expanding it along a soteriological trajectory. The Holy Spirit is preparing creation to become the dwelling of God, which is when Spirit baptism will be finally fulfilled. Proleptically speaking, the Holy Spirit is experienced as the gift of the Father to creation; for the presence of the Holy Spirit is where the full presence of God in and through Jesus Christ finds its fullest expression. The gifts of the Holy Spirit are not merely personal endowments for purposes of witness or individual self-improvement; they become a sanctifying work within creation. Sanctification is the work of the Holy Spirit, but it is not limited to individual moral improvement, but it includes an aspect of justification. Justification is completed when the presence of the Spirit is felt not only in the inner life of the believer, but when the entire created order is in communion with God and each other. The Holy Spirit sanctifies creation—including the individual believer and the church—by bringing it into a proper relationship with God: this is the essence of justification. On the other hand, neither theologian gives much room to discussion of the gifts or the fruits of the Spirit. Our theologians have developed a formal content of Pneumatology so that future generations can give proper material content to the use of the gifts and the fruits of the Spirit. If the Holy Spirit is the agent who perfects love, and in a sense, divine communion, then the gifts and fruits of the Spirit should promote and create a divinely intended and ordered communion.

Ted Peters explains that "the work of the Holy Spirit is the work of God personally in each one of our lives through the theological virtues of faith, hope, and love."[14] As noted, our theologians do not devote much time to the gifts or fruits of the Spirit in respect to the lives of the believers. Macchia does accent the experiential nature of Spirit baptism as a means to move the individual towards justification and sanctification through personal experiences of God's presence. But like Gunton, Macchia is concerned with the formal role of Pneumatology, so that when the Spirit is discussed it is within the framework of God's activity of creation, redemption, and the final con-

---

14. Peters, *God—the World's Future*, 249.

summation. Instead of focusing on the personal effects of the Holy Spirit within the lives of believers, the focus is on the work of the Holy Spirit *in all of* God's activities: the external works of God are indivisible. This means that our discussion of God is not complete until we locate the presence of the Holy Spirit in all theological *loci*, and not simply sanctification. So when the believer experiences a special gifting from the Holy Spirit, it must be thought of as a special gifting from the Father in Jesus Christ by the Holy Spirit. Calvin says that "moreover, as it is for the sake of his Son that God bestows the Holy Spirit upon us, and yet had deposited him in all his fulness with the Son . . . he is called at one time the Spirit of the Father, at another the Spirit of the Son."[15] Calvin understood that any gifts that are associated with the Holy Spirit must be conceived in light of the work of Christ and the will of the Father. This way, when Pneumatology is conceived in a Trinitarian framework, the individual gifts are not what defines the Holy Spirit, but the relation that the Spirit has with the Father and the Son. This explains why our theologians are reticent in exploring the gifts of the Spirit to individuals; the gifts are the eschatological work of the Spirit for the purposes of reconciling creation back to God. It is a work within the individual to bring about a participation in the divine communion of the Trinity so that the individual will be part of the new community.

Therefore, the Holy Spirit does work in the individual to perfect him/her towards their divine *telos* that is located in the loving will of the Father and the grace of Jesus Christ. As Macchia has expressed, the individual experience is not an isolated experience but one that takes place within the divine communion as expressed in the community. The experience of the Holy Spirit's presence and work must not be separated from the Son, whose presence is mediated in his Church by the Spirit. When the individual experiences reconciliation with God's creation in the renewed community, then the presence of the Holy Spirit is there conforming reality to God's divine purpose of *koinonia*. The Holy Spirit is not known only by his effects, but by his relation with the Father and the Son as witnessed in the economy. This way, the Holy Spirit is an active divine person who takes part in our salvation, and the redemption of all creation. The Holy Spirit's personhood and divinity is a fact not established by substantive metaphysics alone, but by his eternal divine relationship with the Father and the Son.

---

15. Calvin, *Institutes of the Christian Religion* 3.1.2.

Christology: From Spirit Christology to Trinitarian Christology

In continuation of established patterns, our theologians have defined Christology in such a way that the Holy Spirit becomes an essential agent in the event of the Incarnation. This stress on Pneumatology led them to develop a Trinitarian account of the Incarnation which goes beyond viewing it as a transaction that solely involves the obedience and humiliation of the eternal *Logos* and his assumption of a human nature. The Incarnation is viewed as an act of the *Triune* God such that theology must explicate the role of each divine person in relation to the Incarnation. With the resurgence of Trinitarian theology generally and Pneumatology in particular, at the minimum, Christology should move forward from a Logos-Christology. So we find that our theologians have each developed a formal Spirit Christology, which materially is a Trinitarian Christology.

Formally speaking, our theologians made use of the Chalcedon definition as a regulatory device providing the normative principle when discussing Jesus Christ. Sarah Coakley observes "that a 'regulatory' reading of Chalcedon's terms is correct so long as we understand (*a*) that the terms themselves are not 'defined' in a precise way, and (*b*) that this approach in no way implies lack of ontological commitments."[16] Gunton and Macchia both follow the regulatory scheme of Chalcedon, both have created a type of Spirit Christology, which is faithful to Chalcedon without denying the ontological commitments underlying the propositions behind the creed. Since Gunton's model is more radical than Macchia's on this score, I will use his version to further elucidate this point.

As stated earlier, Gunton basically identifies the divine nature of the Incarnation with the Holy Spirit, while claiming that it is the Son who is incarnate because he provides the *hypostasis* for the human nature. This move allows him to avoid the charge of creating a model where the Spirit is perceived as becoming incarnate. One of the ontological commitments for Chalcedon is the pre-existence of the Son, which in turn assumes the pre-existence of God as Triune. Gunton, by identifying the divine nature with the Holy Spirit, grounds the Incarnation in the pre-existing and eternal Trinity. The Holy Spirit is not simply Jesus' God-consciousness come to life, but actually the pre-existing Holy Spirit who is completing the pre-existing Father's will to send his pre-existing Son to earth. Whether or not one agrees with Gunton's adoption of Edward Irving's Christological model, Gunton has established that the Holy Spirit must have a more prominent

---

16. Coakley, "What Does Chalcedon Solve and What Does It Not?," 160.

role in the Incarnation than simply as a momentary source of inspiration or empowerment.

Our theologians argue that Spirit Christology cannot imply that Jesus' human nature is inspired or empowered by the Holy Spirit in such a way that the Son has little or nothing to do except maintain the union. Also, any Spirit Christology which resembles Lampe's model is also to be rejected. Gunton was further motivated to move beyond Owen because of Owen's belief that the Holy Spirit was the motive force behind Jesus' human nature: Owen's attempt is laudable, but falls short. Gunton defines the work of the Holy Spirit as liberating the human nature to be what God intended it to be. In other words, the Holy Spirit sanctifies Christ's human nature at conception so that the fallen nature can be redeemed through Christ's obedience to the Father. This way, the Son offers human nature to the Father through a life of obedience.

Where Chalcedon does not define "person" or "nature," Gunton's model defines "person" based on relations, and "nature" as an attribute that inheres in a "person." Oliver Crisp says that "one strategy for preserving the integrity of the hypostatic union . . . is to side with Anselm and claim that the Son assumes his human nature into his divine person, not the divine nature, which is shared with the other persons of the Trinity."[17] The problem is that Gunton has to accept some type of kenotic Christology because in his model it is the person of the Son who is incarnated and assumed human nature, while the Holy Spirit is the divine agent who empowers the human nature: the Son willingly forgoes aspects of his divine nature. Regardless, the advantage of his model is that the Holy Spirit is always with Jesus, sanctifying his fallen human nature so that it is always in a relationship with the Father, enabling it to willingly yield to the Father's will. The Holy Spirit is not the direct motive force on the human nature, but is the direct liberating force enabling the Son's human nature to have the capacity to be received by the Son, become the Son's human nature, and remain in a continual relationship with the Father. Macchia distinctively understands the Holy Spirit as a gift from the Father, who baptizes the human nature so that Jesus can become victorious to baptize creation with the Spirit. The point is that Christology must not be limited to a transaction between the Father and the Son, but it must take into account the immanent relations and economic action—especially in the narratives of Scripture—of the Holy Spirit in relation to the Father and the Son.

Our theologians have attempted to define Christology from within the economy of salvation. Materially speaking, God's omnipotence is defined as

17. Crisp, "Incarnation," 160–75.

the ability to become man, and yet remain God. So the Son's omnipotence for Gunton is seen in that he can assume human nature and provide the *hypostasis* without relying on his divine nature *as* the Son of God. Omnipotence is also seen in the Son's eternal relationship with the Holy Spirit as witnessed in the economy by liberation and communion. When the Holy Spirit is defined in the incarnation as liberating or sanctifying the human nature, then those special moments of empowerment are easier to understand. For example, at the baptism of Jesus, there is not necessarily a reception of the Holy Spirit by Jesus that did not exist from his conception. Rather, the Holy Spirit is establishing the eschatological communion of Christ with the rest of creation by establishing the means of communion with his future followers: Christ is the firstborn of his brothers and sisters of the new community. Using Macchia's metaphor, the Holy Spirit baptizes Christ so that Christ can baptize his followers into a new community. The point is that a Christological model must evince the relationship of the Son with the Spirit from conception, to Christ's life and death, to the resurrection, and the ascension.

This model is not without flaws. Gunton's model has created a situation where the person of the Son is seemingly separated from his own divine nature. It is difficult at times to understand how the divinity of the Son bears upon his own human nature. Even though Gunton would probably respond that Jesus' divine nature is displaying divine omnipotence by maintaining the *hypostatic* union by providing personhood to the *anhypostatic* nature. But it is still conceptually ambiguous to understand Jesus' existence as a single person without more account given to his divine nature. With that said, the goal for our theologians is to define the Incarnation as an event of the Father, Son, and Holy Spirit so that in Jesus "all the fullness of Deity dwells in bodily form."[18] The incarnation still focuses upon the second person because it is the second *person* who becomes the human *person* Jesus Christ, the Son of God. Yet, the full weight of the deity is to be found in the incarnation: the Father wills, the Son obeys, and the Holy Spirit sanctifies and perfects. The triune economy is an expression of the eternal Trinity.

By grounding the Incarnation in the immanent Trinity instead of the dual natures of Jesus, our theologians have decided to align themselves with post-Barthian theology. God creates and redeems because of his good pleasure—surely out of love—and not because of something outside of his existence. Stressing the role of the Holy Spirit in the Incarnation requires that a stress is also placed on the freedom of the Triune God. This way, it is God who elects to become incarnate based on his own divine communion. This places our theologians on the side of the supralapsarians, holding to the opinion

---

18. Col 2:9.

that God would have become incarnate regardless of the fall. For Gunton, the Holy Spirit liberates and perfects the divine communion; and for Macchia, the Holy Spirit is the One who establishes the eternal dance of love between the Father and Son. This same divine action of the Spirit is also witnessed in the Incarnation; for here the Holy Spirit liberates and perfects the Son's human nature, which is also baptized by the Spirit as an expression of their intimate relationship in the eternal Godhead. The personhood of the Spirit is radically secured in that he is the eternally existent divine person and not simply Jesus' superlative God-consciousness. So a stress on the Pneumatological element in Christology broadens theology to the point that the entire Trinity must be considered when discussing the Incarnation.

Materially, the stress on the Holy Spirit has an effect on the doctrine of atonement. Traditionally, atonement has typically been viewed as the work of the Son. Crisp explains that "we might say that 'the Incarnation' is shorthand for the whole work of Christ that obtains in eternity, unfolding in time from the first moment at which his human nature begins to exist to his death on the cross, and beyond that too, including his resurrection, ascension and current intercession for the saints at the right hand of God the Father."[19] This is still a true statement for our theologians, but they would add that the whole saving work of Christ includes his pouring out or giving the Holy Spirit to his community. It is also well known in Christian theology that the Father's love for his creation is the origin of the Son's mission to redeem, as well as the mission of the Holy Spirit. There must be a sense that the Holy Spirit is willfully participating in the atonement by giving himself to complete the Son's work of restoring the relationship between God and humanity. The traditional view of atonement places the stress on the inseparability of the divine nature; the essential unity of the divine substance. That is, since the divine nature is one in the strictest since; and since each person of the Trinity has the fullness of the divine nature; and since the Son is the second person of the Trinity; then when the Son saves, it is really God who saves. For our theologians, this is not sufficient. Gunton especially tends to stress the divine persons over the divine substance, so that it is not enough to rely on the divine substance, for the persons must also be located in the atoning work. By stressing the active role of the Holy Spirit in the atonement, all three divine persons are active in atoning for humanity's sins. Atonement takes place because the Son, whose human nature is uniquely sanctified, is victorious over sin and death. By that victory, which takes place in full cooperation with the Holy Spirit, the Son can promise us that same victory through the gift of the Father, that is, the gift

---

19. Crisp, *Revisioning Christology*, 112.

of the same Holy Spirit. It is only a real promise because Jesus Christ experienced the same human existence as us, yet without sin, because of his eternal relationship with the Father through the Holy Spirit. If Jesus relies on his own divine nature *qua* Son to accomplish obedience to the Father, then he has an eternal advantage that we cannot hope to possess. But as a human who fully relied upon the Holy Spirit as a gift from the Father, he promised to give us that same gift. The Father is vindicated because Jesus Christ's life of obedience to death on the cross demonstrates that God's creation is good. The problem was and is in the rebellious will of humanity. There is still room for penal substitution or satisfaction models, but they must account for the role of the Holy Spirit in atonement in order to satisfy fully the Christological requirements of our theologians.

Therefore, our theologians have expanded Christology so that the Holy Spirit is an explicit and essential element in the Incarnation event. In Jesus Christ, God has revealed himself in his full Triune communion as the God who redeems. The Triune God created the heavens and the earth; the same Triune God participated in the Incarnation; and in that event, the same Triune God atones for the sins of his people. I put forward that to call our theologians' Christology a Spirit Christology falls short. By stressing the role of the Holy Spirit, our theologians have completed the Holy Communion between the three divine persons in the economy and the immanent life of God. Chalcedon remains a valid rubric for Christology, but it should be supplemented with a more robust Trinitarian framework that explicitly recognizes the active work of the Holy Spirit—a Pneumatological Christology or even a Trinitarian Christology results.

Ecclesiology: The Koinonia of the Spirit

Neil Ormerod states that "no single theologian could hope to develop a completely systematic ecclesiology, if only because the Church, as a historical community, is not a static body and so continues to offer us new insights through the process of its own ongoing self-constitution."[20] This statement is applicable to our theologians: neither has developed a completely systematic account of ecclesiology, but they have offered us models that incorporate their Trinitarian and Pneumatological insights. Their respective insights serve to guide and reconstitute ecclesiology in order to incorporate the Pneumatological claims as presented in this paper. Our theologians are part of the recent surge in ecclesiological development

---

20. Ormerod, *Re-Visioning the Church*, 3.

from theologians such as Moltmann, Pannenberg, Küng, and Zizioulas.[21] What we will find is that our theologians have set the agenda for Ecclesiology that attempts to remain faithful to the edict of *ecclesia reformata et semper reformanda secundum verbum Dei* ("the church reformed, always in need of being reformed according to the Word of God.")[22] In order to accomplish this task, the attributes and marks of the Church are structured around the divine communion of the Trinity with an emphasis on the perfecting work of the Holy Spirit.

Our theologians have framed ecclesiology so that it is delimited by the other theological *loci* which ultimately reflects God's self-revelation as a communion of love. In a way, *communion* exists as an ontological reality prior to the church because it is located within God's divine triune life of love: the Church cannot exist apart from God's own *koinonia*. The structure of the church does not have logical priority and neither is the church the place where individuals find grace within a certain structure. *Koinonia* is a gift given by God the Father, through his Son, and then perfected by the Holy Spirit. The Church's very existence is based from the communion of God and exists as a communion given by the Triune God. The Church is not a collection of individuals who exist as justified individuals who only then assemble together periodically for worship. The Church is not the clergy who in turn extend grace to the laity for the purposes of justification. The Church is the concrete expression of God's economic activity expressed as a work of the Father, Son, and Holy Spirit. For Gunton, God has revealed himself through love; and for Macchia, God is experienced soteriologically as love from the Father, through the Son, by the Spirit. Ultimately, ecclesiology should begin with an accent of the constitution of the church prior to discerning of it attributes, marks, and issues of governance.

Our theologians are integrating ecclesiology into a wider theological scheme by closely associating God's relationship with humanity in the church. Timothy Ware says that "the Church as a whole is an icon of God the Trinity, reproducing on earth the mystery of unity in diversity."[23] The Holy Spirit is the one who perfects the divine communion; the one who perfected creation *ex nihilo* and is perfecting creation towards its divine *telos*; the one who perfected the Incarnation by creating and sustaining a body for the Son; and the one who perfects *koinonia*. So it follows that the Holy Spirit is the one who perfects the Father's call and the Son's institution of

---

21. See Moltmann, *The Church in the Power of the Spirit*; Pannenberg, *Systematic Theology*; Küng, *The Church*; Zizioulas, *Being as Communion*.

22. Migliore, *Faith Seeking Understanding*, 423.

23. Ware, *The Orthodox Church*, 240.

the Church by constituting the Church. Our theologians have determined that the Church is not merely a collection of like-minded individuals, but is something that is called out by the Triune God to be his servant. The Church is the body of Christ because of the divine action of the Holy Spirit that constitutes the Church by creating a community from the diversity of believers. The Reformers were concerned with issues of church governance and soteriology due to the overpowering authority of the clergy. Our theologians are not that concerned with church governance issues since a Church that is constituted by the Holy Spirit to be a communion-in-diversity should not place too much emphasis and authority in a select few—this would not be a community-in-diversity, but a community-in-the-few. In explaining Eastern Orthodox ecclesiology, Kärkkäinen, says that "the christological aspect guarantees stability while its pneumatological aspect gives the church a dynamic character."[24] The Spirit gave life to creation, and the same Spirit gives life to the Church. The work of the Son and the Spirit are inseparable in instituting, constituting, and sustaining the Church. Gunton's ontological commitments—based on the revelation of God as a divine communion—caused him to envisage God's redemption in relational terms so that the Church becomes a preview of the future restoration of community in creation. In a similar manner, Macchia's experiential commitments results in a vision of Spirit baptism as restoring the communion between God and his creation, which also creates a horizontal communion within creation. So the Church is a communion that is brought about by the Holy Spirit as a preview of the full communion that will take place at Christ's return.

By expressing the Pneumatological aspect of the Church, our theologians have also determined that particularity must be given equal weight in respect to the universal nature of the church. This means that a proper doctrine of the Church must take into account that the local church is *the* Church of Christ. The universal Church is also the church of Christ, but it does not have a logical priority over the local church. The Holy Spirit creates one Church—the local and universal. An ecclesiology which is faithful to the Pneumatological aspect will also include an ecumenical element. Our theologians have both expressed interests in the Ecumenical movement as an outworking of their unity-in-diversity motif. The Holy Spirit perfects the relationship of the distinct persons in God; he perfects the relationship between two distinct realities of God and creation; and he perfects the relationship between distinct persons in the community. This same action is also to be seen between distinct local churches. The Spirit must be conceived

---

24. Kärkkäinen, *Introduction to Ecclesiology*, 24.

as bringing the unity between distinct bodies while each body maintains their particular distinction.

Neither of our theologians addresses those issues that are unique to each body; those issues which may lead to disharmony. Issues such as the nature of the sacraments, and the clergy, disagreements over the *ordo salutis*, and liturgical practices are some of the roadblocks to unity which must be addressed. It seems that even though our theologians have not explicitly addressed these issues, there must be a drive by the churches towards a unity in Christ which is being mediated and brought about by the Holy Spirit: Ecclesiology must be closely associated to Pneumatology. The Church's unity is due to the Spirit's action of bringing individual members into a particular community to be that community as an expression of his particularizing action. The visible Church is the Church, and the invisible Church is simply the eschatological Church that God's Spirit is bringing about. For Gunton, the Spirit liberates the individual believer to freely join the new community; and for Macchia, the Spirit baptizes the individual believer so that he/she may enjoy the *koinonia* of the new community. The Protestant belief in the priesthood of all believers is a call to mutual service of the believers to each other. Luther says, "the fact that we are all priests and kings means that each of us Christians may go before God and intercede for the other. If I notice that you have no faith or a weak faith, I can ask God to give you a strong faith."[25] Also, Cyril Eastwood states that for Calvin "the believer is adopted by God into a believing community."[26] So for Calvin, the priesthood of believers in intimately related to Christ as our Mediator, and our union with him. What this means is that for Luther and Calvin, there was an element of community where the priesthood of the believer was to find its concrete expression. Our theologians are in harmony with the Reformers when they express that the Holy Spirit is creating a new community that is the local Church. The community is comprised of individuals in mutual relationships that is based on the unity found in Jesus Christ and the particularity that is given by the Holy Spirit.

What is evident is that our theologians derive their ecclesiology from the doctrine of God as a being-in-communion. This is of no surprise since both theologians were influenced by John Zizioulas. For example, the sacraments are not viewed as a debate between Luther and Zwingli to determine the location of the body of Christ. The sacraments, especially the Eucharist, serves to bring about the unity of the community. The sacraments serve as

---

25. George, *Theology of the Reformers*, 97.

26. Eastwood, *The Priesthood of All Believers; an Examination of the Doctrine from the Reformation to the Present Day*, 73.

an indication that this particular community is the church of Jesus Christ. The sacraments are bonded to faith, but they also serve the visible community. The visible community performs a visible and material act as a referent to the risen Christ for the purposes of associating this particular historical community with the historical Christ. Gunton says "that we have inherited a very individualistic conception of baptism as rather that which is performed on the individual to save him or her from an inherited stain or a hellish fate than that by which a person is brought into a new relation with God through the medium of the covenant community."[27] Macchia reacts against the sacraments as mediating grace by stating that "more of an emphasis on the charismata will open the sacraments up as wellsprings of a communal life that involve all the people of God as active participants."[28] What this means is that Ecclesiology is a reflection of the Trinity in that God has revealed himself as a Triune redeemer who redeems and creates trinitarily. So the sacraments reflect God's Triune action in that they incorporate the life of the community into the redeeming action of God. The sacraments do not mediate salvation to the individual, but the Spirit uses the sacraments as a means to bind the individual to Christ in and through the new community. The sacraments serve as a concrete expression pointing back to Christ, using concrete elements of creation in order to establish a concrete local community. The sacraments serve the Church that is constituted and liberated by the Spirit as a community that freely participates in the sacraments established by Christ. So the divine action, which is commensurate in establishing the Church, also gives the sacraments their effectiveness—the Holy Spirit is essential in all aspects of ecclesiology.

Finally, through the doctrine of the Church, we recognize the overall systematic approach of our theologians to construct a theology that gives due weight to the Holy Spirit. In doing so, they adumbrate a Pneumatology that is more formal than material. Even in Ecclesiology, the formal content suggests a proper Pneumatological aspect of Ecclesiology, so that future theologians can construct the material content in light of the Triune God. The doctrine of God, Pneumatology, and Christology express God's loving desire to have a relationship with us, and that we reciprocate the love with him and the rest of creation. So our theologians interpret Protestant ecclesiology through the lens of a Pneumatology that is based on a recovery of persons-in-communion, or particularity-in-community. This is the culmination of the Spirit's work to perfect creation towards its telos as the community that will be the dwelling place of God. The individual can at

---

27. Gunton, *Father, Son, and Holy Spirit*, 205.
28. Macchia, "Rediscovering the Church's Charismatic Structure," 29.

times get lost in this scheme when so much stress is laid on the community. But that is not the goal. The goal is to enhance the individual by recognition of their individuality which is truly expressed within a community: the otherness finds its ultimate expression in the face of an other. Therefore, Ecclesiology must be shaped by a Pneumatology that is defined as eschatologically perfecting the individual as a part of the reconciled community, which is also perfected as the people of the Triune God.

Bibliography

Achtner, Wolfgang. "Time, Eternity, and Trinity." *Neue Zeitschrift für systematische Theologie und Religionsphilosophie* 51, no. 3 (2009) 268-88.
Anderson, Allan. *An Introduction to Pentecostalism: Global Charismatic Christianity.* Cambridge: Cambridge University Press, 2004.
Aristotle. *Metaphysics.* Translated by Hugh Lawson-Tancred. Penguin Classics. London: Penguin, 1998.
Athanasius of Alexandria. *De Decretis or Defence of the Nicene Definition.* Translated by John Henry Newman and Archibald T. Robertson. In *A Select Library of the Nicene and Post-Nicene Fathers of the Christian Church,* edited by Philip Schaff and Henry Wace, 4:150-72. New York: Christian Literature, 1892.
———. *On the Incarnation of the Word.* Translated by Archibald T. Robertson. In *A Select Library of the Nicene and Post-Nicene Fathers of the Christian Church,* edited by Philip Schaff and Henry Wace, 4:36-67. New York: Christian Literature, 1892.
Augustine. *On the Free Choice of the Will, on Grace and Free Choice, and Other Writings.* Edited by Peter King. Cambridge Texts in the History of Philosophy. Cambridge: Cambridge University Press, 2010.
———. *The Trinity (De Trinitate).* Translated by Edmund Hill. Hyde Park, NY: New City, 1991.
Ayer, A. J. *Language, Truth and Logic.* London: Penguin, 1990.
Baillie, D. M. *God Was in Christ: An Essay on Incarnation and Atonement.* New York: Scribner's Sons, 1948.
Barth, Karl. *The Church Dogmatics.* 14 vols. Edited by Geoffrey W. Bromiley and Thomas F. Torrance. Translated by George Thomas Thomson and Harold Knight. Peabody, MA: Hendrickson, 2010.
———. *Protestant Theology in the Nineteenth Century: Its Background & History.* London: SCM, 1972.
Basil of Caesarea. *On the Holy Spirit.* Translated by Blomfield Jackson. In *A Select Library of the Nicene and Post-Nicene Fathers of the Christian Church,* edited by Philip Schaff and Henry Wace, 8:1-50. New York: Christian Literature, 1895.
Bavinck, Herman. *Reformed Dogmatics.* 4 vols. Edited by John Bolt. Translated by John Vriend. Grand Rapids: Baker Academic, 2004.
———. *Reformed Dogmatics: Abridged in One Volume.* Edited by John Bolt. Grand Rapids: Baker Academic, 2011.
Bender, Kimlyn J. *Karl Barth's Christological Ecclesiology.* Aldershot, UK. Ashgate, 2005.
Berkhof, Louis. *Systematic Theology.* London: Banner of Truth Trust, 1959.

Blocher, Henri. "Calvin's Theological Anthropology." Chap. 4 In *John Calvin and Evangelical Eheology: Legacy and Prospect*, edited by Sung Wook Chung, 66-84. Louisville: Paternoster, 2009.

Braaten, Carl E. "Classical Christology and Its Subsequent Criticism." In *Christian Dogmatics*, edited by Carl E. Braaten and Robert W. Jenson, 497-515. Philadelphia: Fortress, 1984.

Bruce, Alexander Balmain. *The Humiliation of Christ, in Its Physical, Ethical, and Official Aspects*. Cunningham Lectures. Edinburgh: T. & T. Clark, 1876.

Bruner, Frederick Dale. *A Theology of the Holy Spirit: The Pentecostal Experience and the New Testament Witness*. Grand Rapids: Eerdmans, 1970.

Brunner, Emil. *The Christian Doctrine of God*. Vol. 1 of *Dogmatics*. Translated by Olive Wyon. Philadelphia: Westminster, 1950.

———. *The Mediator: A Study of the Central Doctrine of the Christian Faith*. Philadelphia: Westminster, 1947.

Caird, G. B. *The Language and Imagery of the Bible*. London: Duckworth, 1980.

Calvin, Jean. *Institutes of the Christian Religion*. 4 vols. Translated by Henry Beveridge. Grand Rapids: Christian Ethereal Library, 1845.

Chan, Simon. "Mother Church: Toward a Pentecostal Ecclesiology." *PNEUMA The Journal of the Society for Pentecostal Studies* 22, no. 2 (2000) 177-208.

———. "Whither Pentecostalism?" In *Asian and Pentecostal: The Charismatic Face of Christianity in Asia*, edited by Allan Anderson and Edmond Tang, 550-75. Oxford: Regnum, 2005.

Childs, Brevard S. *Biblical Theology of the Old and New Testaments: Theological Reflection on the Christian Bible*. Minneapolis: Fortress, 1992.

Coakley, Sarah. "'Persons' in the 'Social' Doctrine of the Trinity: A Critique of Current Analytic Discussion." In *The Trinity: An Interdisciplinary Symposium on the Trinity*, edited by Stephen T. Davis, Daniel Kendall, and Gerald O'Collins, 123-44. Oxford: Oxford University Press, 1999.

———. "What Does Chalcedon Solve and What Does It Not? Some Reflections on the Status and Meaning of the Chalcedonian 'Definition.'" In *The Incarnation: An Interdisciplinary Symposium on the Incarnation of the Son of God*, edited by Stephen T. Davis, Daniel Kendall, and Gerald O'Collins, 143-64. Oxford: Oxford University Press, 2002.

Cobb, John B., Jr. "Alfred North Whitehead." In *Founders of Constructive Postmodern Philosophy: Peirce, James, Bergson, Whitehead, and Hartshorne*, edited by David Ray Griffin, 165-95. Albany: State University of New York Press, 1993.

Coffey, David. "The "Incarnation" of the Holy Spirit in Christ." *Theological Studies* 45, no. 3 (1984) 466-80.

Craig, William Lane. *Time and Eternity: Exploring God's Relationship to Time*. Wheaton, IL: Crossway, 2001.

Crisp, Oliver D. "Incarnation." In *The Oxford Handbook of Systematic Theology*, edited by J. B. Webster, Kathryn Tanner, and Iain R. Torrance, 160-75. Oxford: Oxford University Press, 2007.

———. "John Owen on Spirit Christology." *Journal of Reformed Theology* 5 (2011) 5-25.

———. "Problems with Perichoresis." *Tyndale Bulletin* 56, no. 1 (2005) 119-40.

———. *Revisioning Christology: Theology in the Reformed Tradition*. Farnham, UK: Ashgate, 2011.

Cullmann, Oscar. "Immortality of the Soul or Resurrection of the Dead?" In *Immortality and Resurrection: Four Essays by Oscar Cullman, Harry A. Wolfson, Werner Jaeger, and Henry J. Cadbury*, edited by Stendahl Krister, 9–53. New York: MacMillan, 1965.

Cumin, Paul. "The Taste of Cake: Relation and Otherness with Colin Gunton and the Strong Second Hand of God." In *The Theology of Colin Gunton*, edited by Lincoln Harvey, 65–85. London: T. & T. Clark, 2010.

Cupitt, Don. *Taking Leave of God*. London: Xpress Reprints, 1980.

Cyprian of Carthage. *On the Unity of the Church*. Translated by Robert Ernest Wallis. In *The Ante-Nicene Fathers*, edited by James Donaldson Alexander Roberts and A. Cleveland Coxe, 5:421–29. Buffalo: Christian Literature, 1886.

Dabney, D Lyle. "'Justified by the Spirit': Soteriological Reflections on the Resurrection." *International Journal of Systematic Theology* 3, no. 1 (2001) 46–68.

Dods, Marcus. *On the Incarnation of the Eternal Word*. London: R. B. Seeley and W. Burnside, 1831.

Dorries, David W. *Edward Irving's Incarnational Christology*. Fairfax, VA: Xulon, 2002.

Doyle, Robert C. *Eschatology and the Shape of Christian Belief*. Carlisle, UK: Paternoster, 1999.

Dulles, Avery. *The Catholicity of the Church*. Oxford: Oxford University Press, 1987.

Dunn, James D. G. *Christology in the Making: A New Testament Inquiry into the Origins of the Doctrine of the Incarnation*. London: SCM, 1980.

Eastwood, C. Cyril. *The Priesthood of All Believers; an Examination of the Doctrine from the Reformation to the Present Day*. Minneapolis: Augsburg, 1962.

Emery, Gilles. *The Trinitarian Theology of Saint Thomas Aquinas*. Oxford: Oxford University Press, 2007.

Ferguson, David. "Eschatology." In *The Cambridge Companion to Christian Doctrine*, edited by Colin E. Gunton, 226–44. Cambridge: Cambridge University Press, 1997.

Forsyth, Peter Taylor. *The Justification of God: Lectures for War-Time on a Christian Theodicy*. London: Duckworth, 1916.

Frankenberry, Nancy. "Hartshorne's Method in Metaphysic." In *The Philosophy of Charles Hartshorne*, edited by Lewis Edwin Hahn, 291–312. La Salle, IL: Open Court, 1991.

Fuchs, Lorelei F. "Communion Terminology in the Lutheran-Roman Catholic International Dialogue in Light of the Koinonia Language of the Canberra Statement." *Journal of Ecumenical Studies* 39, nos. 3–4 (2002) 248–75.

———. *Koinonia and the Quest for an Ecumenical Ecclesiology: From Foundations through Dialogue to Symbolic Competence for Communionality*. Grand Rapids: Eerdmans, 2008.

George, Timothy. *Theology of the Reformers*. Nashville: Broadman, 1988.

Gibson, James. *Locke's Theory of Knowledge and Its Historical Relations*. Cambridge: Cambridge University Press, 1968.

Green, Bradley G. *Colin Gunton and the Failure of Augustine: The Theology of Colin Gunton in Light of Augustine*. Eugene, OR: Pickwick, 2011.

———. "Colin Gunton and the Theological Origin of Modernigy." In *The Theology of Colin Gunton*, edited by Lincoln Harvey, 165–81. London: T. & T. Clark, 2010.

Green, Clifford J. *Karl Barth: Theologian of Freedom*. Making of Modern Theology. San Francisco: Collins, 1989.

Gunton, Colin E. *Act and Being: Towards a Theology of the Divine Attributes*. Grand Rapids: Eerdmans, 2002.

———. *The Actuality of Atonement: A Study of Metaphor, Rationality, and the Christian Tradition*. Edinburgh: T. & T. Clark, 1988.

———. *Becoming and Being: The Doctrine of God in Charles Hartshorne and Karl Barth*. London: SCM, 2001.

———. *A Brief Theology of Revelation*. Warfield Lectures. London: T. & T. Clark, 1995.

———. *Christ and Creation: The Didsbury Lectures*. Eugene, OR: Wipf & Stock, 1992.

———. "The Church on Earth: The Roots of Community." In *On Being the Church: Essays on the Christian Community*, edited by Colin E. Gunton and Daniel W. Hardy, 48–80. Edinburgh: T. & T. Clark, 1989.

———. "Election and Ecclesiology in the Post-Constantinian Church." *Scottish Journal of Theology* 53 (2003) 212–27.

———. *Enlightenment and Alienation: An Essay Towards a Trinitarian Theology*. Edinburgh: Eerdmans, 1985.

———. *Father, Son, and Holy Spirit: Essays toward a Fully Trinitarian Theology*. London: T. & T. Clark, 2003.

———. *The One, the Three, and the Many: God, Creation, and the Culture of Modernity*. Cambridge: Cambridge University Press, 1993.

———. *The Promise of Trinitarian Theology*. Edinburgh: T. & T. Clark, 1991.

———. *The Promise of Trinitarian Theology*. 2nd ed. London: T. & T. Clark, 2003.

———. *Revelation and Reason: Prolegomena to Systematic Theology*. T. & T. Clark Theology. London: T. & T. Clark, 2008.

———. *Theology through the Theologians: Selected Essays, 1972–1995*. London: T. & T. Clark, 1996.

———. "The Trinity in Modern Theology." In *Companion Encyclopedia of Theology*, edited by Peter Byrne and J. L. Houlden, 937–57. London: Routledge, 1995.

———. *The Triune Creator: A Historical and Systematic Study*. Edinburgh Studies in Constructive Theology. Grand Rapids: Eerdmans, 1998.

———. *Yesterday and Today: A Study of Continuities in Christology*. London: Darton, Longman & Todd, 1983.

Guthrie, W. K. C. *A History of Greek Philosophy*. Vol. 1, *The Earlier Presocractics and The Pythagoreans*. Cambridge: Cambridge University Press, 1962.

Hägglund, Bengt. *History of Theology*. St. Louis: Concordia, 1968.

Haight, Roger. "The Case for Spirit Chirstology." *Theological Studies* 53 (1992) 257–87.

———. "Logos Christology Today." In *From Logos to Christos: Essays in Christology in Honour of Joanne McWilliam*, edited by Kate Merriman, Ellen M. Leonard, and Joanne McWilliam, 91–111. Waterloo, OT: Wilfrid Laurier University Press, 2009.

Harnack, Adolf von. *History of Dogma*. Translated by Neil Buchanan. Vol. 2. Boston: Little, Brown, 1907.

———. *History of Dogma*. Translated by Neil Buchanan. Vol. 3. Boston: Little, Brown, 1901.

Harvey, Lincoln. "The *Double* Homoousion: Forming the Content of Gunton's Theology." In *The Theology of Colin Gunton*, edited by Lincoln Harvey, 86–99. London: T. & T. Clark, 2010.

Harvey, Lincoln, ed. *The Theology of Colin Gunton*. London: T. & T. Clark, 2010.

Havel, Václav. *Open Letters: Selected Writings, 1965–1990*. New York: Knopf 1991.

Heppe, Heinrich. *Reformed Dogmatics*. Edited by Ernst Bizer. Translated by G. T. Thomson. London: Wakeman Trust, 2002.
Heron, Alasdair I. C. *The Forgotten Trinity*. London: British Council of Churches, 1989.
Hill, William J. *The Three-Personed God: The Trinity as a Mystery of Salvation*. Washington, DC: Catholic University of America Press, 1988.
Hocken, Peter. "Theology of the Church." In *The New International Dictionary of Pentecostal and Charismatic Movements*, edited by Stanley M. Burgess, 544–51. Grand Rapids: Zondervan, 2002.
Höhne, David A. *Spirit and Sonship: Colin Gunton's Theology of Particularity and the Holy Spirit*. New Critical Thinking in Religion, Theology, and Biblical Studies. Farnham, UK: Ashgate, 2010.
Hollenweger, Walter J. *The Pentecostals*. London: SCM, 1976.
Hunsinger, George. "Jesus as the Lord of Time According to Karl Barth." *Zeitschrift für Dialektische Theologie* 4, Supplement (2010) 113–27.
Irenaeus of Lyons. *Irenaeus against Heresies*. In *The Ante-Nicene Fathers: Translations of the Writings of the Fathers Down to A.D. 325*, edited by Alexander Roberts, James Donaldson, and A. Cleveland Coxe, 1:315–525. Buffalo: Christian Literature, 1885.
Irving, Edward. *The Collected Writings of Edward Irving in Five Volumes*. Vol. 5. London: Strahan, 1865.
Jacobsen, Douglas G. *Thinking in the Spirit: Theologies of the Early Pentecostal Movement*. Bloomington: Indiana University Press, 2003.
Jenson, Robert W. "A Decision Tree of Colin Gunton's Thinking." In *The Theology of Colin Gunton*, edited by Lincoln Harvey, 8–16. London: T. & T. Clark, 2010.
———. *God after God: The God of the Past and the God of the Future, as Seen in the Work of Karl Barth*. Minneapolis: Fortress, 2010.
———. *Systematic Theology*. Vol. 2. Oxford: Oxford University Press, 1999.
———. *The Triune Identity: God According to the Gospel*. Philadelphia: Fortress, 1982.
Johnson, William Ernest. *Logic*. Vol. 1. Cambridge,: Cambridge University, 1921.
Jüngel, Eberhard. *God's Being Is in Becoming: The Trinitarian Being of God in the Theology of Karl Barth. A Paraphrase*. Translated by J. B. Webster. 2nd English ed. Edinburgh: T. & T. Clark, 2001.
Kariatlis, Philip. "Affirming Koinonia Ecclesiology: An Orthodox Perspective." *Phronema* 27, no. 1 (2012) 51–65.
Kärkkäinen, Veli-Matti. *Introduction to Ecclesiology: Ecumenical, Historical & Global Perspectives*. Downers Grove, IL: InterVarsity, 2002.
———. *Pneumatology: The Holy Spirit in Ecumenical, International, and Contextual Perspective*. Grand Rapids: Baker Academic, 2002.
———. *The Trinity: Global Perspectives*. 1st ed. Louisville: Westminster John Knox, 2007.
Kasper, Walter. *The God of Jesus Christ*. New York: Crossroad, 2005.
———. *Jesus the Christ*. New York: Paulist, 1977.
Kelly, J. N. D. *Early Christian Doctrines*. New York: Harper, 1960.
Kenny, Anthony. *A New History of Western Philosophy*. 4 vols. Oxford: Clarendon, 2004.
Knight, Henry H., III. "Reflections on Frank Macchia's Baptized in the Spirit." *Journal of Pentecostal Theology* 16, no. 2 (2008) 5–8.
Kotarbinska, Janina. "On Ostensive Definitions." *Philosophy of Science* 27, no. 1 (1960) 1–22.

Küng, Hans. *The Church*. Garden City, NY: Image, 1976.
Kuyper, Abraham. *The Work of the Holy Spirit*. Grand Rapids: Eerdmans, 1975.
Lampe, G. W. H. "The Holy Spirit and the Person of Christ." In *Christ, Faith and History: Cambridge Studies in Christology*, edited by S. W. Sykes and J. P. Clayton, 111-30. Cambridge: Cambridge University Press, 1972.
Letham, Robert. *The Holy Trinity: In Scripture, History, Theology, and Worship*. Phillipsburg, NJ: P & R, 2004.
Locke, John. *An Essay concerning Human Understanding*. 27th ed. London: Tegg and Son, 1836.
Lowe, E. J. "Metaphysics." In *The Routledge Companion to Twentieth-Century Philosophy*, edited by Dermot Moran, 438-68. London: Routledge, 2008.
Lyle, Randal C. "Social Trinitarianism as an Option for 21st Century Theology: A Systematic Analysis of Colin Gunton's Trinitarian Paradigm." PhD diss., Southwestern Baptist Theological Seminary, September 2003.
Macchia, Frank D. *Baptized in the Spirit: A Global Pentecostal Theology*. Grand Rapids: Zondervan, 2006.

———. "Baptized in the Spirit: Reflections in Response to My Reviewers." *Journal of Pentecostal Theology* 16 (2008) 14-20.

———. "Baptized in the Spirit: Toward a Global Theology of Spirit Baptism." In *The Spirit in the World: Emerging Pentecostal Theologies in Global Contexts*, edited by Veli-Matti Kärkkäinen, 3-20. Grand Rapids: Eerdmans, 2009.

———. "Justification and the Spirit: A Pentecostal Reflection on the Doctrine by Which the Church Stands or Falls." *Pneuma* 22, no. 1 (2000) 3-21.

———. "Justification by Faith: A Case of Hearing the One Gospel through Historically Dissimilar Traditions." In *The Bible as a Human Witness to Divine Revelation: Hearing the Word of God through Historically Dissimilar Traditions*, edited by Randall Heskett and Brian Irwin, 223-34. New York: T. & T. Clark, 2010.

———. "Justification through New Creation: The Holy Spirit and the Doctrine by Which the Church Stands or Falls." *Theology Today* 58, no. 2 (2001) 202-17.

———. *Justified in the Spirit: Creation, Redemption, and the Triune God*. Pentecostal Manifestos. Grand Rapids: Eerdmans, 2010.

———. "The Kingdom and the Power: Spirit Baptism in Pentecostal and Ecumenical Perspective." In *The Work of the Spirit: Pneumatology and Pentecostalism*, edited by Michael Welker, 109-25. Grand Rapids: Eerdmans, 2006.

———. "Pentecostal Theology." In *The New International Dictionary of Pentecostal and Charismatic Movements*, edited by Stanley M. Burgess, 14-20. Grand Rapids: Zondervan, 2002.

———. "Pinnock's Pneumatology: A Pentecostal Appreciation." *Journal of Pentecostal Theology* 14, no. 2 (2006) 167-73.

———. "Rediscovering the Church's Charismatic Structure." *The Living Pulpit* (2000) 28-29.

———. "The Spirit and Life: A Futher Response to Jürgen Moltmann." *Journal of Pentecostal Theology* 5 (1994) 121-27.

———. "Toward a Theology of the Third Article in a Post-Barthian Era: A Pentecostal Review of Donald Bloesch's Pneumatology." *Journal of Pentecostal Theology* 10, no. 2 (2002) 3-17.

———. "Tradition and the *Novum* of the Spirit: A Review of Clark Pinnock's *Flame of Love*." *Journal of Pentecostal Theology* 13 (1998) 31-48.

———. *The Trinity, Practically Speaking*. Downers Grove, IL: InterVarsity, 2010.
Mackintosh, H. R. *The Doctrine of the Person of Jesus Christ*. New York: Scribner's Sons, 1912.
MacLeod, Donald. "The Doctrine of the Incarnation in Scottish Theology: Edward Irving." *Scottish Bulletin of Evangelical Theology* 9, no. 1 (1991) 40–50.
Macmurray, John. *Persons in Relation*. London: Faber, 1991.
Marías, Julián. *History of Philosophy*. New York: Dover, 1967.
Mariña, Jacqueline. "Christology and Anthropology in Friedrich Schleiermacher." In *The Cambridge Companion to Friedrich Schleiermacher*, edited by Jacqueline Mariña, 151–70. Cambridge: Cambridge University Press, 2005.
Martin, Gottfried. *Kant's Metaphysics and Theory of Science*. Manchester: Manchester University Press, 1955.
May, John D'Arcy. "Visible Unity as Realised Catholicity." *Swedish Missiological Themes* 92, no. 1 (2004) 55–61.
McCall, Thomas H., and Michael C. Rea. *Philosophical and Theological Essays on the Trinity*. Oxford: Oxford University Press, 2009.
McDonald, Suzanne. "The Pneumatology of the 'Lost' Image in John Owen." *Westminster Theological Journal* 71, no. 2 (2009) 323–35.
McDonnell, Kilian. *The Other Hand of God: The Holy Spirit as the Universal Touch and Goal*. Collegeville, MN: Liturgical, 2003.
McFarland, Thomas. *Coleridge and the Pantheist Tradition*. Oxford: Clarendon, 1969.
McFarlane, Graham. *Christ and the Spirit: The Doctrine of the Incarnation according to Edward Irving*. Carlisle, UK: Paternoster, 1996.
McGrath, Alister E. *Iustitia Dei : A History of the Christian Doctrine of Justification*. 3rd ed. Cambridge: Cambridge University Press, 2005.
McIntyre, John. *The Shape of Pneumatology: Studies in the Doctrine of the Holy Spirit*. London: T. & T. Clark, 2004.
McLeod, Donald. "The Basis of Christian Unity." In *Ecumenism Today: The Universal Church in the 21st Century*, edited by Francesca Aran Murphy and Christopher Asprey, 107–19. Aldershot, UK: Ashgate, 2008.
Mesle, C. Robert. *Process-Relational Philosophy: An Introduction to Alfred North Whitehead*. West Conshohocken, PA: Templeton Foundation, 2008.
Migliore, Daniel L. *Faith Seeking Understanding: An Introduction to Christian Theology*. 2nd ed. Grand Rapids: Eerdmans, 2004.
Miller, Donald E., and Tetsunao Yamamori. *Global Pentecostalism: The New Face of Christian Social Engagement*. Berkeley: University of California Press, 2007.
Modiano, Raimonda. "'Naturphilsophilosophie' and Christian Orthodoxy in Coleridge's View of the Trinity." *Pacific Coast Philology* 17, nos. 1–2 (1982) 59–68.
Moltmann, Jürgen. *The Church in the Power of the Spirit: A Contribution to Messianic Ecclesiology*. San Francisco: Harper & Row, 1977.
———. *God in Creation: A New Theology of Creation and the Spirit of God*. Gifford Lectures. 1st Fortress Press ed. Minneapolis: Fortress, 1993.
———. *The Spirit of Life: A Universal Affirmation*. 1st Fortress Press ed. Minneapolis: Fortress, 1992.
———. *The Trinity and the Kingdom: The Doctrine of God*. Minneapolis: Fortress, 1993.
Neander, August. *The History of the Christian Religion and Church during the First Three Centuries*. Vol. 1. Translated by Henry John Rose. London: Printed for C. J. G. and F. Rivington 1831.

Neumann, Peter D. *Pentecostal Experience: An Ecumenical Encounter.* Princeton Theological Monograph. Eugene, OR: Pickwick, 2012.

Newbigin, Lesslie. *The Household of God: Lectures on the Nature of the Church.* London: SCM, 1953.

Nola, Robert. "The Young Hegelians, Feuerback, and Marx." In *The Age of German Idealism*, edited by Kathleen Marie Higgins and Robert C. Solomon, 6:290–329. Routledge History of Philosophy. London: Routledge, 1993.

Oliphant, Mrs. *The Life of Edward Irving, Minister of the National Scotch Church, London.* Vol. 2. London: Hurst and Blackett, 1862.

Ormerod, Neil. *Re-Visioning the Church an Experiment in Systematic-Historical Ecclesiology.* Minneapolis: Fortress, 2014.

Owen, John. "A Declaration of the Glorious Mystery of the Person of Christ." In *The Person of Christ*, 3–274. Grand Rapids: Sovereign Grace, 1971.

———. "A Discourse concerning the Holy Spirit." In *The Holy Spirit*, 15–365. Grand Rapids: Sovereign Grace, 1971.

———. *The Holy Spirit, His Gifts and Power: Exposition of the Spirit's Name, Nature, Personality, Dispensation, Operations and Effects.* Grand Rapids: Kregel, 1960.

———. *Pneumatologia: Or, a Discourse concerning the Holy Spirit.* Vol. 1. Glasgow: Macaulay, 1792.

Pannenberg, Wolfhart. *Basic Questions in Theology: Collected Essays.* 2 vols. Translated by George H. Kehm. Philadelphia: Fortress, 1971.

———. *Jesus—God and Man.* Translated by Lewis L. Wilkins and Duane A. Priebe. Philadelphia: Westminster, 1975.

———. *Systematic Theology.* Vol. 3. Translated by Geoffrey William Bromiley. Grand Rapids: Eerdmans, 1998.

———. *Systematic Theology.* Translated by Geoffrey William Bromiley. Vols. 1–2. T. & T. Clark Academic Paperbacks. London: T. & T. Clark, 2004.

Parker, T. H. L. *John Calvin: A Biography.* Rev. ed. Louisville, KY: Westminster John Knox, 2007.

"Perspectives on Koinonia." *Pneuma: Journal of the Society for Pentecostal Studies* 12, no. 2 (1990) 117–42.

Peters, Ted. *God—the World's Future: Systematic Theology for a New Era.* 2nd ed. Minneapolis: Fortress, 2000.

Pinnock, Clark H. *Flame of Love: A Theology of the Holy Spirit.* Downers Grove, IL: InterVarsity, 1996.

———. "Review of Frank D. Macchia's *Baptized in the Spirit: A Global Pentecostal Theology.*" *Journal of Pentecostal Theology* 16 (2008) 1–4.

Pippin, Robert B. *Modernism as a Philosophical Problem: On the Dissastisfactions of European High Culture.* Cambridge, MA: Blackwell, 1991.

Placher, William. "The Triune God: The *Perichoresis* of Particular Persons." In *Theology after Liberalism: A Reader*, edited by J. B. Webster and George P. Schner, 87–112. Oxford: Blackwell, 2000.

Plato. *Plato's Timaeus.* Translated by Benjamin Jowett. Rockville, MD: Serenity, 2009.

Plato. Translated by Robin Waterfield. Introduction and ntoes by Andrew Gregory. *Timaeus and Critias.* Oxford World's Classics. Oxford: Oxford University Press, 2008.

Prestige, George Leonard. *Fathers and Heretics: Six Studies in Dogmatic Faith with Prologue and Epilogue.* Bampton Lectures. London: SPCK, 1940.

Rahner, Karl. *The Trinity*. Translated by J. F. Donceel. New York: Crossroad, 2004.
Reardon, Bernard M. G. *Religion in the Age of Romanticism: Studies in Early Nineteenth Century Thought*. Cambridge: Cambridge University Press, 1985.
Richard of Saint Victor. *On the Trinity: English Translation and Commentary*. Edited and translated by Ruben Angelici. Eugene, OR: Cascade, 2011.
Robeck, Cecil M., Jr. "The Achievements of the Pentecostal-Catholic International Dialogue." In *Celebrating a Century of Ecumenism: Exploring the Achievements of International Dialogue: In Commemoration of the Centenary of the 1910 Edinburgh World Missionary Conference*, edited by John A. Radano, 163–94. Grand Rapids: Eerdmans, 2012.
Rogers, Eugene F. *After the Spirit: A Constructive Pneumatology from Resources Outside the Modern West*. Radical Traditions. Grand Rapids: Eerdmans, 2005.
Russell, Bertrand. *A History of Western Philosophy*. New York: Simon and Schuster, 1945.
Sanford, David H. "Determinates vs. Determinables." *The Stanford Encyclopedia of Philosophy*. 2011. http://plato.stanford.edu/archives/spr2011/entries/determinate-determinables/.
Schaeffer, J. H. F. *Createdness and Ethics: The Doctrine of Creation and Theological Ethics in the Theology of Colin E. Gunton and Oswald Bayer*. Berlin: de Gruyter, 2006.
Schwöbel, Christoph. "The Shape of Colin Gunton's Theology. On the Way towards a Fully Trinitarian Theology." In *The Theology of Colin Gunton*, edited by Lincoln Harvey, 182–208. London: T. & T. Clark, 2010.
Sheppard, Gerald T. "The Nicean Creed, *Filioque*, and Pentecostal Movements in the United States." *Greek Orthodox Theological Review* 31, no. 3 (1986) 401–16.
Simmons, Ernest L. *The Entangled Trinity*. Minneapolis: Fortress, 2014.
Solomon, Robert C. *Continental Philosophy since 1750: The Rise and Fall of the Self*. A History of Western Philosophy. Oxford: Oxford University Press, 1988.
Spence, Alan. *Incarnation and Inspiration: John Owen and the Coherence of Christology*. T. & T. Clark Theology. London: T. & T. Clark, 2007.
———. "The Person as Willing Agent: Classifying Gunton's Christology." In *The Theology of Colin Gunton*, edited by Lincoln Harvey, 49–63. London: T. & T. Clark, 2010.
———. "The Significance of John Owen for Modern Christology." In *The Ashgate Research Companion to John Owen's Theology*, edited by Kelly M. Kapic and Mark Jones. Surrey, UK: Ashgate, 2012.
Stark, Rodney. *The Rise of Christianity: A Sociologist Reconsiders History*. Princeton: Princeton University Press, 1996.
Stauffer, Richard. *Dieu, la Création et la Providence dans la Prédication de Calvin*. Basler und Berner Studien zur Historischen und Systematischen Theologie. Bern: Lang, 1978.
Stephenson, Christopher A. *Types of Pentecostal Theology: Method, System, Spirit*. Academy. New York: Oxford University Press, 2013.
Studebaker, Steven M. "Integrating Pneumatology and Christology: A Trinitarian Modification of Clark H. Pinnock's Spirit Christology." *Pneuma* 28, no. 1 (2006) 5–20.
Synan, Vinson. "Pentecostal Roots." In *The Century of the Holy Spirit: 100 Years of Pentecostal and Charismatic Renewal, 1901–2001*, edited by Vinson Synan, 16–37. Nashville: Nelson, 2001.

Terry, Justyn. "Colin Gunton's Doctrine of Atonement: Transcending Rationalism by Metaphor." In *The Theology of Colin Gunton*, edited by Lincoln Harvey, 130–45. London: T. & T. Clark, 2010.
Tertullian. *On Baptism*. Translated by S. Thelwall. In *Ante-Nicene Fathers*. edited by Alexander Roberts, James Donaldson and A. Cleveland Coxe, 3:669–79. Buffalo: Christian Literature, 1885.
———. *On Modesty*. In *The Ante-Nicene Fathers*, edited by James Donaldson Alexander Roberts, A. Cleveland Coxe, 4:74–101. Buffalo: Christian Literature, 1885.
Thomas Aquinas. *Basic Writings of Saint Thomas Aquinas*. Vol. 1, *God and the Order of Creation*. Translated by Anton C. Pegis. Indianapolis: Hackett, 1997.
Torrance, Thomas F. *The Christian Doctrine of God, One Being Three Persons*. Edinburgh: T. & T. Clark, 1996.
———. *Trinitarian Perspectives: Toward Doctrinal Agreement*. Edinburgh: T. & T. Clark, 1999.
Trueman, Carl R. *John Owen: Reformed Catholic, Renaissance Man*. Great Theologians. Aldershot, UK: Ashgate, 2007.
Turretin, Francis. *Institutes of Elenctic Theology*. Vol. 2. Translated by George Musgrave Giger. Phillipsburg, NJ: P & R, 1994.
Twesten, A. D. C. "The Trinity." *Bibliotheca Sacra and Theological Review* 4, no. 13 (1847) 25–67.
Varkey, Wilson. *Role of the Holy Spirit in the Protestant Systematic Theology: A Comparative Study between Karl Barth, Jurgen Moltmann, and Wolfhart Pannenberg*. Carlisle, UK: Langham Monographs, 2011.
Volf, Miroslav. *After Our Likeness: The Church as the Image of the Trinity*. Sacra Doctrina. Grand Rapids: Eerdmans, 1998.
Vondey, Wolfgang. *Beyond Pentecostalism: The Crisis of Global Christianity and the Renewal of the Theological Agenda*. Pentecostal Manifestos. Grand Rapids: Eerdmans, 2010.
Wacker, Grant. *Heaven Below: Early Pentecostals and American Culture*. Cambridge, MA: Harvard University Press, 2001.
Wainwright, Geoffrey. *Doxology: The Praise of God in Worship, Doctrine, and Life: A Systematic Sheology*. New York: Oxford University Press, 1980.
Ware, Timothy. *The Orthodox Church*. London: Penguin, 1993.
Warrington, Keith. *Pentecostal Theology: A Theology of Encounter*. London: T. & T. Clark, 2008.
Webster, John. "Systematic Theology after Barth: Jüngel, Jenson, and Gunton." In *The Modern Theologians: An Introduction to Christian Theology since 1918*, edited by David Ford, 249–64. Malden, MA: Blackwell, 2005.
Weinandy, Thomas G. *In the Likeness of Sinful Flesh: An Essay on the Humanity of Christ*. Paperback. ed. London: T. & T. Clark, 2006.
Whitney, William B. *Problem and Promise in Colin E. Gunton's Doctrine of Creation*. Boston: Brill, 2013.
Williams, J. Rodman. "Baptism in the Holy Spirit." In *The New International Dictionary of Pentecostal and Charismatic Movements*, edited by Stanley M. Burgess, 354–63. Grand Rapids: Zondervan, 2002.
Wilson, Dwight J. "Pentecostal Perspectives on Eschatology." In *The New International Dictionary of Pentecostal and Charismatic Movements*, edited by Stanley M. Burgess, 601–5. Grand Rapids: Zondervan, 2002.

Yoder, John Howard. *The Politics of Jesus: Vicit Agnus Noster.* 2nd ed. Grand Rapids: Eerdmans, 1994.

Yung, Hwa. "Pentecostalism and the Asian Church." In *Asian and Pentecostal: The Charismatic Face of Christianity in Asia*, edited by Allan Anderson and Edmond Tang, 37–58. Oxford: Regnum, 2005.

Ziegler, Philip G. "Stumbling upon Peter? The Question of the Church in Ecumenical Dialogue." In *Ecumenism Today: The Universal Church in the 21st Century*, edited by Francesca Aran Murphy and Christopher Asprey, 17–28. Aldershot, UK: Ashgate, 2008.

Zizioulas, John D. *Being as Communion: Studies in Personhood and the Church.* London: Darton, Longman and Todd, 2004.

———. "Communion and Otherness." *St. Vladimir's Theological Quarterly* 38, no. 4 (1994) 347–61.

Author Index

Achtner, Wolfgang, 28, 28n48
Anderson, Allan, 117n1, 118, 119, 119n8, 121, 121n19, 145
Aquinas, St. Thomas, 20, 27n45, 42, 43, 83, 159
Aristotle, 90, 90n91
Augustine, 28n48, 41–47, 41n9, 42n10, 43n16, 54, 78, 78n46, 97n107, 153–54, 154n18, 159, 162, 162n43, 179–80, 179n44, 199, 206, 209

Barth, Karl, ix, ixn1, xiv, xivn16, xx, xxn30, 2, 2n6, 15–16, 16n11, 28, 33, 33n69, 41n8, 51, 51n46, 55, 55n60, 60–61, 60n77, 79n48, 88–89, 89n85, 89n87, 110, 117, 136–37, 136n40, 137n43, 144, 144n74, 155, 155n21, 161, 171, 171n18, 178, 204, 214
Basil of Caesarea, xn5, 92
Bavinck, Herman, 13, 13n1, 106n24, 142n66
Brunner, Emil, xx, xxn31, 92n99, 126, 126n40, 204–5, 204n4,

Calvin, John, 29n52, 53–55, 53n54, 54n55, 54n56, 211, 211n15, 219
Chalcedon, xxi, 65, 76, 80, 82, 84, 87, 91–95, 91n97, 91n98, 92n99, 97, 110, 155, 162–65, 212–13, 212n16, 216
Chan, Simon, 117n1, 120, 136
Coakley, Sarah, 153, 212

Coffey, David, 150, 156–62
Coleridge, Samuel Taylor, 56, 56n64, 56n68
Crisp, Oliver, 75–76, 75n36, 95, 95n103, 213, 213n17, 215, 215n19
Cumin, Paul, 3, 3n8, 97n107
Cupitt, Don, 39–40, 39n3

Dabney, D. Lyle, 123
Descartes, Rene, 4–6
Dunn, James, 67

Forsyth, P. T., 40n7

Gibson, James, 5, 5n18
Green, Bradley, 17, 42, 42n10, 97n107

Harnack, Adolf, 101–2, 102n9, 106, 107
Hartshorne, Charles, 88, 88n84, 89
Harvey, Lincoln, xi, 35, 97n107
Hegel, Georg Wilhelm Friedrich, 51, 22n27
Heppe, Heinrich, 35n77, 142
Heraclitus, 17, 20n20
Höhne, David, 38
Hollenweger, Walter J., 119, 119n11

Irenaeus of Lyons, 15, 31n62, 42, 101
Irving, Edward, 11, 66, 68, 75n34, 76–78, 78n45, 79, 79n48, 80, 80n49, 81–87, 91, 91n95, 91n96, 92, 96n105, 97n107, 212

Jenson, Robert, 36, 41n9, 51, 51n46, 60, 63n89, 100, 174, 174n29
Johnson, W. E., 6, 6n22, 6n24, 7
Jüngel, Eberhard, 19n18, 89

Kant, Immaneul, xviii, 4, 22n27, 30, 30n56, 30n58, 32, 87n76, 192
Kärkkäinen, Veli-Matti, 154, 157, 218
Küng, Hans, 137–39, 142, 217
Kuyper, Abraham, 70

Locke, John, 5, 5n18, 6, 8, 87, 87n76
Luther, Martin, x, 53, 54, 54n56, 55, 93, 219

Macchia, Frank, ix, xi, xiv, xv, xvi, xvii, xviii, xix, xx, xxi, 10, 117, 117n1, 118, 118n3, 118n5, 119–26, 126n40, 127–58, 160–66, 166n1, 167–70, 170n11, 171–85, 185n64, 186–93, 193n7, 194–96, 196n18, 197–207, 208n11, 209–215, 217, 218–20
Macmurray, John, xviii, 52, 87
Marías, Julián, 16
McFarlane, Graham, 82, 83
McGrath, Alister, 54, 170
Moltmann, Jürgen, 36–37, 117, 124–25, 140, 143–44, 150–52, 152n10, 178, 196n18, 197–98, 206, 209, 217

Novatian, 100, 104, 106–8

Origen, 101

Owen, John, 11, 66, 68, 68n7, 69, 70–75, 75n34, 76–77, 80, 84–85, 87, 91, 100, 213

Pannenberg, Wolfhart, x, xn4, xvi, 61, 62, 86n72, 142, 158, 160, 162–64, 193, 193n7, 195, 205, 208, 217
Parmenides, 17, 20, 28
Pinnock, Clark, xiv, 184–86
Plato, 19n18, 20n20, 28, 29

Richard of St. Victor, 41–42, 43n15, 43n17, 45n22, 53, 57, 62
Rogers, Eugene, 179, 179n47

Schleiermacher, Friedrich, 4, 5, 28, 85n72, 91n97, 155
Schwöbel, Christoph, 3, 19, 42

Tertullian, 100–101, 104, 104n18, 105, 105n20, 106–8
Torrance, T. F., 24, 29n52, 79n48
Turretin, Francis, 70

Volf, Miroslav, 132, 137–39, 147

Warrington, Keith, 122
Webster, John, xiv, 41, 97n107

Yoder, John Howard, 100, 111–16

Zizioulas, John, xviii, 18n18, 19n18, 23, 24, 52, 100, 109, 117, 178, 196, 197, 217, 219

Subject Index

autonomy, 23, 23n32, 39, 58, 91

baptized in the Spirit. *See* Spirit Baptism
becoming, 52, 58, 88n84, 89–92, 109, 142
being-in-communion, 11, 13, 19, 19n18, 24, 26, 36–37, 42, 52, 65, 99, 101, 203, 219
being-in-relation, 14, 22–23, 33, 35, 108
Bond of love, 11, 44, 46–48, 50, 54, 64, 155, 167, 179–82, 179n44, 195, 198–200, 206–7, 209

charisma, 118, 119n8, 120–21, 121n19, 131, 132, 134, 144, 220
charismata. *See* charisma
charismatic. *See* charisma
Christology, ix-xxi, 1–2, 8n28, 10–11, 54–55, 60, 64–69, 67n2, 67n4, 67n5, 68n7, 73n31, 75n36, 76–77, 79n48, 80, 82–87, 83n61, 85n72, 91–92, 91n97, 91n98, 94–95, 96n104, 96n105, 97n107, 99–100, 103, 109–113, 121, 126–27, 149–73, 190, 202–3, 208–216, 220
communal, communion, community, xiii, xvi, xviii, xix, xxi, 9–12, 18, 18n18, 19, 19n18, 20, 21, 23n32, 24–25, 25n39, 26, 27, 35, 37–42, 46, 47, 49, 51–54, 57–59, 59n73, 60, 64, 65–66, 74, 98–109, 111, 115–16, 120, 123, 127–31, 133–36, 138–39, 142, 144–49, 153, 167, 169, 171–72, 174–78, 180–81, 181n53, 183n58, 187–89, 191–92, 194, 196–99, 202, 204, 208–211, 214–21
creation, x-xi, xii-xiv, xvi, xvii, xviii-xx, 1, 3, 8–21, 23–25, 25n39, 26, 27, 27n44, 28, 31, 31n62, 32–35, 37–40, 40n5, 48, 51, 53–66, 70, 73, 74, 77, 80–81, 98, 108, 117, 122–24, 124n29, 125, 125n32, 127, 130, 132, 134, 138–40, 148–52, 156, 158, 158n32, 159–61, 163, 165–70, 170n11, 171–73, 175–77, 180–86, 186n69, 187, 187n72, 188–92, 194–99, 201, 203, 204, 208, 210–11, 213–18, 220

ecclesiology, ix, xviii-xix, xxi, 2, 11, 84, 99, 100–116, 121, 127–42, 143, 146, 148–49, 167, 174, 181n53, 190, 197, 202–3, 208, 216–21
ecumenical, xiv, xv, 129, 131, 133–35, 140, 141–43, 146, 148, 156, 162, 168n4, 218
election, doctrine of, 55, 74, 110, 141, 171, 183, 199–200, 205
enlightenment, ix, 22n27, 39, 201
epistemology, xx, xxi, 1–4, 6, 8–10, 19, 21, 25n40, 63n89, 111–12, 122, 124, 126–28, 145–46, 156–57, 160, 162, 166, 188, 190, 202–3

237

SUBJECT INDEX

eschatology, ix, xi, xiii, xiv, xvii, xviii, xx, 16, 27n44, 31, 31n62, 33, 54n56, 55, 55n61, 56, 60–61, 64, 103, 106, 109, 124, 127, 142, 146n78, 169, 184–86

eternity, 15–16, 19–20, 27, 27n45, 28, 28n48, 29, 29n52, 30–33, 35, 51, 51n46, 55, 55n60, 56, 60–62, 78, 110–12, 114, 194–95, 215

filioque, 49, 158, 209

freedom, 11, 19, 22n27, 26, 27n44, 31, 35, 40, 42, 45, 53–62, 63n89, 64, 73, 85, 91, 92, 97, 103, 114, 116, 137, 144, 151, 163, 184, 187–89, 198,

God
    taxis, 31, 39, 49, 62, 152, 160, 170, 208–9
    The Father, ix-xiv, xvi-xx, 2–3, 8–12, 14–16, 18n18, 19, 19n18, 20, 23, 24, 26, 32–38, 43–55, 57–59, 59n73, 60–63, 63n89, 64–70, 72–74, 74n32, 75, 77–78, 80–82, 84–86, 89, 91, 96n91, 92–94, 96–99, 101–5, 110–11, 113, 116–17, 123–24, 126–28, 132–34, 142, 145–46, 148–52, 152n10, 153, 154–58, 158n32, 159–62, 164–66, 166n2, 170, 172–83, 183n58, 184, 186–93, 193n7, 193n9, 194–96, 196n18, 197–200, 200n34, 201–207n11, 208–217

Holy Spirit
    perfecting cause, x-xi, xiii, xiv, xviii, xix-xxi, 3, 11, 19, 27, 27n44, 34, 37, 49–51, 53–61, 64, 68, 74–75, 80, 89, 92–93, 96, 98–99, 103, 108, 110, 148, 169, 171, 176, 186, 189, 210, 217, 221

hypostasis, 18n18, 23, 67, 72, 75, 85, 96, 208n11, 212

hypostatic union, 66, 70, 75, 75n34, 76, 80, 84, 85, 93, 94, 95, 157, 160–61, 213, 214

incarnation, xi, xii, xiv, xx, xxi, 3, 10, 14–16, 20, 34, 38, 60–62, 65–69, 69n10, 70, 72, 74–84, 86–87, 91–96, 96n105, 97, 97n107, 98, 109, 111–12, 124, 126–27, 140, 149–50, 152, 155–61, 163, 172, 175–76, 180–82, 184, 191, 194, 199–200, 212–17

individual, ix, xii, xviii, 18, 25n39, 25n40, 38, 40, 53, 54, 72, 87, 105, 132, 135, 192, 220, 221

individualistic. *See* individual

individuality. *See* individual

indwelling, xvii, 36, 144, 169–73, 175–78, 180, 182–83, 187–88, 191–92, 194, 196, 199

Jesus Christ, xii, xiii, xvi, xvii, xviii, xxi, 3, 8–11, 15, 25, 49, 57, 58, 60, 61, 62, 63, 63n89, 66–67, 69–75, 75n34, 78, 79n48, 80, 81, 84–85, 86, 86n72, 89–90, 91n96, 94, 96, 96n105, 97n107, 98, 99, 108–116, 120, 123–27, 131, 133, 136, 140, 141, 143, 145, 147, 148, 149, 150–51, 153–55, 157–65, 171, 173, 175–77, 181, 183, 184, 185, 186n69, 187, 190, 192–93, 195–96, 198, 201, 203, 205, 206, 209–216, 219, 220

God the Son, ix-xvi, xvii, xix-xx, 2–4, 8–11, 14–16, 18, 18n18, 19–20, 24, 26, 32, 33–38, 43–45, 47–55, 57–59, 59n73, 60–67, 67n4, 68–74, 74n32, 75–78, 78n45, 80–87, 89, 91, 92, 93, 95, 96, 96n104–5, 97, 97n107, 98–99, 103–5, 109–113, 123–24, 126–28, 132–34, 145, 147–48, 150–52, 152n10, 153–58, 158n32, 159–64, 166n2, 168–70, 172, 174–77, 179, 179n44, 180–93, 193n7, 193n9, 194–96, 196n18, 197–99, 199n32, 200, 200n34, 201–2, 205–7, 207n11, 208–218

The Word, x, xvi, xviii, xxi, 12, 15, 16, 31n62, 59, 69, 69n10, 70, 73, 76, 77, 83–86, 93, 97, 112,

SUBJECT INDEX

125–26, 136–38, 150, 157, 164, 172, 182, 190, 195–96, 217
justification, xvi, 54, 54n55, 55, 117, 125, 125n32, 132, 144, 149, 154–56, 158, 163, 166n2, 167–68, 168n4, 169–70, 170n11, 171–74, 174n29, 175, 188, 191–93, 205, 210, 217

kenosis, 75, 76, 78, 78n45, 96, 84, 94, 96n104, 96n105, 213
kenotic. *See* kenosis
kingdom of God, xi, 36, 64, 119, 137–40, 149–52, 156, 166, 183, 184, 195–96
koinonia, xviii, xix, xxi, 18n18, 96, 125n32, 127, 130–36, 138–39, 142, 144–50, 153–54, 166n2, 167, 169, 172, 174–75, 177–83, 188–89, 191, 197–200, 202, 211, 217, 219

liberation. *See* liberty
liberty, xiii, 11, 31, 35, 53, 54n55, 55, 57–60, 62, 63n89, 66–67, 86, 93, 96, 99, 103, 108–111, 113, 115–16, 133, 151–52, 172, 181, 187–89, 213–15, 219–20
Logos Christology, 65–68, 91, 98, 108–9, 163–64, 164n50, 212
Logos, 65–72, 75, 76, 78, 80, 85, 86, 91–94, 97n107, 98, 109, 110–11, 113, 157, 160, 163–65, 212
love, x, xiii, xvi, xx, 11, 35, 36, 40, 40n7, 42, 42n10, 43–46, 46n28, 46n29, 47–57, 59, 64, 73, 74n32, 77–78, 81, 86, 92, 98, 110, 121, 124, 126, 126n40, 129, 130, 133, 142, 145–46, 148, 154–55, 158–61, 166n2, 167, 170–71, 174–79, 179n44, 180–82, 186, 188–89, 191, 195–201, 206–7, 209, 210, 214–15, 217, 220

mediation, 3, 4, 10, 18, 63n89, 73, 97n107, 123, 172, 182
metaphysics, 5, 8n29, 19n18, 28, 43, 63n89, 87, 88–89, 184, 204–5, 211

modernity, 17, 22, 22n27, 23n32

(Neo)Platonic, 18, 19n18, 28n48, 102, 103, 137
nominalism, 5

one and the many, xiv, 16–20, 22–24, 27, 27n44, 28, 32–33, 35, 56, 100, 103
open transcendentals. *See* transcendentals.
ostensive definition, 5, 6, 6n22, 7–9
ousia, 23, 113, 154, 208

Pantheism, 25, 56, 63, 87
participation, 10, 24, 123, 129–30, 133, 135, 143, 145, 156, 166n2, 169, 172, 173–75, 179, 181, 188, 198–99, 211
particularity, 19, 26–27, 27n44, 29, 35, 38–40, 40n4, 41–42, 49–50, 64, 66, 73, 85, 90–91, 100, 105, 109, 116, 130, 207, 218–20
Pelagianism, 55
pentecostal, pentecostalism, xiv, xv, xvn19, xvii, xviii, xix, xxi, 117–20, 118n3, 118n6, 118n7, 119n8, 119n11
perichoresis, 11, 17, 24–27, 32–35, 35n77, 36, 36n81, 94, 134, 176, 177, 189, 196, 206, 207
personhood, ix, xviii, xix, 17, 23, 19, 25n40, 40, 50, 52–53, 59, 63n89, 72, 84, 86–87, 90, 92–93, 95, 97, 130, 161, 163, 176, 179, 187, 191, 196–99, 207–9, 211, 214–15
Pneumatology, ix, x, xi, xiii, xiv, xv, xvi, xvii, xviii, xix, xxi, 1–3, 10–12, 19–20, 26, 36–37, 39, 41, 47–49, 53, 55–56, 58, 60, 64–66

redemption, ix, x, xi, xii, xiii, xiv, xvii, xix, xx, 12, 15–16, 20, 29, 31, 33–34, 37, 40, 40n5, 64, 67, 77–78, 80n49, 86, 98, 124–26, 124n29, 149, 151–52, 158n32, 159, 165–66, 168, 169, 170, 170n11, 172, 175, 180, 184–86, 188, 191, 204–5, 208, 210–11, 218

239

Reformation, ix, x, xn4, 59n73, 219n26
relatedness, relational, xviii-xix, xxi, 6, 10–11, 19, 22–23, 23n32, 24–28, 25n40, 27n44, 31–37, 36n81, 40, 48, 52–54, 58, 64–66, 72, 74, 87–88, 88n82, 90, 92, 99, 108, 128, 130, 133, 135, 137, 156, 162, 169–70, 178–79, 188, 196–97, 202–4, 209, 218
relational ontology, xviii-xix, 74
relationality, xviii, 11, 19, 22, 23, 23n32, 24, 25, 25n40, 26, 27, 27n44, 28, 31, 34, 35, 36, 36n81, 37, 40, 53, 58, 65, 90, 99, 135, 197, 203
revelation, xi, xviii, xx, xxn30, xxi, 2–5, 5n16, 7–13, 15, 16, 19, 20, 36, 38–39, 40n7, 44, 56, 63n89, 65, 69, 72, 76, 89, 89n85, 101–2, 104, 108, 111–12, 121–24, 124n29, 125–27, 161, 164, 168, 192–93, 193n9, 195, 199–205, 208, 217–18

salvation, xiii, xv, xvi, xvii, xviii
sanctification, ix, x, xn4, xii, 70, 71, 75, 77, 96, 125, 145, 171, 175, 191, 210–11
soteriology, x, xi, xviii, xxi, 1, 36, 40, 64, 82, 106, 121, 123, 127, 149, 156, 166–69, 172, 174–76, 192–93, 196, 199, 203, 218
Spirit Baptism, xv, xvi, xvii, xxi, 118, 119, 119n11, 120, 121, 123, 124, 124n29, 125–27, 129–35, 139, 141–53, 156–58, 160–61, 164, 166, 166n1, 167–76, 180–82, 184–86, 188–96, 199–201, 207, 209–210, 218
Spirit Baptizer, xvi, 126–27, 132, 141–42, 149–52, 154, 156, 160–63, 165, 170–73, 176, 181–83, 189–90, 194, 196, 199–201
Spirit Christology, xxi, 11, 65–67, 67n4, 76–77, 84, 87, 91–92, 97n107, 98, 150, 163, 165, 212–13, 216
substantiality, 17, 27n44, 35, 36n81, 38, 90, 206

temple of the Spirit, 109, 130, 142
time, xii, 7, 15, 20, 25n39, 27, 27n45, 28, 28n48, 29, 29n52, 30, 30n58, 31–35, 49, 55–56, 58, 60–62, 71, 77, 78n45, 87–88, 89n85, 91n96, 97, 100, 104–6, 112–13, 118n5, 129n7, 136, 141, 144n75, 154, 158n32, 170n11, 173, 177, 181, 199, 210–11, 215
tongues, 119, 119n11, 120, 144–45, 147, 173
transcendental idealism, 30, 30n56
transcendentals, 14–21, 25n39, 25n40, 26, 27, 30–33, 35–36, 36n81, 37, 101, 206
open transcendentals, 14, 16, 17, 21, 26, 33, 35, 62, 101
Trinity, x, xi, xii, xiv, xvi, xvii, xviii, 1, 1n3, 14–16, 18, 19, 19n18, 22, 23n32, 24, 25n39, 26, 32, 34, 36, 39, 40–43, 45–46, 48–49, 51, 51n46, 52, 56–57, 60, 64, 69, 72–74, 78n45, 81–82, 86, 103, 105, 109, 121, 124–26, 128, 130, 132–35, 151–53, 158, 160, 161, 169, 178, 179n44, 182, 187, 191, 193, 196, 198, 200–201, 203, 205–206, 208, 211–15, 217, 220

universals, 5, 30

www.ingramcontent.com/pod-product-compliance
Lightning Source LLC
Chambersburg PA
CBHW050438240426

43661CB00055B/2426